D1338215

STRANGE PEOPLE I HAVE KNOWN

STRANGE PEOPLE I HAVE KNOWN

... AND OTHER STORIES

ANDY McSMITH

Biteback Publishing

First published in Great Britain in 2023 by
Biteback Publishing Ltd, London
Copyright © Andy McSmith 2023

ISBN 978-1-78590-805-7

10 9 8 7 6 5 4 3 2 1

A CIP catalogue record for this book is available from the British Library.

Set in Minion Pro and Trade Gothic

Printed and bound in Great Britain by
CPI Group (UK) Ltd, Croydon CR0 4YY

FSC
www.fsc.org
MIX
Paper | Supporting
responsible forestry
FSC® C171272

*To Tamsin Almeida, whose arrival coincided
with events described here in Chapter 18*

CONTENTS

PREFACE

As the past is another country, I am a foreign visitor in today. I come from a land where money is measured shillings, pence and half-crowns, brown ten-shilling notes and green pound notes. Five pounds will fill the petrol tank in your car and leave you with some change. The Queen is young enough to add one more prince to the royal bloodline; there is a John Wayne movie showing this week at the Odeon; and The Beatles are top of the Hit Parade again. You can listen to their singles, EPs or LPs on that bulky piece of furniture that holds your gramophone, but if it's an LP, don't forget to switch from 45 to 33 rpm. In the poor, half-hidden suburbs you sometimes see a black person, but the only black people you see on television are the blacked-up singers on *The Black and White Minstrel Show*.

I also have a blurred recollection of a place where there were ration books, and my mother would walk us to the local community hall to pick up a half-pint bottle of milk, and we would sit together to watch *The Woodentops*, or *Muffin the Mule*, on a black and white television that gave off a smell of burning rubber if it was switched on for too long. Children were not encouraged to listen to or watch the news, but at school, we would be excited to hear about it when another murderer was to be hanged.

Since, I have travelled through times filled with such novelties as colour television, cash machines, dishwashers, phones not attached to a wall and the world wide web.

It was a clever Dane who observed that 'life can only be understood backwards; but it must be lived forwards'. Looking backwards, I see a life strewn with good fortune. Yet at times, I contrived to think I was hard done by as I stumbled through a privileged private school education, which eased me into Oxford University and into a profession that I loved. So I am in no way qualified to write a misery memoir about life on society's underside; but in late adolescence a heavy cloud of gloom enveloped me. I broke off contact with everyone I had known at school, and almost everyone I had known at university, and then walked out of journalism. But then I wished to return to the trade and had to bluff my way back, at the age of forty, by pretending to be much younger. Along this jagged journey I met some very rare and interesting specimens of the human race. This memoir describes some of them.

A PERSON OF RENOWN

Bratsk. I believe I was the only one in our party who had heard of the place, and what I thought I knew about it was wrong. There was no such town as Bratsk in the 1940s. It was an old Cossack fortress, and a labour camp whose inmates were dragooned into the construction of the Trans-Siberian Railway. It became a place you could find on a map in the 1950s, when construction workers dammed the Angara River, created one of the world's largest man-made lakes and built a hydroelectric power station and a town to house its workforce. That was Bratsk.

We landed there because our aircraft had to refuel between London and Tokyo. The Russians knew that there was a person of great renown aboard our craft and insisted that we disembark and be greeted in the airport's VIP suite. The formalities were conducted in one room, where the Mayor of Bratsk officiated, while most of our party waited in the adjoining lounge. The floorboards were bare, the refreshments were nil, but there was one extraordinary luxury – a large television screen on the wall, showing Sky TV.

To understand how strange this was, consider that no one in Britain had ever seen satellite television until Sky began broadcasting in February 1989. This was September 1989. We were 3,000 miles east of Moscow, watching Elton John perform 'I'm Still Standing' in a Siberian town that used to be part of the gulag. It was the first time I realised that programmes could be broadcast simultaneously across continents.

A connecting door opened and Margaret Thatcher entered, having completed her audience with the Mayor of Bratsk, and walked slowly in my direction, smiling, head tilted a little to one side. People look smaller in real life than on television. This extraordinary woman had to, literally, look up to almost every man she met, even if they figuratively looked up to her.

She recognised me as one of the journalists accompanying her but either had forgotten or did not care that I was from the Labour-supporting *Daily Mirror*. I guess that she reckoned that whoever I was, I was more interesting than the Mayor of Bratsk. Not a high bar, perhaps. Momentarily, I had the Prime Minister's undivided attention. All I needed was to think of something to say. The best I could manage was to ask how the meeting with the mayor had gone. A slight raising of the eyebrows told me that it had been less than gripping.

'But did you see the Elton John video on Sky?' I enquired.

'No! They were showing the Green Party conference,' she exclaimed indignantly. 'That man was saying there is litter in the streets. He can't say that in a programme that's being broadcast all over the world.'

That was it. A Downing Street official had spotted the Prime Minister in conversation with a hack and scuttled across the room, drawing a predatory pack of journalists in his wake. Still, it was enough for an exclusive on the lines of 'Furious Maggie Lashes Out'.

Every thinking adult in the UK had an opinion about Margaret Thatcher. She was recognisable like no other Prime Minister since Winston Churchill. I was in a corridor by the open door at the back of a classroom in Tokyo full of Japanese girls aged about fourteen when Thatcher paid them a visit. I could not see her from where I was standing, but I knew exactly when she entered the room because the entire class started screaming with uncontrolled excitement. I doubt that there was any other head of government anywhere who could have provoked that kind of reaction among children in a country halfway across the globe.

In June 1990, Thatcher visited Leninakan, an Armenian city, since renamed Gyumri, which had been partially destroyed by an earthquake two years earlier. An immense crowd poured into the centre of town, filling every square foot of public space. People were waving from windows and standing on the roofs. Behind Thatcher, amid this heaving crowd, was her devoted press secretary, Bernard Ingham, who came from Yorkshire and prided himself on being always on the same wavelength as the man in the pub in Hebden Bridge. There was a risk that Thatcher might be crushed in the melee. With no time to think or choose partners, British and Soviet officials had to link arms in a protective ring around her, and I was vastly amused to see Bernard Ingham arm in arm with a man in the uniform of a high-ranking KGB officer.

Nearby, a line of chauffeur-driven ZiLs waited to take the officials away. I suspect that every government car in Armenia was in that line. A Kremlin doctor and a Georgian photographer were loitering by the vehicles. From them, I learnt that the temperature that day was 90 degrees Fahrenheit (32 degrees Celsius) and that the KGB had estimated the size of the crowd at 150,000. Given the number who had moved out after the earthquake destroyed their homes, that suggested that the entire population of Leninakan plus others from the countryside had come for a glimpse of the British Prime Minister.

Thatcher was recognised everywhere she went but not universally loved, especially not in the north-east of England, where I was living when she assumed office in 1979. Working-class communities were already at the sharp end of deindustrialisation before she took office, and she set about doing all she could to make matters worse. I was invited by the Workers' Educational Association to give a talk in Consett, in County Durham, a town built around its 140-year-old steelworks. It was a lively audience, made up of men who knew where they stood, whose weekly pay packets made sure that their families were never without the basic necessities. A few days after I met them, they all learnt that they were to be thrown onto the dole. The Thatcher government had imported a Scottish American businessman named Ian MacGregor from the USA, at vast public expense, to fatten up the steel industry, ready for privatisation. The Consett steelworks made a small profit, but MacGregor decided it was not enough. In his office 200 miles to the south of Consett, he signed the death certificate of the old steelworks and threw 4,500 people out of work. The knock-on effect hit every business in Consett, where unemployment reached 36 per cent. It was a pattern repeated across the region. Factory buildings turned into empty husks, industrial estates made up of nothing but warehouses, pit villages facing dereliction, hundreds of thousands of people – men predominantly – who had been breadwinners all their adult lives thrown out onto the dole without a realistic prospect of ever finding paid work again. That was Thatcher's gift to the north-east.

Most politicians try to convince the public that they are well-meaning public servants and not ruthless at all. Not Margaret Thatcher. As a woman having constantly to assert her authority over men, she cultivated her reputation as the 'Iron Lady', who was not for turning. She would lecture the nation on how to behave. When challenged about the north-east's shocking level of unemployment during a rare visit to the region, she told the locals to stop being 'moaning minnies'.

Yet in private, when not being challenged, she could be thoughtful and kind. One of the perks enjoyed by the corps of parliamentary journalists known as 'the lobby' was the right to dine with politicians in expensive central London restaurants and reclaim the cost. I was joined one lunchtime by Angela Rumbold, the Minister for Education, who arrived looking flustered and told us about an ordeal she had been through that morning. She had had to report personally to Thatcher on some item of policy, on which she had no doubt spent hours ensuring that she was briefed to the eyeballs and able to answer every question the boss might ask, but as she entered Thatcher's office, she was hit by an unseen catastrophe: the minister and the Prime Minister were wearing identical dresses.

'Did she say anything?' I asked.

'She did. She said, "It looks much better on you."'

That same tactfulness was on display the first time I saw Margaret Thatcher in person. During the general election of February 1974, the Conservatives in Slough had booked a hall for a public rally, to which the press were invited. So were the voters, but, almost without exception, they chose to give it a miss. When three of us journalists arrived together, we almost doubled the head count. Thatcher, the Secretary of State for Education, the only woman in Edward Heath's Cabinet, was there, accompanied by the young candidate, smartly turned out in suit and tie, looking as if he wished the floor would swallow him up. As Thatcher spotted the presence of journalists, she said in a loud voice, 'What a lovely hall this is!'

It was a bog-standard sort of hall, and almost empty, but the humiliated candidate must have inwardly blessed her tact. Even without a public, the show had to go on. The candidate's speech bristled with fury, supposedly directed at the Labour Party, though perhaps provoked by the absence of listeners. His best line was that a Labour government would 'pump them and dump them'. Thatcher's speech was delivered with good humour, as if it were a pleasure to speak to rows of unoccupied chairs. One thing I remember her saying was that she was 'jealous' of Sir Keith Joseph, Secretary of State for Social Services, because his department's budget was the only one bigger than hers. Thatcher the public spending slasher was as yet unborn.

Parliament is a graveyard of ambition. So many people have gone there thinking that they could make an impact on the life of the nation and come away knowing that they have not. For some, the disappointment is so hard to bear that they have to pretend. There was an MP whom it would be cruel to name, whose body language was a symphony of self-regard, which I could not resist observing in the social setting of Parliament's subsidised cafes. He was tall and would walk slowly, head up, rarely looking around to see who else was in the room, as if he expected all eyes to be on him. He would sit upright, elbows on the table, hands clasped together close to his chin. If someone to one side spoke to him, he would move his eyes to show that he was listening but would not turn his head. If he replied, he would continue looking straight ahead as he spoke. He was in Parliament for thirty years; his party was in and out of power, but no Prime Minister thought to make him a minister; no opposition leader invited him to be a shadow minister. Still, he believed he had enough political wisdom to fill a book that someone was persuaded to publish. I went to his book launch, in the hope of picking some political intelligence, and discovered I was one of just six people who turned out. Even then, he was protected by his carapace of self-importance from thinking that his long political career had amounted to nothing. I know, because when I met him later, he was good enough to tell me that he never read anything that I wrote because so many newspapers and magazines came to his office – he listed them all – but he was too busy to read them. Anyone who has time to tell you how busy they are isn't.

Margaret Thatcher must have come up against men like that by the dozen on her rocky road to Downing Street. It surprised me, as it surprised many others, when the Conservatives chose a woman to lead them in 1975. From the Conservative councillors and office holders in the Slough area, I knew that many of them wanted to be rid of Heath and rather regretted that sending for Enoch Powell was out of the question. Sir Keith Joseph was the first to challenge Heath, but his candidature self-imploded, making way for Thatcher. I asked a Slough councillor named Mr Lawless whether the Conservatives would really countenance being led by a woman. He could be quite sardonic about the prejudices of his fellow Tories. His reply was short and blunt, 'They'd rather have a woman than a Jew.'

Something that can certainly be said for Margaret Thatcher is that she was free of antisemitism, though that was a Conservative speciality, back then. And even when she was one of the world's most recognisable individuals, she did not walk around in a manner that exuded importance. I know, because I was almost caught out, the second time I encountered her. It was in a narrow corridor behind the Speaker's chair in the House of Commons, a few weeks after she had won her third successive general election. It was soon after the conclusion of Prime Minister's Questions. There was a woman in the corridor, coming in the opposite direction. It was not wide enough for us to pass each other by without risking brushing against one another. At first, I took her for a member of staff. To my surprise, she stopped and, looking amused, raised a finger and moved it in an arc, as if she were aping the movement of a windscreen wiper. It was Margaret Thatcher, giving me a choice of standing aside to the left or to the right, but making it very clear that I was the one who was going to get out of the way. There are many other people I have known who would have accompanied the gesture with an irate 'don't you know who I am look', but she seemed to think it was funny that I did not immediately realise who she was.

In the summer of 1989, she came to a social event organised by lobby journalists, in a room high up in the Commons, near that part of the roof from which a fictional Prime Minister, Francis Urquhart, pushed a journalist to her death in the BBC drama *House of Cards*. As Thatcher arrived, she beamed with pleasure at seeing the lobby chairman, a former *Daily Mail* hack named Geoffrey Parkhurst, who was well plugged in to the Tory Party, and she pretended to buckle at the knees after climbing so many stairs.

In retrospect, the very fact that she was there was extraordinary.

Other Prime Ministers have socialised with journalists but on home ground, in Downing Street, with a special adviser or two at their side to step in if difficult questions were asked. Thatcher was the last Prime Minister who would walk fearlessly into a room full of journalists, unprotected. If Bernard Ingham or another member of staff were present, they would keep a respectful distance, no doubt trying to hear what was said but not presuming to interrupt. She seemed to enjoy being surrounded by journalists, because they were too busy asking questions and trying to sniff out a story to talk down to her.

Without a spin doctor to chaperone her, Thatcher could not always know who she was talking to. These lobby receptions were open to correspondents from any recognised British news outlet, regardless of political leanings, including, for instance, the *Morning Star*, the Communist Party's daily newspaper, which relied heavily on a bulk order from the Soviet Union. There could be disputes about what qualified as a news outlet. *Private Eye*, with its large circulation, was never allocated a lobby pass, whereas for a time, there was a recognised correspondent from the *Sunday Sport*, a tabloid whose front page featured such world exclusives as 'Aliens Turned Our Son Into A Fish Finger' or 'Adolf Hitler Was A Woman' or, more recently, 'Putin Shat Himself After Two Pints of Shandy' – until the authorities responsible for allocating lobby passes decided that this was not really a news-gathering operation.

Thatcher enjoyed herself, and stayed so long at that reception that she was still socialising when journalists started drifting. As I left, I looked back and noted that she was down to an audience of two. On one side of her was Mike Ambrose, veteran political editor of the *Morning Star*, and on the other, a woman who styled herself the 'political editor' of *Sunday Sport*. If Thatcher had let slip some government secret in that company, no one would have believed that what they wrote came from a reliable source.

One journalist she knew well and liked was the long-serving political editor of the *Daily Mail*, Gordon Greig. He had a career trajectory that would be impossible in the industry these days. He began as a teenage messenger on a Glasgow newspaper, did his national service, kept the regimental tie, which he would wear around the Commons to encourage old soldiers in the Conservative Party to spill their secrets, and returned to become one of the best tabloid journalists in the trade. He broke the story that Thatcher planned to challenge Edward Heath in 1975. His editor, David English, was immediately sold on the idea of a woman leading the Tories. But how, he asked, could she convince them that she was a Prime Minister in waiting when she had 'a voice like breaking glass'? He ordered Gordon Greig to ask her that very question. It was a Sunday. It was quiet in the *Daily Mail*'s spacious newsroom as Greig rang Mrs Thatcher's home. It seemed to him that everyone in the room was listening, knowing what he had been told to ask and wondering if he would. Denis Thatcher answered and called his wife to the phone. After a brief conversation, she had said enough to reassure Greig that he could write the story without risking a denial. He took a deep breath, and he asked, 'How can you lead the Conservative Party when you have a voice like breaking glass?'

'Breaking glass!' she cried. The way Gordon Greig told it, it was very much like the sound of breaking glass. Thatcher took voice training later but never lost her affection for the journalist who asked her that impertinent question.

As the Prime Minister's plane crossed the Soviet Union on its way back from Japan, the journalists in the party were invited to go in groups of four to talk to her in the front section, while Bernard Ingham and two other Downing Street officials stood back at a respectful distance. Thatcher made a comment about the UK's relations with the European Union, at which Gordon Greig laughed in her face and asked, 'Does Geoffrey Howe agree with that?'

Even I, the newest member of the party, knew the answer to that one. Two months earlier, Thatcher had elbowed Howe out of his job as Foreign Secretary because of their long-running disagreements over Europe, aggravated by personal animosity. But at that level of government, everyone must keep up the public pretence of friction-free unity, so it would have been in order for Thatcher to bat away the question with a few prepared phrases. But that was not how she reacted.

Instead of addressing the question of whether Sir Geoffrey Howe agreed with her or not, she poked Gordon Greig on the lapel and told him, 'Rearrange your ideas, Gordon!' Another old hand in the lobby named Frank Johnson, who, like Greig, had risen from teenage messenger boy to the top of the profession, used to say that truly serious people do not take themselves totally seriously and that Thatcher, who was well-aware of her carefully cultivated Iron Lady image, would indulge from time to time in self-parody. Watching her deal with this round of mental jousting, surrounded by men younger than her, was like being with a flirtatious granny.

People ask what it is like to meet and talk with someone who is world famous. Journalists are not very good at answering that question. Before I had ever interviewed anyone famous, I knew a journalist named David Chipp, who had interviewed Mao Zedong when he was Reuters correspondent in China. Of course, I asked him eagerly, 'What was Mao like?' and was frustrated when he could not give me a descriptive answer. The reason, of course, was that he was so focused on the task of asking the right questions and getting the answers written down in shorthand that there was no space left in his mind to be awed by the thought that 'wow, I'm talking to Mao Zedong'.

There was a moment when speaking to Margaret Thatcher when I was suddenly, forcibly reminded who she was. As that exchange in the plane came to an end, I was the last journalist to leave and had a short one-to-one exchange with her. Talking about relations between the USA and the Soviet Union, I ventured the opinion that the new US President, George Bush (the father, not the son), knew more about world affairs than his predecessor. Thatcher did not like that. Frowning, she replied, 'Oh, but with Ron, it all came from the heart.' It hit me that I was talking to someone who really was on first-name terms with President Ronald Reagan.

But my greatest gasp-of-astonishment moment came after I had been trapped in a traffic jam. It was the worst traffic jam I ever experienced, not just because of how long it lasted. On the day before I was due to board the Prime Minister's plane to Japan, I called into the *Daily Mirror* room in Parliament and found a yellow Post-it note on my screen from the political editor of the Press Association, Chris Moncrieff, saying that the departure time had changed. He gave a time, but I was not sure if he was telling me when the plane was leaving or when journalists were required to be at the VIP terminal in Heathrow, which was always one hour earlier. I could not find anyone who knew the answer, and in those days, no one owned a mobile phone, so as a precaution, I booked a taxi to get me there an hour earlier than Moncrieff had told me I must be there. As we entered the M25, the driver pointed to the fast-moving traffic and assured me we would be there in good time.

Then, suddenly, the M25 stopped being a highway and became a car park. There had been an accident ahead. We waited. At first, I could take comfort in knowing that there was at least an hour and more before the plane took off. But the traffic did not move for more than an hour and the horrible realisation descended on me that we would not be at Heathrow by the time specified on Moncrieff's note and that, for all I knew, the Prime Minister's plane would be up above the clouds while we were motionless below. Trapped in that traffic jam, my whole life seemed to pass before my eyes. I had something unique. I had gone directly from the Labour Party press office into a position as a political correspondent, based in the lobby. No one else has done that in the past forty years or more. I could see my future unfolding. People would laughingly repeat the tale of the press officer who landed this extraordinary job, was given the exceptional privilege of a seat on the Prime Minister's plane, did not get to the airport on time, got sacked and never worked as a journalist again.

When at last the traffic started flowing, my nervous state had infected the driver, who got flustered as I was giving him directions to the VIP terminal and took a wrong turn. Finally, we were at the gate, and a police officer came to the window to check who we were. Had Mrs Thatcher's plane taken off? I asked, dreading his reply. No, he said, her car was forty minutes away.

I floated into the VIP lounge on waves of relief, not caring when a Downing Street official pointed out that I was late and told me to go add my passport to the others, which had been collected and placed in an adjoining room. There I saw that they were in two piles. I did not know to which I was supposed to add mine, so I picked up the top one from a pile, flicked it open and discovered to my amazement that I was holding Margaret Thatcher's passport. I could not have been more astonished if I had been holding an artefact from the tomb of Tutankhamun.

I wonder what would have happened if the civil service had forgotten to pack her passport, or a sneak thief had stolen it to keep as a memento, and she had arrived abroad without it. Would an immigration official have refused her entry? I resisted the temptation to steal Margaret Thatcher's passport and quickly put it back where I had found it.

2

SURVIVING CHILDHOOD

The closest vote in Parliament during Margaret Thatcher's premiership was on 22 July 1986 when the Commons decided by 231 to 230 to ban corporal punishment in state schools. The Labour government later extended that law to private schools. But when I was growing up in the 1950s, young children were expected to be sturdy. Beating them, at home or at school, was thought to do them good.

The risks that parents took in the post-war period, ignoring dangers in the home or on the roads, would in our time warrant a visit from social services. I believe my mother was more alert than most to the possibility that something bad might happen to her brood. As she came to collect her sons from nursery school on 6 February 1952, she saw a group of mothers standing outside with shocked and solemn expressions and immediately felt a stab of cold fear that there had been an accident involving the children. A mother stepped towards her and asked in a hushed tone whether she had heard the news.

'The king has died,' she announced sombrely.

My mother tried to hide her relief. 'I was sorry about the king but so glad nothing had happened to either of you,' she told us later.

And yet my earliest memory is from the age of two, of playing near an unguarded free-standing electric heater, whose bars were glowing red, in the children's bedroom in our home in Thames Ditton. My parents used to call it the 'electric fire', but to me it was a disappointing 'fire', not like the exciting one that burned in the hearth in the sitting room, with its fascinating tongues of dancing orange flame. I did not know the word for flame, but I remember wondering whether this so-called fire contained any of 'those things'. As a test, I draped a towel nappy over it and very suddenly discovered that – yes – you can draw flames out from an 'electric fire'. The cries of alarm brought my parents hurrying into the room. I remember them standing in the doorway, after my brother and I had taken refuge on the side of the bed farthest from the door. The nappy lay smouldering on the green linoleum floor.

It seems shocking now that parents would allow two very small boys to play unsupervised near an unguarded electric heater, but that generation had been through the Blitz and the V-1 and V-2 rockets. My father had survived German bombardment in north Africa. My mother had seen what a bomb could do while she was a volunteer fire warden. Those dangers had passed. This was peace time, a time of austerity and rations, when a mother's primary concern was how to make sure there was food on the table. This was no time to start worrying about hazards in the home or on the roads.

I was aged either four or five when I was told that I could go out and play with a friend who lived nearby. I set off alone, dressed in a new pair of green dungarees. I had not gone far before my dungarees had turned into a suit of armour as worn by the Knights of the Round Table, and I was invincible. As I crossed a road, I saw a car coming and deliberately stopped and stood in its path, knowing that a vehicle could not so much as dent my dungarees. The driver braked and sounded his horn. The noise sent me scuttling to the pavement.

That shock did not put me off cars at all. One of my fondest childhood family memories is of my father's old Chevrolet. It had only two seats, but when the boot lid was down, it revealed a small bench which could hold another two passengers, facing backwards. Thus we would set off on family outings with my parents in the car and my brother and I on this bench, with only fresh air between us and the tarmac. If that Chevy had lurched forwards suddenly... but then again, I doubt that it had the horsepower to do anything suddenly.

When I was eight, I was sent to a boarding school called Wells Court, near Tewkesbury, where we were encouraged to climb the tall trees in the school grounds as high as we dared, a policy that remained in place even after one nine-year-old fell and broke his leg. I witnessed him being carried back into the building in tears. We were also allowed to own sheaf knives with four- or six-inch blades. I pestered my mother to buy one for me. Reluctantly, she did but arranged for her father, who was a builder, to blunt the blade. To my shame and embarrassment, I was the only boy in school whose sheaf knife was not sharp enough to cut anything.

There were a small number of day-boys whose families lived close to Wells Court, who would come in for lessons and go home in the evenings. We despised them, because they did not have to endure what we endured, so they formed their own little gang, whose acknowledged leader, in my time, was a boy named Phillips.

My best friend and I spotted Phillips in a field on his parents' farm as we were returning from a walk one Sunday afternoon. We were having a mock argument, and I thought up a great joke: I told my friend that I was going to send Phillips to beat him up – there being no one and nothing so unthreatening as a day-boy. I was surprised when, fifteen years later, for the first and only time in my life, a letter arrived by post from Wells Court, containing the breathless news that the former day-boy Mark Phillips was to marry Princess Anne.

Wells Court was the junior branch of a school for ten- to thirteen-year-olds called Wells House, located in the beauty of the Malvern Hills, where Edward Elgar taught music. Both establishments were run by a character named Alan Darvall, who liked to be known as 'Beak', who took charge of Wells House in 1933, ran it for thirty-five years and would have thought it most odd if anyone had suggested to him that he could keep order without resorting to the riding crop. He is commemorated in the memoir *Under a Mackerel Sky* by the celebrity chef Rick Stein. I remember Christopher Stein, as he then was – a cheerful, rotund redhead who did not stand out as a future high achiever but seemed content to drift along, doing OK and enjoying himself, although he was obviously more knowledgeable than the average child. When I was eight years old, I walked into a classroom where two older boys were joking, one of whom I presume was called Francis, because the other turned to me and announced, without preamble, 'We're Frankenstein – he's Frank, I'm Stein.' I had, at least, heard the name 'Frankenstein'. Some years later, an older boy pointed to a friend and informed me, 'I'm Toscanini; he's Paganini' – and unless my memory is wrong, that also was Christopher Stein. He must have heard adults at home mention those two names and been amused by their similarity. I had certainly not heard of either.

There was no malice in Stein, but there is a passage in his memoir that I did not like, in which he recalled hearing adults describe Alan Darvall as 'a silly old histrionic queen', and he wrote that 'Beak was unmarried and we were all a little scared of him. He was keen on beating us regularly. I managed to avoid it generally, but others were not so fortunate.' In the book, Stein added, 'Beak never touched or spoke to any of us inappropriately and was a thoroughly good headmaster' – but I do not remember reading that in the excerpt published in the *Daily Mail*.

I do not doubt that Beak was gay, but his sexuality was never relevant and he was never inappropriate with the boys in his charge. He did, though, make regular use of corporal punishment, but it was never my impression that he was 'keen' to beat. He was a religious man who knew his Bible, with its adage that 'he that spareth his rod hateth his son', and would have thought it strange if someone had suggested that it is not necessary or desirable to beat young children.

There was one occasion I remember well when he really did not want to wield the riding crop but duty called. Once a term, on 'Expedition Day', the entire school was sent out on long supervised walks across the Malvern Hills and came back, supposedly, tired out and ready for sleep. On the evening of Expedition Day in the winter of 1960, I was cleaning my teeth in a communal bathroom, when I spotted an unusually large tube of bright pink toothpaste, an unfamiliar brand, possibly belonging to a child whose parents were stationed abroad. It seemed perfect for a prank. I stole it, removed the cap, placed the tube in the bed of a boy with whom I shared a dormitory, named Philip, and persuaded the other inmates to jump on their beds. When Philip returned from the bathroom, I told him that we were having a competition to see who could jump highest. He, of course, joined in with gusto, oblivious to the fat, open tube of toothpaste beneath his feet. After lights out, his cries of surprise and protest were heard by a member of staff, and Philip and I were sent downstairs in dressing gowns and slippers to explain to Beak why there were pink smudges all over his pyjamas and a lump of pink toothpaste in his wiry hair. I took full responsibility. Beak was tired out by the long day's tramping over the hills and really did not want to put himself through the exertion of delivering a beating, no matter how richly deserved. 'This is a terrible ending to Expedition Day,' he exclaimed, with self-pity in his voice. He was still complaining over breakfast the following morning.

Though Philip had been ordered to go straight back to bed while I was dealt with, he bravely waited on the staircase to check that I was all right – which makes me sorry to recall that later he became the target of systematic bullying, in which I took part. There were nine of us in the sixth form in our last year. We would see one another six or seven days a week during three long terms and, being sixth-formers, we mostly kept to ourselves. Within this enclosure of swirling friendships and animosities, there was an inbuilt risk that someone would get victimised. Philip had mildly eccentric ways; he was not good at sport, strove very hard to please the teachers and did not know how to gang up on anyone, and he became the constant butt of taunts and cruel jokes. Someone composed a song that mocked his physical appearance and friendlessness. One of the teachers knew he was being victimised and tried to put a stop to it, but he resorted to shouting and issuing threats of punishment, which only hardened hostility to the victim. I believe that I might have responded if an adult had taken me aside to say that what we were doing was cruel and distressing, because there were moments when I half wanted to be friends with him again, but they soon passed. It was safer and more fun to go with the crowd. The only excuse I can offer is that I was twelve years old. I have no memory of ever being implicated in bullying during my teens.

Meanwhile fourteen miles away at Wells Court, where the boys were younger, there was a headmaster who was not a bachelor or 'histrionic queen' but married to an elegant, softly spoken woman, much loved by the pupils, and with a son my age. This family man did something that Beak would never do: he would deal with particularly bad breaches of discipline by making a child pull down his trousers and pants to receive a beating on bare skin. During one communal bath time, he stood at the door, watching and waiting, until a boy named W stepped out of the bath, whereupon he was ordered to proceed to an adjoining room, naked and dripping wet. He reported that a leather strap on wet skin stung worse than a bed of nettles. These beatings were, of course, a regular topic of conversation. I can recall one meal where a boy, who would have been aged nine, made a joke too obscene to be reproduced in print.

Yet he too was a good and kindly headmaster, with a lively sense of humour. He would joke about the beatings he administered, saying that it turned boys into 'striped tigers', which made us laugh. It is wrong to suppose that only sadists or fanatics used to beat young children. The uncomfortable truth was that caring teachers did it, believing without question that it was good for a child's character – and in so doing, they provided cover for others who were not so well intentioned.

One day, when I was twelve or thirteen, I could not help but notice that one of my friends at Wells House had a swelling on his forehead almost the size of half a golf ball. A junior teacher had lost control and hit another boy during class. My friend objected, saying that if the master were to hit him, he would complain to Beak, so the master did just that, with the kind of force that could have concussed a child, then dared him to complain. He took heed and said nothing.

Other teachers would hit the children without fear of being called to account. There was a former colonel at Wells Court who made us address him by his old army rank, who would call a child to the front of the class to be publicly slapped on the back of the leg, so hard that it usually drew tears. There was another who taught mathematics and sport and liked boys who excelled on the sports field but struggled in class. I was the cleverest in the maths class, and hopeless on the rugby pitch, so he really did not like me. We were cleaning up in the washroom when I accidentally spilled paint on another boy, which threw the teacher into a rage. He forced me down over the basin and delivered a vigorous kick on the arse. I did not howl or cry, which only angered him the more. He delivered a second kick. Still no reaction. There he stopped. Perhaps it crossed his mind that injuring me might harm his career.

He had a special favourite, named Richard, whom I thought of as being a reincarnation of Richard III, because he was a bully, but he had the dual virtues of being stupid and good at sport. One evening, that teacher, who had a bachelor's bedroom next to one of the boys' dormitories, heard Richard's voice, talking after lights out. The correct procedure would have been to report the offence to the headmaster, but instead he marched his pet pupil into his bedroom, to chastise him with a cricket stump. In that school, where the oldest pupils were aged ten, and none of us knew anything about adult sexuality, we instinctively understood as the story went around the school that he had acted in that strange way precisely because Richard was his special favourite.

Wells House had a deputy headmaster, Mr Hall, known as 'Stubbs', who claimed that he had killed a German soldier in face-to-face combat during the war. When Beak was absent, or when he pleaded that a sprained shoulder or some other ailment prevented him carrying out the duty of beating, he would hand the responsibility over to Stubbs, who claimed to dislike performing this delegated task; I can remember him telling us that we were wrong to picture him 'grinning behind his cane'. But it was revealing that he felt he had to issue a denial and in such vivid language. Stubbs was short but very powerfully built, and his beatings were greatly feared.

Stubbs ran the school for one whole term while Beak was away and discovered that maintaining discipline was not as easy as it seemed. One Sunday, the whole school was supposed to have walked to a specified destination and back, but the majority decided not to bother going the full distance. All the culprits were ordered to own up and present themselves outside the headmaster's study. Dozens joined the line, with a shame-faced prefect at the front. Stubbs marched angrily along this long queue, spotted one boy laughing and lost his temper. He ordered the child into the study for a beating. Those of us in the long queue heard each blow as it hit its target. The sound of human flesh being struck with a cane can be sickeningly loud. I can still picture that child on his way out, staggering past the long line of his fellow pupils, rubbing his behind, in tears, in pain and publicly humiliated, because he had picked the wrong moment to laugh.

Rick Stein mentioned a feature of Wells House life, that on sunny summer days, we would congregate in the school's outdoor swimming pool, to swim naked, watched over by male staff. This was not as sinister as it may sound, but it meant that any boy who had been beaten in the previous few days would necessarily be displaying the evidence. There was a boy, call him A, who was so unhappy at that school that he made one attempt to run away. At other times, he shielded his happiness behind flippancy, answering every comment directed at him with what sounded like an attempt to make a joke. This habit greatly annoyed Stubbs. When given the opportunity to beat A, he set about it with a vigour that would have had any child screaming in pain. Afterwards, A was obliged to join us for a swimming session. He had wrapped a towel around himself but drew a curious crowd of boys pleading to be able to see whether the beating had really been as severe as was rumoured. With that unhappy smile that was almost always on his face, he reluctantly removed the towel and turned about to display a riotous tapestry of scarlet, black, yellow and blue welts and bruises, which drew cries of wonder and admiration. We had never seen a boy's bum so richly decorated. If Beak had been in charge, he would have put a stop to this show, but Stubbs said nothing. Silently approaching, hands in pockets, he too took a close-up look. I did not have much respect for him. Above the surrounding noise, I exclaimed, 'Aren't they *lovely*, sir?' He walked away slowly, hands deep in his pockets.

This was a school for privileged boys whose parents were paying for their education and knew what was happening but thought it normal and correct. It was excellent cover for the truly sadistic abuse that was taking place in homes for children in care, who had no protection. Fathers tolerated their sons being beaten because they had been beaten when they were boys. A cliché of that time was the adult who proclaimed, 'It never did me any harm.' Some children were terrified by the prospect of a beating, but most treated it as a rite of passage, like having to start the day with a cold bath. 'Did you blub?' was a common question addressed to the victim. He gained kudos if he had emerged dry-eyed. Some boys even boasted that it did not really hurt, it just stung a bit. I heard this from older boys when I first arrived at Wells Court, so when a fellow new boy had been the first of our intake to undergo this experience, I asked if it was true that it did not hurt, it only stung. The child, who was eight, did not know the correct reply and exclaimed truthfully, 'It hurt a jolly lot!'

It took decades to turn public opinion against beating children. Two cultural landmarks of 1968 were the publication, for the first time, of the unexpurgated text of George Orwell's memoir of his time at a preparatory school called St Cyprian's, *Such, Such Were the Joys*, and the cult film *If...*, directed by Lindsay Anderson, which included a depiction of a sadistic beating inflicted by prefects. It was filmed in Cheltenham boys' college, Anderson's old school, where I was also a pupil, so I should add that beatings at Cheltenham were very rare and never carried out by prefects. In 1984, Roald Dahl pitched in with a grim and bitter memoir of his school days.

I was working on *The Journal*, in Newcastle, in 1976, when parents objected after two teenage girls were beaten by the headmaster of a local comprehensive school, as the law allowed. The future Tory

MP Piers Merchant was a fellow reporter, known for his off-colour humour. He remarked, 'If I'd known that it gave me the right to beat little girls on their bottoms, I'd have taken up teaching.'

He was joking, but he illuminated a truth. It was not just the pain involved that made this practice obnoxious; what was every bit as sinister was the pleasure some people found in doing it.

3

THE END OF PIERS

There is a cliché that all political careers end in failure, but not many fail as spectacularly as that of my aforementioned colleague, Piers Merchant. Now that his name has cropped up, I will complete his story.

I did not take to him when I first saw him across the open-plan newsroom at *The Journal*, in Newcastle upon Tyne, when he was twenty-four, the youngest journalist on the subs' table. He was keen, alert and anxious to please the editor and anyone else in authority. There had been a journalists' strike at my previous newspaper, in Slough, so well supported that the editor was going to have to produce a newspaper single-handed, until to his surprise, one subeditor, a member of the National Union of Journalists, crossed a picket line to join him. Piers had a tight, thin, pointed face, just like that sub's. I guessed that if there were ever an NUJ strike at *The Journal*, he would break it.

I was wrong. There was a strike after I left, and Piers did not merely support it, he led it, as Father of the NUJ Chapel. Leading a strike can be a gamble. The union representative might be swept away in the next round of redundancies, or his skills as a leader and negotiator might make such a big impression that he is promoted. Piers advanced quickly from strike leader to news editor.

I liked him once I came to know him. I had an unusual reason for being very grateful to him. My twenty-eighth birthday had sent me into a spiral of gloom. Twenty-eight seemed old, too old ever to advance onto a national newspaper. I feared that I was trapped in provincial journalism for life. Living alone in a single rented room, I went through long nights of sleeplessness, mornings when lead weights seemed to hold me in bed, days permeated with a feeling of failure. I struggled to keep working as normal in the office, where no one seemed to notice that anything was wrong, except Piers, who took one look as I was walking past the subs' desk, exclaimed that I looked terrible and asked what was the matter. I lied. I said that I was fine, but I never forgot that moment of observant kindness.

We discovered a shared interest in politics. During long conversations, the opinions he expressed were tolerant and middle of the road. When the Social Democratic Party was launched a few years later, it struck me as being the place for people like Piers. By then, I had been out of touch with him for a while and did not know that he was an active Conservative. At certain times in his political career, he talked the talk of an English nationalist and borderline racist, yet I do not believe he was either. I think, fundamentally, he was frivolous. There are people who think that politics is all a game. Piers was one of them. That was his undoing.

He had terrible judgement, which took him across the thin border between edgy humour into bad taste, or worse. He liked to pretend to be a Gestapo officer and would conduct mock investigations into his fellow reporters on *The Journal*, always concluding that they were subversives who should be shot. One Christmas, during an office pantomime, he announced, in a mock German accent, 'You know I haff vays of making you laugh: I just haven't found them yet.' While he was a reporter, most of his peer group found his humour amusing, if peculiar. It was not funny when he was news editor. One evening, he forgot to lock the filing cabinet reserved for his personal use, and journalists on the night shift discovered personal files Piers kept on his staff. One was described as 'manic depressive', another as a 'plagiarist'. The municipal correspondent, Bryan Christie, was said to be unable to 'dig for stories' – in recognition of which, when he left soon afterwards, his colleagues presented him with a garden spade. The worst discovery, by far, was a cartoon Piers had drawn of himself as a Nazi concentration camp guard watching as his staff were marched into a gas chamber. One of them had Polish anteced- ents. Two were Jews.

During the 1983 general election, I volunteered to act as press officer for the Labour Party in the marginal seat of Newcas- tle Central. The Labour candidate was a lifelong friend named Nigel Todd, a Newcastle councillor whose daughter, Selina Todd, achieved eminence as a historian, academic, writer, socialist and feminist, and who was targeted by trans activists months before J. K. Rowling entered that bear pit. The Conservative candidate was, by coincidence, Piers Merchant. It was a bonus for the Tories to have this media-savvy candidate, who had once led a strike, in a region where unions were strong and Conservatives were thin on the ground. But while the election was under way, someone turned up an old piece of campaign literature, dating from 1970, when an ultra right-wing fringe party had contested a seat in Piers's home town of Nottingham. By law, election leaflets have to bear the name and address of the election agent. The name on this tatty leaflet was P. R. G. Merchant; the address was his parents' home.

The possibility that he had had links with the far right was investigated thoroughly, without turning up any evidence, apart from that old leaflet. He flatly denied knowing how his name came to be on it. The connection appears to have been through Air Vice-Marshal Don Bennett, a man with a very fine war record and a very dubious penchant for supporting far-right fringe groups. Piers had met him while he was a student at Durham University and, having more curiosity than judgement, must have let himself be drawn in to something he should have avoided. In a normal year, the mere suspicion of a link to the far right could have ended his chances of ever entering Parliament, but this was 1983, when Labour was losing seats to the Conservatives like never before, and he was elected.

His four years on the back benches were spent in semi-obscurity, except for one occasion when he made the national news, by mistake. He was interviewed by a local television station in September 1985 and made a few unexceptional comments about the level of unemployment in the north-east. By sheer mischance, this was the day when Margaret Thatcher paid a rare visit to the region, and when challenged about the rising jobless figures, she retorted sharply that the way to attract investment to the region was by 'not always standing there as moaning minnies. Now stop it!' Inevitably, the bulletins cut away from her to Piers Merchant's conciliatory platitudes, making it appear that he was deliberately contradicting his leader, which he never intended. In those few minutes, his chances of being a minister in her government went down the plug hole.

After losing Newcastle Central in 1987, he made a comeback in

1992 as MP for Beckenham, a solidly safe Tory seat in south London, which, with a little more care, he could have held for the rest of his life. I was glad to see him back in the Commons, because I was short of contacts in the Tory Party and Piers loved to gossip. He never achieved any office higher than being an unpaid parliamentary private secretary to a middle-ranking minister – but just as it was all over for the Conservative government, he rocketed to fame.

Apparently, the first hint of danger came at a rally addressed by Piers Merchant and Eric Forth, Tory MPs from neighbouring south London constituencies. A young woman in a short skirt was in the front row, giving them admiring looks. Afterwards, Forth remarked to his fellow MP, 'That woman is trouble!'

Generally, a highly sexed, adolescent woman is 'trouble' for a middle-aged man only if he actively wants to be troubled, which Piers evidently did. As the 1997 general election was in full flow, *The Sun* ran six pages of photographs of him with this seventeen-year-old 'nightclub hostess' in a park, in his constituency, in the midst of the campaign, looking for all the world as if he was enjoying fellatio in the fresh air.

For the rest of his life, Piers asserted that the camera lied, that he and the teenager were only being affectionate and that *The Sun* had paid her to entrap him. I think he was telling the truth. It was obviously a set-up: tabloid photographers do not randomly lurk in bushes in public parks hoping to capture MPs having rumpy-pumpy out in the open with campaign volunteers. There is no reason to doubt that the young woman was bribed by *The Sun* to simulate sex, but it is not plausible that she would risk arrest by actually performing a sexual act, knowing there was a camera nearby. Even so, Piers's behaviour was staggeringly foolish. For months, ever since John Major had launched an unfortunate campaign slogan 'Back to Basics', which, according to the accompanying spin, was to include an emphasis on sexual morality, the tabloids had delighted in exposing the extra-marital goings-on of Tory MPs. The Piers story was a classic of that genre: a Tory MP seemingly so horny that he could not resist having sex with a teenager in a public place in his constituency in mid-election. 'What on earth does he think he's doing?' is the reaction that John Major recorded in his memoirs, where he added that 'a few million other Britons, over their breakfast newspapers, must have been spluttering in similar vein'.

Not for the first time, I had Piers to thank for adding to the gaiety of my life. Of all the stories arising from the 1997 general election that I covered for *The Observer*, this was by a very long way the most fun. The Beckenham Conservative Association was advised from on high to deselect Piers and find another candidate promptly, but its officers had no intention of doing what they were told and were remarkably willing to say so, even to a journalist from the liberal press. After a special meeting on a Saturday afternoon, Piers emerged triumphant, with his wife Helen at his side, and with his constituency sticking by him, he was comfortably re-elected in a year when so many other Tory MPs went down to defeat.

I rang him a few months later to suggest that we meet up during the Conservative annual conference. He was disappointingly vague about whether he would even be there. Later, I understood why.

A month after the election, he heard from a journalist that the teenager who featured in those damning photographs was full of regret, angry with *The Sun*, wishing she could meet him to explain. They met and somehow, together, they decided that since the whole country thought that they had been having an affair, they may as well do that. But they needed somewhere private, so Piers turned for assistance to an old acquaintance, an antiques dealer named Anthony Gilberthorpe.

Gilberthorpe was a known liar. He once sued a news agency and three newspapers who had reported that he was being treated for HIV. Unusually, the journalists claimed that their information came from Gilberthorpe himself, who had made an unprompted call to the news agency to tell them that he was receiving treatment in New York. Gilberthorpe denied making the call, denied that he was ill and denied that he was gay. The jury believed him and awarded damages, but a year later, the case took an unusual turn when the newspapers appealed and produced three witnesses to testify that Gilberthorpe was indeed gay and had therefore lied in court. The verdict was overturned.

That was not the only strange story about him to have appeared in print, and yet it was to this erratic liar that Piers Merchant entrusted his reputation. When his wife thought he was away in Blackpool, at the Conservative annual conference, he was actually holed up in Gilberthorpe's flat in York indulging in the delights of the flesh with a willing teenager.

He emerged to the shock of his life. A *Sunday Mirror* reporter confronted him with a verbatim record of his and the young woman's pillow talk, with accompanying pictures. Piers told me that he went cold with horror when he saw the transcript, because it was so 'chillingly accurate'. Gilberthorpe had instilled a recording device in the room Piers and the young woman were using. He sold the story for a reputed £25,000.

There was worse. A television channel owned by the *Mirror* had a film of the couple, which they broadcast, without regard to the impact this must have had on the teenager whose naked body they were putting on display.

Piers was concerned enough about her to insist that she return to south London with him, so that he could help protect her from the tabloid hordes, who staked his house and would have staked out hers if she had gone back alone. When he or his wife left home, they slipped out by the back and climbed across neighbours' gardens to avoid the press pack at their front door – a story I used four years later when I wrote the novel *Innocent in the House*. Piers even offered to show me their route, for added authenticity.

He told me without self-pity that he would never live this story down. He immediately resigned from Parliament, which did not deter the *Sunday Mirror* from running its exposé for another two weeks. He must have foreseen that it was not going to be easy to find another job as he joined an already crowded field of unemployed former Tory MPs searching for work, in a year that the market value of access to Conservative politicians had never been lower. Hoping to return to journalism, he wrote an account of his travails for the *Daily Mail*. When he opened the newspaper, he discovered that his prose had been rewritten. He told me that upset him more than giving up his seat. He managed to land one good job in the City but then lost it and was in and out of work. He was reduced to asking me to act as his referee, which I agreed to do.

Suddenly, in 2004, Piers found a new niche, as chief executive of the UK Independence Party. He organised UKIP's startlingly successful campaign in the 2004 election to the European Parliament, during an interlude when Nigel Farage had been supplanted as leader by a former Conservative MP named Roger Knapman. This might seem to indicate that Piers was on the anti-EU right wing of the Tory Party all along, but I do not think so. The Maastricht Treaty was the issue that divided left from right in the Conservatives under John Major. The crucial vote was on 22 July 1993, when the Tory rebels joined Labour in inflicting a defeat on the government, which set off a confidence vote that might have forced a general election. On that occasion, Piers loyally voted with the government, as he almost always did. I think he took the UKIP job because he was on good terms with Knapman, his convictions were forever flexible and he needed the salary.

During the July 2009 European election, I thought it might be worth talking to Nigel Farage, who by now had been reinstated as UKIP's leader. I was working for *The Independent* and was not sure that he would want to spend time with someone from a liberal, pro-EU newspaper, but I rang him anyway. He asked where I was. I said I was in the Commons. He replied that he was in a pub a few minutes' walk away and invited me to join him. After consuming an ocean of alcohol, we took a train to the south coast, where Farage went into the streets to waylay passing shoppers and share his opinions about the evils of the EU. After a ride back to London, he invited me to meet the staff at UKIP's head office. But there was no sign of Piers Merchant. When I asked after him, Farage's chatty friendliness dropped for a moment, as he told me brusquely that Piers had been exposed as a 'political intriguer'.

I was keen to hear the story from the other side, anticipating that Piers, being an inveterate gossip, would willingly give me all manner of dirt on Nigel Farage. I phoned, I texted, I sent an email. I was mystified that my old friend did not reply – until I learnt that he was in a hospice, dying of cancer.

The initial story that broke during the election was sensational – it was a talking point – but it was not a matter of public interest if a candidate and an unpaid volunteer on his campaign chose to have a kiss in a public park. The second story was more to Piers's discredit, not just because this time he undoubtedly was having an illicit, secret affair with someone scarcely a third his age but because it was reported that he had hired her as an assistant, for which, if true, she would have been paid from public funds, though not for long.

But to put it in perspective, there is no reason she was tricked or coerced into joining him for that ill-fated tryst in County Durham. There have been too many stories of young women, and some young men, who have secured jobs in Parliament, only to have to deal with the unwanted advances of a lecherous employer, but this was not an example of that. Piers Merchant was a fool but not a villain. It speaks well of him that he was concerned for the teenager's welfare as his political career came down in flames. This was a titillating story because it was at the edge of what is acceptable in the judgement of a permissive society.

This story would be considered even more salacious in the misnamed 'Swinging Sixties', where even something as innocuous as a romance between people of different ethnic backgrounds encountered stern disapproval, except possibly in the seedier parts of London, as I learnt when I was seventeen.

4

SEX, RACE AND PUBLIC SCHOOLS

When sexual intercourse began, in 1963, it was too late for Philip Larkin but too soon for British public schools, who housed their charges in dormitories for thirty-nine weeks of the year, denied them contact with the opposite sex and warned that they could do themselves permanent damage if they masturbated, alone or in company.

It was not that college boys were kept in ignorance of how to make babies. Far from it. Our syllabus at Cheltenham College included nine hours of lectures from a visiting psychiatrist named Dr Matthews, subversively known as the Dirty Doc, who used slides to explain the physical differences between men and women and drew a diagram to illustrate how male and female psychology differed. The diagram was a circle, representing the home. Inside was the woman, the domesticated cave dweller; outside was man, the hunter. He also told us that we all passed through five stages from infancy to adulthood – love of mother, love of self, love of I forget what, love of friends of the same sex and love of someone of the opposite sex. Stage four was the dangerous one. The reason some people became gay, he explained, was that they had engaged in forbidden sex during stage four and were stuck on it for ever, like sinners in the fires of hell, because everyone's first sexual experience left a permanent imprint. Pre-marital sex was dangerous and cruel, he warned: dangerous because if your first experience of sex was furtive and guilt-ridden, then for the rest of your life you would be hooked on furtive, guilt-ridden sex; and to demonstrate its cruelty, the Doc showed us a photograph of the hollow-eyed face of a wretched baby born outside wedlock. The good news: sex within marriage was the heaven-like reward for those who waited.

Beyond the boundaries of the college, there was rock music, fashion and free love. Within the boundaries of the college, sexuality was as in Victoria's reign.

In the autumn of 1964, a scandalous report reached the school authorities. One of the kitchen staff – known in the local slang as a 'college maid' – had struck up a friendship with one of the boys. She had probably left school at fourteen to work in a kitchen; he was receiving an elite education at his parents' expense. The prefect in charge of our boarding house gave us a homily at our evening assembly. 'Personally,' he said, 'I can think of nothing more disgusting than a college maid.'

I do not know what happened to the girl, whether she was sacked, or perhaps warned never to look twice at a college boy again, on pain of dismissal. She did not identify the offending youth, but the school authorities had a good idea who it was. He was a quiet, strong-willed, introverted fifteen-year-old who hated boarding school and hated being told what to do, but whose brooding looks exerted a fascination over teenage girls. His name was Dai.

The following summer, it was reported that a youth wearing the uniform of a college boy had been spotted across town, within the grounds of Cheltenham Ladies' College. That institution was famous for the care it took to protect the virginity of its young charges. Its founder was Dorothea Beale, a renowned Victorian pioneer of female education. The girls knew a rhyme about her and that other trailblazer, Frances Buss. There are different versions of the rhyme, but the one they told me went:

> Miss Beale and Miss Buss, they were not like us.
> Miss Buss and Miss Beale love's pangs did not feel.

There was a recording made in 1962 of a song about how 'I went to school in Cheltenham, at a fashionable ladies' college', sung with a cut-glass English accent by a Chinese actress named Tsai Chin, who later appeared in a couple of Bond films. If the lyrics of the song were to be believed, Cheltenham Ladies' College was a den of refined sexual licentiousness and criminality.

The joke, of course, was that nowhere was so free from vice as Cheltenham Ladies' College. Its inmates were not allowed to venture beyond the school boundaries alone. They could go into specified parts of town, dressed in their pea-green uniforms, provided they went in pairs and were never further apart than the width of Cheltenham High Street. They were emphatically not allowed visits from young men. In the summer of 1966, a few months after I had left Cheltenham, a member of staff at the ladies' college heard a suspicious noise one evening, searched the dormitories and found that two senior girls were missing. The principal, Margaret Hampshire, rang David Ashcroft, headmaster of the boys' college, and at her insistence, he rang the masters in charge of the nine boarding houses, ordering that each was to be searched for any sign of girls. The truants were discovered having coffee and conversation with two eighteen-year-olds, both of whom I knew well. The young women were expelled and sent home. Hampshire demanded that Ashcroft inflict the same penalty on the young men, which he did. One returned to a disturbed domestic set-up: his father had been sent to prison for embezzlement, his mother was suing for divorce and relatives had clubbed together to pay his school fees. Whether they got money off for his truncated final term, I could not say.

Dai was never caught having a forbidden liaison with anyone from the ladies' college. He was accused of being the mystery youth spotted on their premises but denied it. He was lying. I know because I once accompanied him. The girls slept two to a room on the ground floor, so we climbed through the window and sat on their beds, and they sat up in bed, in their nightdresses. It was very exciting and very innocent. The authorities were also convinced that he was lying, but since they could not prove it, he was asked directly whether he was the youth who had been seen hanging around the previous year with a 'college maid'. He owned up to that. When the interrogation was over, he came to me, with tears welling, to say that he had been expelled. The next day, he was put on a train home to Aberystwyth.

That drama was played out in the same year – 1965 – that Hampshire and Ashcroft decided on something revolutionary: they agreed to organise a school dance. Young ladies in their final or penultimate school year would be transported by coach to the boys' college, where an equal number of young gentlemen would be waiting. The dancing would take place in the college dining hall. The young men were told that they would be permitted to take their dance partners out to sample the evening air, so long as they did not stray off college grounds or into any other building.

Public school boys were encouraged to compete all day, in every way, and in that spirit, the school dance was looked upon as a kind of sports day, where the winners would claim the best-looking girls. While others were excited, I was dreading the evening. I had never made the effort to compete. I had not felt that I needed to, because of my unusual status as a scholarship boy. Every day, I encountered physical reminders that I was special. The peg on which I hung my coat, where I sat during the quiet hour in the early evening or where my bed was positioned in the shared dormitory all reflected my status as a scholar.

Before I arrived, the head of the mathematics department had persuaded David Ashcroft to let him experiment by taking a child out of the normal streaming system and giving him one-on-one tutoring from the age of thirteen, so that he win a mathematics scholarship to one of the Oxbridge colleges at sixteen. It would be a good advertisement for the school. I was the first on whom this scheme was tried out – most unsuccessfully, in my case. Public opinion revered the school's sporting heroes above all others; nothing was more prestigious than to be in the Rugby First XV, competing against teams from rival public schools. The kindest word that could be used to describe my sporting ability would be 'mediocre', but I was officially just about the cleverest boy in the school, so what did it matter? I got out of playing cricket by volunteering to act as scorer for the First XI, on the grounds that I could add up faster than our top batsman could score runs.

Cheltenham had a strong military tradition, which they upheld by making the boys all dress up as soldiers and march here and there every Wednesday afternoon. Fortuitously, I managed to escape that too, because when I was fifteen, a petrol lorry ran over my right leg, which put me in Cheltenham General Hospital for three weeks, where I was treated with great kindness by staff and adult patients. The person closest to me in age was Student Nurse Bailey. One day, she mischievously ruffled my hair. Another day, as I was being taken to surgery for one of five operations I underwent, I asked her to do it again, which she did, giving me a naughty, twinkling grin. Sadly it landed her in trouble with matron, who gave her a ferocious telling-off as they wheeled me into surgery, ostensibly because her mask was not fitted properly but actually, I suspect, because she was not supposed to be so familiar with a patient.

I could not help but notice that these people were not like public school boys, constantly competing. By the time I hobbled back to school on crutches, I had lost interest in the whole scheme of advancement that the head of mathematics had planned for me. I did not want to be their prize exhibit who took the Oxbridge entrance at sixteen: I wanted to go to university with people my own age. I was also armed with a solid excuse for getting out of the activities I most disliked. A friendly consultant gave me a chit saying that because of my damaged foot, I should not be made to wear rugby or army boots. Cheltenham could not have me marching around in ordinary shoes, so I played no further in any competition to be the school's smartest, fittest soldier.

But there was no avoiding the competition that the school dance would surely turn out to be. We assembled under starter's orders on one side of the dining hall floor. It was a huge room with a high ceiling, not dissimilar to the dining hall in Hogwarts, as depicted in the Harry Potter movies, minus the owls and, on this occasion, minus the tables. We were dressed smartly casual, with green jackets instead of dark suits. The girls filed in nervously. They had been allowed to discard their green uniforms and had gone to great pains to dress up. The music struck up and there was a thunder of feet on wood as the more confident of the boys raced across the floor to grab the prettiest dancing partner. I watched, as if I was there only as a spectator, too cowardly to enter the race, and was mildly amused to spot that one particularly stunning girl, who was obviously aware of her good looks, was approached not by a prefect or a member of the Rugby First XV but by a lad with nothing much to commend him other than a self-assured disrespect for authority. He took her by the hand and marched to the centre of the room where everyone could see his prize. Others were not far behind. Soon, the floor was a mass of young bodies straining to enjoy themselves.

I could not spend all evening standing in the shadows. There were still a few disappointed girls waiting for one of the cowards to pluck up courage and ask them to dance, but I was in the firm grip of indecision and wandered around the darkened edges of the hall, hoping not to be noticed. Suddenly I spotted a gorgeous teenager, beautifully turned out, with a rose in her hair, sitting on her own, back to the wall, looking angry and exasperated. No one was talking to her; no one had asked her to dance; no one was likely to. She was black.

There were no black boys in the dance hall. It was not that David Ashcroft operated a full colour ban. His successor, Richard Morgan, did. In 1989, I was invited back to talk to the school about journalism and noted that the audience was exclusively white. I mentioned this to Morgan, who told me, without a trace of embarrassment, that the school had applications from around the world to send black or Asian boys to be educated there, but they turned them all down, because, he said, if he let one in, they would soon flood the place. Very soon after he shared this pearl of wisdom with me, the Cheltenham Conservative Association went into convulsions because the party chairman, Chris Patten, was determined to see a black Conservative returned to Parliament for the first time and had imposed a barrister named John Taylor, the son of Jamaican immigrants, as the prospective candidate in Cheltenham. Some of Cheltenham's long-standing, paid-up Conservatives had no compunction about expressing their disgust, on camera. In 1992, the Conservatives were defeated by a Liberal Democrat in Cheltenham, for the first time in eighty-two years.

David Ashcroft was more laissez-faire. He let each housemaster decide, boarding house by boarding house, whether to operate a colour bar. Our house, Cheltondale, was whites only. Jews were accepted, though they had to put up with the constant antisemitism. In school slang, the word 'jew' was a verb, meaning to cheat – as 'he was caught jewing in exams'. At meal times, boys were free to choose where they sat, but if a senior arrived late and wanted a place already taken by someone junior, he would tap the younger boy on the shoulder and order him to move. This procedure was known as 'jewing out'. Other houses had opened their doors to a limited number of boys from wealthy Asian families, including a reputed morganatic son of the King of Thailand. During my time, the housemaster in charge of Christowe house announced that, for the first time, a non-white pupil would be joining them in the coming year. As he relayed this news, someone at the back exclaimed, 'Oh god!' I knew the youth who shouted that. He was a nice lad, who played guitar in Cheltenham College's first rock band, who only wanted to be popular. In the 1960s, even nice people were racist.

There she was, this lovely teenager, who had taken such care over her appearance, who might just as well have been invisible for all the chance she had that anyone would appreciate her. I wish I could truthfully record that this was the moment when I stepped forth to take a stand against racism – a word that was not then in common usage. The truth was that I did not have any formed opinions on the subject. But spotting her gave me an idea: I thought I could ask her for the first dance and use the time to work out a plan to get me through the rest of the evening. She needed no persuading: once asked, she was out of her seat and onto the dance floor like a released spring.

My early attempts at socialising with teenage girls were often crashing disasters, because I tried too hard to impress or else suffered a collapse of confidence that left me red-faced and barely coherent. But on this occasion, I was assuming we would share one dance and go our separate ways, so did not try to make conversation. I was not aware that I was being closely scrutinised. She broke the silence by telling me her name and asking mine. Neither of her names sounded English. I asked her nationality. She told me she was Nigerian.

We danced on.

'Which are you interested in? Sport or cars?'

'Why?'

'I was told that all boys are interested in sport or cars.'

'I'm sorry. I'm not interested in either.'

That earned an approving nod. If she had asked, I might have told her that I was fascinated by nineteenth-century Russian novels, particularly anything by Tolstoy. Luckily, she did not ask. Instead, after another pause, the exchanges moved on to round three.

'I heard that the boys are having a competition to see who can go furthest tonight? Is that true?'

It was interesting that she should ask. If she had heard that rumour, presumably it had gone all around the ladies' college, but I doubted that there were many other girls on that dance floor – if any – with the nerve to ask their dancing partners about it.

I told her that there was a competition going on around us. I probably conveyed that I was not trying to take part in it, without actually saying so.

She must have been dreading this event more than I was, but unbeknown to me, she had now worked out a way to make it bearable. While I was wondering how I was going to fill the rest of the evening, this strong-willed girl had resolved that I was spending it with her. She asked if I wanted to continue dancing or sit and talk. I opted for conversation and found her take on life so interesting that I forgot my intention to abandon her to search for another dance partner. It was a mild summer evening. I suggested a stroll around college grounds. We were walking by one of the boarding houses when some younger boys leant out of a window and shouted stupid comments. I reacted angrily, but she said I should ignore them.

We made our way to a walled-off vegetable garden on college grounds that almost no one visited, where we could lie comfortably on a grass path. Doc Matthews had told us that women did not experience any form of physical attraction to men and that such pleasure as they derived from sex was emotional, not physical. I now found out that the Dirty Doc was not the expert he claimed to be. And I made another discovery that evening, for which I had

had no forewarning. I learnt that if a young male is powerfully stimulated, his testicles become full and swollen, and if they do not discharge their payload, the effect can be quite painful. As we were saying farewell beside the coach that was returning our guests to the ladies' college, I suddenly emitted a loud groan and almost doubled up. She asked in alarm what was wrong. I was too embarrassed to explain.

The evening held other incidents that were neither funny nor pleasant. Just before the ladies were escorted to their waiting coaches, we were all required to reassemble in the dining hall and file out in couples, so that David Ashcroft could bid us goodnight. He did not have a high opinion of me. I suspect he was worried about the school's financial situation, which would explain his strange decision to give the film director Lindsay Anderson permission to use the premises as a set for the film *If...*, to make what he must have known would be a derogatory portrayal of the public school system. From the school reports which my mother kept in a file, I can infer his growing anger that the school was not getting its money's worth from the scholarship I had been awarded. They bristled with comments such as 'he is too lazy and too moody to make full use of his abilities'.

The master in charge of our boarding house, Gordon Wallace-Hadrill, respectfully disagreed with the headmaster. He was new to this role. One of his first responsibilities was to arrange for Cheltondale to perform a play in front of the whole school. It was important to him that it was a success, and he asked me to read as many playscripts as I could and advise him on a suitable choice. As usual, I did not do exactly as asked. After the summer holidays, I returned with a script I had written and suggested we perform it. It was a childish effort but went down a storm with the school. A handful of boys who had left came back to watch the performance. One of them, who was earning good money in the City, hired a hotel room and bought a bottle of whiskey. After the performance, I drank so much of it that I was ill, and to this day, the smell of whiskey makes me nauseous. But Wallace-Hadrill was delighted that he had something to boast about that no other housemaster could match.

But Ashcroft was not impressed. I was supposed to be studying mathematics with my scholarship, not dabbling in literature. When he learnt that I had also written a novel about college life that was being passed around, he read it and summoned me to his grace-and-favour home to tell me what a shoddy piece of work it was, a 'worm's eye view of worms'. My novel was, indeed, as childish as the play, but teenagers have done worse things than write bad plays and bad novels.

Why I ever cared about that arrogant man's opinion is beyond me, but as we were saying goodbye at the end of the dance, I hoped for a hint of his approval that I had had the good manners to not leave the only black girl in the hall to sit alone all evening. Instead, he bestowed a beaming smile on the couple ahead of us in the queue, which suddenly disappeared when he saw the two of us together. I thought I saw a flash of anger. He shook my hand coldly and turned to bestow a nice smile on the next couple in the queue.

Earlier, there had been a more serious portent of trouble to come. As we were leaving the privacy of that walled garden, we encountered someone else who had persuaded his dance partner to sample the evening air. This character – call him W – was a bully. It amused him to target a younger Asian boy, whose name, if I remember correctly, was Kassim. He tested Kassim's sense of humour by bombarding him with racist insults, which the younger boy was supposed to accept as witty banter. One day, W arrived in Cheltondale shaking with laughter, because while walking along College Road, he had spotted an Asian boy on the far side, whom he took to be Kassim, and had shouted, 'Fuck off, you black bastard' – then noticed that he was addressing a complete stranger. He shared this hilarious tale with anyone who would listen. When W spotted us, he grinned triumphantly and his shoulders shook with silent laughter. It was another fine joke for him to spread around. I overheard him declaring, 'The funniest thing I have ever seen was Andy Mac coming out of the cabbage garden with *a very dishevelled* …!' The sentence ended with a monosyllabic and highly offensive noun. And he was lying about her being 'dishevelled'.

Not everyone's reaction was at that level of ignorance. I was touched when one of the school's sporting heroes, who was due to be captain of the Rugby First XV, took me aside to say quietly that he could not see anything wrong in having a black girlfriend. But that was unusual. In no time, my dance companion had a new nickname. She was 'Limpopo', after the reference in Rudyard Kipling's *Just So Stories* to 'the great grey-green, greasy Limpopo River'. The height of the season's wit was to ask me, jauntily, 'How's Limpopo?' By the end of the summer term, I was so battered by sneering comments that when one boy caught my eye and smiled at me in a crowded room, I cut him dead, thinking that he was about to make some obnoxious comment. Only later did it occur to me that, for all I knew, he was just being friendly. During the summer holiday I was at a party in Hitchin, a hundred miles from Cheltenham, when someone I barely knew asked if it was true that I had spent the school dance in the company of a black girl. There was a ladies' college student living nearby, spreading the news. The '60s may have been swinging, but in British society, racism was so normal that there was not even a word for it in common usage, until the civil rights marches in the USA threw up the term 'racialist'.

I was hoping my dance partner and I could meet during the holiday, though inviting her to Hitchin was out of the question. If my father had known in 1965 that I was exchanging gushing love letters with a Nigerian teenager, he would have delivered a stern homily on why separate races should stay separate. Almost every middle-class parent would have reacted in the same way, in the 'Swinging '60s'.

A better idea, it seemed, would be to meet in London, where my dance companion's family lived. I suggested this by letter. She wrote back, regretfully, to say that her father had prohibited it.

The only remaining possibility was to invite her to tea with me in Cheltondale during my final school term, thereby making her, perhaps, the first black African to enter that old building, but I did not know if I could risk it. It was a large building, with a long narrow corridor on the ground floor. The small study allocated to me was at the far end, around a corner, opposite the shower room and next to the small gym where boys changed for games. Although the loud-mouthed W had left, I feared that if she were made to walk that long gauntlet, someone might make some audible sneering comment, or while she was in my study, one of the younger boys might shout 'Limpopo', or worse, through the closed door.

So I took the coward's road. I wrote to her, calling an end to our short romance, offering some threadbare explanation. I did not refer to her race; it was not a subject we ever mentioned. I got a sweet letter in reply, thanking me for my tact, and had an awkward encounter with her weeks later, browsing in W. H. Smith. I did not know what to say, because I was heartily ashamed that I had allowed the fear of ridicule to destroy our relationship. She remarked that we seemed to have nothing to say any more. We never spoke again.

Three years later, I was in London with a girlfriend named Mandy, who suggested that we call on her aunt and uncle. When we arrived at their door, she was told via the intercom to come in by herself, leaving me to kick my heels on the pavement for what seemed like an interminable wait. When I was eventually admitted to their sitting room, the atmosphere was uncomfortably tense. After we left, Mandy reluctantly explained the problem. On her previous visit, she had brought along a black boyfriend. I had been left outside firstly so that her uncle and aunt could check that I was white, and secondly to tell Mandy how deeply offended they were that she had contaminated their sitting room. The only thing about this story that surprised me was how daring Mandy had been to introduce a black man to members of her family.

That was in 1968, the year when Martin Luther King was assassinated and Enoch Powell delivered an inflammatory speech in Birmingham.

5

ENOCH AND SIR EDWARD

Once every few years, someone crawls out of the woodwork to assert that 'Enoch was right' – usually in blissful ignorance of what the late Enoch Powell stood for. Nigel Farage told the magazine *Total Politics* in October 2008 that Powell was not 'racist in any way at all', as he explained why Powell was his political hero. I also remember the story of a quietly unambitious, not very sociable journalist named Nigel Hastilow, who covered the 1987 general election as political editor of the *Birmingham Post* and was adopted as Conservative candidate for Halesowen – until, in 2007, David Cameron made him resign for having written in a local newspaper that Powell had rightly warned about the impact of 'uncontrolled immigration'.

Powell did not become a household name by telling immigration officers to smarten up their act. He advocated something much nastier. Ethnic cleansing is a modern name for Powellism. He was sly enough to avoid saying how it was to be done, but he was proposing that the government should see to it that thousands of non-white immigrants departed British shores. He and his kind did not use the harsh word 'deported'. To soften the impact of what they planned, they said their victims were to be 'repatriated' or 'resettled' – but the meaning was the same: they were to be got rid of. Speaking in Eastbourne, in November 1968, seven months after he had delivered his infamous 'rivers of blood' speech, Powell proposed that there should be a Ministry of Repatriation, whose task would be 'the resettlement of a substantial proportion of the Commonwealth immigrants in Britain ... on the scale which the urgency of the situation demands' – because, he maintained, someone whose skin was brown or black could never be English. 'The West Indian or Asian does not, by being born in England,' he said, 'become an Englishman. In law he becomes a United Kingdom citizen by birth; in fact he is a West Indian or an Asian still.'

The polite fiction was that this programme would be 'voluntary', as if thousands of immigrants were ready to take the plane back to the Indian subcontinent or the Caribbean islands, if only the government would pay their fare. After 1970, Edward Heath's government did in fact offer immigrants cash inducements to return to their countries of origin. Four years after the scheme's introduction, Parliament was informed that the offer had been taken up by 144 families, made up of 491 people, at an average cost to the Exchequer of £654 per family. One beneficiary, Mohammed Khan, had accepted the government's money, returned to Pakistan, changed his mind and was back in the UK.

It was well understood at the time that if the government was going to make any serious inroads into the number of immigrants in the UK, they would have to use force. Late in 1973, I went to a meeting at which a local councillor made his pitch to be adopted as Conservative candidate for Eton and Slough in the impending general election. The meeting was organised by the Monday Club, which was then the largest organised group within the Conservative Party. Knowing his audience, the wannabe candidate began by praising General Pinochet and the Chilean Army officers who had risen up and cornered their elected socialist President, Salvador Allende, who committed suicide, and interned thousands of his supporters. He went on to express keen support for the government's policy of repatriation – but added that it should be 'voluntary'. That was when the jeering and barracking began. He had lost the room and lost the nomination.

It would be wrong to think that Powell's support was confined to a racist fringe. At middle-class drinks parties you would hear Powell's name pronounced with a reverence matched by no other politician. I had a long talk with a neighbour, a gentle, tolerant man, a loving husband and father, who had spent time in Africa, who was in awe of the 'courage' of Enoch Powell. I was twenty years old, he was more than twice my age, but he was at least prepared to listen as I struggled to put the case that British society would be the better for the contribution made by immigrants, to which he responded, 'If they have something to contribute, why can't they do it in their own countries?' In the end, he chuckled and said, 'I'm a terrible old racialist.'

Someone like that would have been repelled by a street thug shouting racist slogans, but Powell was not a rabble rouse, like Oswald Mosley, who founded the British Union of Fascists. Powell was austere, intelligent and a skilful public speaker who could make racism sound reasonable and rational. That was what made him so pernicious.

In October 1972, I was invited as a journalist to a dinner in Slough, at which Powell would be guest speaker. I wanted to bring a partner but was told that this event was for men only. The hosts were in the property business, so were benefiting from an unprecedented inflation in house prices, stimulated by the arrival of the post-war baby boomers into the housing market. Parliament was told in that same month that the average price of a newly built house had leapt by 37 per cent in two years. Local councils were under contact pressure to release land for housing. Agricultural land was cheap, but if you owned ten acres and could get planning permission to develop them, you became richer by £100,000, which was equivalent to being a millionaire at today's prices. The villain, in the popular mind, was the 'property speculator' who bought a farmer's field for next to nothing, leant on the council to change its designation and sold to a builder at a vast profit, adding nothing to anyone's wealth but his own. Powell came to Slough to speak up in defence of property speculators.

It was intriguing to watch him address an audience which he described as 'naturally biased in my favour'. He was not chummy with them: he was distant, like an oracle. He had a face like a sloping bank of hard, grey and unsightly gravel, and the body language of a ventriloquist's dummy, as if his mind did not belong inside something so mundane as a human body. He gave the impression of someone who had never known a moment's joy. He once said, on *Desert Island Discs*, that he would have liked to have been killed in the war. Privately, I nicknamed him as 'sackcloth Enoch'.

There was a biography of Powell by Andrew Roth, whose weekly newsletter *Westminster Confidential* had been the first to report the scandalous relationship between the Minister for War, John

Profumo, and Christine Keeler. Roth had had to flee the United States because J. Edgar Hoover suspected him of being a communist fellow traveller, yet Powell publicly commended that that biography was the best book that had been written about him. Roth believed that Powell's unhappiness was rooted in deeply repressed homosexuality.

Powell gave one of the most skilfully constructed political speeches I have ever heard. His classical training had taught him to use words clearly and precisely, and he was no longer inhibited by any prospect of holding public office. His argument was that house prices were not affected by the price of building land. Even if an eccentric landowner gave away his land for nothing, the price of the properties built on it would be set not by him but by the market. By pressuring councils to release more land for building, the speculator was doing a public service by helping to increase supply. This argument was laid out so clearly that I can remember it without difficulty, fifty years later. He made my job all the easier by comparing property speculators to mothers-in-law. Mother-in-law jokes were very much in fashion that year; Powell suggested that they and property speculators were equally unfairly maligned, thereby supplying the obvious introduction for my report in the *Evening Mail*. He departed to a standing ovation and shouts of 'Enoch Powell for Prime Minister'.

Ronald Bell, MP for Beaconsfield, which adjoined Slough, was said to be jealous of Powell, seeing him as a late arrival on the outside right of the Conservative Party. Bell did not even pretend to believe in 'voluntary repatriation'. He supplied the foreword to a Monday Club pamphlet calling for people to be 'repatriated' at a rate of 50,000 a year. Bell was another accomplished speaker, a barrister whom I heard address a public meeting in his constituency, called to protest about the noise of aircraft taking off from Heathrow. He argued that planes should be diverted over the heavily populated parts of Slough, because people who live in towns are used to noise, but people who have bought expensive properties in the surrounding villages expect the area to be quiet. He was speaking a couple of years after a passenger plane had crashed just outside Staines, killing 118 people. When someone in the audience asked about race, Bell said that 'voluntary repatriation' was not going to achieve its intended aim of clearing out the ethnic minorities. Heads nodded in agreement. No one challenged him.

Bell died in 1982, causing a by-election held at the height of the Falklands War, the only by-election in a Conservative-held seat in the 1980s in which they increased their share of the vote – a lesson about the impact of war on public opinion that was not lost on the defeated Labour candidate, Tony Blair. What went unreported at the time was why Sir Ronald died so suddenly. The inestimable Andrew Roth let me into a secret well known in Westminster but rarely reported. At the age of sixty-seven, Bell was enjoying a bout of nookie with a female employee in his Commons office when the exertion brought on a fatal heart attack. This could have been seriously embarrassing, because in those days the Westminster coroner had no jurisdiction in the Palace of Westminster. Fortunately, the ambulance staff were persuaded to record that he died on the way to hospital, rather than within the grounds of the palace. When Margaret Beckett was Leader of the House of Commons, I asked her what would have happened if the paramedic had registered him as dead before he was removed from his office. With tears of laughter rolling down her face, she hypothesised that the only person with the authority to preside over the inquest would have been HM the Queen. So, it can be said of Sir Ronald Bell QC MP, as of the Thane of Cawdor, that nothing in his life became him like the leaving it.

Against such a background, a word needs to be said in defence of the much-maligned Edward Heath. He immediately sacked Enoch Powell from the shadow Cabinet for making the 'rivers of blood' speech, and when the Ugandan dictator Idi Amin deported nearly 80,000 Asians whose families had been transported to east Africa to help run the British Empire, Heath defied right-wing opinion in his own party, and a very large section of public opinion, by announcing that 29,000 of the deportees would be allowed to settle in Britain. By contrast, when Kenyan Asians faced a similar threat, the Labour Home Secretary, James Callaghan, hastily cobbled together legislation to deny entry even to those with valid British passports.

One of the joys of covering parliamentary matters during the Thatcher years was seeing Heath at his place on the front bench below the aisle, glowering with a resentment that smouldered fiercely through the years. There was a brief interlude after the fall of Thatcher, when he was prepared to give John Major a certain grudging loyalty, but it did not last. Heath seemed to delight in the news, in 1993, that the Conservative Party in Canada had been defeated in every constituency but two. Speaking at events outside Parliament, Heath speculated that perhaps the British Conservatives too might be reduced to a rump of two MPs – 'and as I look around, I ask myself: who will the other one be?' According to his aide, Mike McManus – who stuck by Heath when almost every other active Conservative avoided him as if they feared they would catch something – he stopped thinking this was funny as the 1997 election approached, as he saw his majority in Old Bexley and Sidcup shrinking dangerously.

Heath did not find contentment in old age, though he certainly looked happy on the day when it was announced that he had been awarded a knighthood. Surrounded by a pack of journalists out on the Victoria Embankment, he beamed with delight as he was interviewed on camera. When that was done, he turned to the newspaper journalists, expecting more questions, but we had all the quotes we needed from his television interview. 'You're just a lazy bunch of parasites, aren't you?' he said, still smiling jovially.

Luckily, he was not alive to hear himself being ignorantly accused by the Chief Constable of Wiltshire of having been a paedophile, during that strange period of hysteria in 2017, when similar false accusations were levelled against others, some of whom were alive. Heath was gay: I don't think that is open to serious doubt, but to be attracted to men is not the same as being a threat to children, even if some people struggle to grasp the distinction. For the first fifty-two years of Heath's life, homosexuality could land a man in prison, and for the rest of his time in politics, it would have been enough to destroy him politically. He cared too much about his career to take such risks and was celibate all his life.

Once a year, Heath would play host to a gaggle of journalists at his home, Arundells, close to Salisbury Cathedral. The invitation list would be drawn up by Mike McManus, whose loyalty did his political career no good but helped establish him as a writer, with a biography of Heath and a stage play *Maggie and Ted* about Heath's antagonistic relations with Thatcher.

Arundells was a beautiful house. Heath was monumentally vain, and his home was a sanctuary, full of trophies that reminded the visitor what an important person he was. There was a grand piano, whose surface was covered to capacity with photographs of him in the company of the powerful and the famous, including more than one Pope, and more than one Chinese communist – though there were no pictures of Margaret Thatcher or Enoch Powell. It was said that his loathing of Thatcher was powered by misogyny. My impression was that Heath valued women, when they were cooking, keeping house or otherwise making him comfortable. What he found intolerable was that a woman should be in charge of the Conservative Party.

In 1998, the young new Conservative leader William Hague tried to break the permafrost by persuading Heath and Thatcher to be sitting on the platform, side by side, during the party's annual conference. On the eve of this event, Heath held court for some journalists in Arundells, one of whom asked him when he last spoke to Thatcher. I wish I had made a contemporaneous note of his reply. From memory, it went thus. Heath took his time, as if taking care to be absolutely accurate, then speaking slowly, ponderously, he told us, 'I last spoke to Margaret Thatcher on January...' and gave an exact date, which I cannot recall.

I was impressed. This was only nine months ago, I thought. That seemed to be the general reaction around the room.

Heath allowed it to sink in, then added, '1978.'

There was a man who knew how to hold a grudge.

6

THE MEANING OF GAY

The first man who was openly gay and proud that I ever saw was standing on a box in Speaker's Corner, in Hyde Park, London, in the early 1970s. Most of the orators on that famous corner were essentially talking to themselves and getting only cursory looks from people wandering by, but there was one who had drawn a vocal, hostile crowd. He was about my age, dressed inexpensively, in a woollen shirt, jeans and soft lace-up shoes, and had the long hair that was fashionable then. There was a friend at his side giving silent support. He was not camp. No one would have guessed that he was gay, but he stood up on his box to announce that he was, that there was no shame in it and to exhort any secret gay individuals in the crowd not to live in fear. I could hardly believe that I was hearing this. I must have listened, transfixed, for the greater part of an hour.

He needed to speak over a continuous stream of insults, taunts, jokes and expressions of disgust. Three youths in high spirits who were mildly drunk joined the crowd and quickly picked up what was happening. One shouted out a well-known homophobic joke, the very same joke delivered earlier by someone else, who had since got bored and moved on. For once, the speaker interrupted his flow. 'We've had that one!' he announced.

Though he was pretending not to care, his strained and harassed face told me that the unremitting hostility was hurting but that he knew he must expect more, and still he kept going. Too cowardly to say anything, I left without a word.

That speaker would have been a teenager in 1967, when sexual acts conducted in private by consenting males over the age of twenty-one ceased to be a criminal offence meriting a prison sentence in England and Wales. But the legal reform did not make homosex-uality socially acceptable. At best, gay people were required to be harmlessly, ridiculously camp, like John Inman's character in the TV series *Are You Being Served?* – someone the majority could laugh at, tolerate and look down on.

Tom Robinson was the first paid performer that I am aware of to tell an audience that he was gay, and proud. A few months after the Tom Robinson Band had released 'Glad to Be Gay', in 1978, with its grim lyrics about the ignorance, discrimination and violence directed at gay individuals, I was surprised to get a call from him. He was coming to Newcastle and had heard that I was involved in setting up a new left-wing bookshop. He volunteered to perform a solo, fundraising gig.

On the evening in question, I had a moment's anxiety just before the show began when I noticed that a leading shop steward from a small engineering factory on the Scotswood Road had taken a front row seat, flanked by his wife and children. In other circumstances, I would have been pleased that the bookshop we planned to open was supported by local trade union representatives, but this particular shop steward was a hard-line communist whose views on sexuality were likely to be similar to Joseph Stalin's.

After a few opening songs, Tom Robinson warned that his next number would be 'Glad to be Gay' and added with mock solemnity, 'I know that there are people who are repelled and disgusted by this subject, and to anyone who feels like that, I would just like to say...' Then, when it sounded as if he was on the cusp of an apology, he defiantly raised two figures and blew a raspberry. From where I was sitting, he seemed to be looking directly at the union man in the front row.

Incidentally, before the performance, Tom mentioned that the band had been jeered during a concert in Sheffield, not by homophobes but by radical feminists, who objected to another of his political songs, 'Right On Sister', which was a tribute to feminism. They argued that the women's movement did not need an endorsement from a band of men. Tom noted that the Stranglers, whose repertoire included such titles as 'Bitching' and 'Bring on the Nubiles', had performed at the same venue without any such interruption.

Like the speaker I saw in Hyde Park, Tom too was in his teens when homosexuality was partially decriminalised. Older men like Joe Orton, or Tom Driberg, who were proud to be gay, were rare. Driberg was doubly rare, because he thrived as an MP despite it being well known around Westminster that he was gay. By contrast, one Tory, a future Cabinet minister, chided that fine journalist, Andrew Roth, for describing him in print as a 'confirmed bachelor', which his constituency association interpreted as code for gay. With an election looming, the man had felt compelled to marry in haste.

In my own teenage years, I liked to explore London on my own, oblivious to the thought that there might be danger in town. On 14 August 1964, I made a note in a diary:

> I went to London for the day, visited many famous sights, and encountered a queer in a news theatre. He was a stubby man, shorter than I, with pointed features, grey hair, and a slight accent – German I think. He started talking to me in the theatre, making childish comments on the film, and I suspected immediately that he might have unnatural tastes. As I got up to go, I said to myself – 'If he follows me now, he's a queer.' He followed me.

I regret the expressions 'queer' and 'unnatural' – but I had had a bad fright. I was sixteen. It was the first time I had knowingly encountered a gay man. When he suggested that we both go to watch a film at his expense, I rashly agreed. When he started feeling me up, in the darkness, I froze. I did not know how to make him stop and broke into a cold sweat such as I had never experienced before – an icy cold forehead and large globules of water flowing from the hairline. I was smoking a cigarette, which I should not have been at that age. The brand was Peter Stuyvesant. Afterwards, the sight of a white and red Peter Stuyvesant packet made me nauseous. As he realised that he was getting no response, he withdrew, and we went our separate ways, but I was flustered enough to board the wrong train at King's Cross and had to ring my parents, in Hitchin, to be rescued from Hereford Station. My father was not pleased. I did not dare tell him what had happened.

Before I was much older, I learnt that men making these approaches had more reason to be afraid of me than I needed to be of them. They were taking a risk. I never felt threatened after that first experience, but I did wonder, sometimes, 'Why me?' And it was, sometimes, annoying. Once I was on the train home, standing because all the seats were taken, when a well-dressed man stood next to me started a conversation. 'The young don't know how lucky they are,' he declared. It was a common complaint of those whose youth had been taken away by war. Having implied that I owed him something, he placed a furtive hand where it did not belong, but I simply turned and stared, and he left me alone.

During my last year at university, when I was on my way to London, I thumbed a lift off a man in a sports car. He asked me what my plans were. I told him I was thinking of journalism, and suddenly he became very interested and talkative and suggested that I break the journey to have lunch in his home in a village called Ibstone, near High Wycombe. His name was David Chipp. He had recently been appointed editor-in-chief of the Press Association, which, he explained, was an agency that provided a news service to which virtually every newspaper in the land subscribed. Chipp was possibly the most effective head that PA ever had.

Over the next few years, I was a frequent visitor to his converted country cottage. When we first met, I was twenty-one, he was forty-two. I was struck by the contrast between the curt, somewhat intimidating boss I would hear talking on the phone, and the bachelor who fussily cooked our meals and sometimes acted as if there was a pubescent teenager entombed inside his middle-aged body. In between regaling me with stories about his time in China, or expounding knowledgeably, he would make schoolboyish remarks about sex, dropping hints that I pretended not to notice. Reluctantly, I turned down his offer to take me to Bayreuth for a week, to watch Wagner's Ring Cycle. I did once bring a female friend with me to Ibstone, and David was so struck down by shyness that he sat in awkward silence like a boy in the presence of an unfamiliar adult. Before we left, he whispered, 'Is she your wife?' I replied that actually she was somebody else's.

He was terrified of coming out – terrified, it seemed, of admitting his sexuality even to himself. We were watching television, and when that wonderful actor John Gielgud appeared on screen, David roared with laughter and made some comment that I did not understand and which he did not seem to want to explain. It made sense only later, when I learnt that Gielgud had been arrested and fined for cottaging, as a public warning to all gay individuals. Until he was forty years old, David would have needed to be caught just once to be ruined for life.

Some of his earlier timidity had worn off when he turned up in Newcastle on my twenty-eighth birthday and invited me out to dinner. I was restless, wanting to get out of provincial journalism and fearful that I had left it too late. He suggested that I should apply to the Press Association. When I said that I was not sure I wanted to join an organisation as the boss's favourite, he laughed and told me not to worry about that. Two Press Association executives later turned up in Newcastle, for a retirement party for their long-serving northern correspondent, with instructions from David Chipp to interview me. After the interview, I joined a group of journalists, including the old fellow from PA who had had his leaving party the previous evening. Someone asked him why his bosses were still in town. He replied, in a venomous tone, 'They're here to interview some laddie Chipp picked up.'

I decided not to take the job.

I saw David Chipp occasionally after that, until one day in 2008 when I turned to the obituary pages and saw to my sorrow that he had died.

• • •

Public attitudes to homosexuality improved slowly during the 1970s but took an abrupt turn for the worse early in the next decade, with the arrival of the AIDS epidemic. Though it brought horrific fear and suffering into the lives of gay men, a large section of public opinion was not sympathetic but actually blamed them for causing the problem. I remember there was a gay man working at Labour Party headquarters, who had been employed there for several years, when a secretary demonstratively refused to sit near him, claiming she might catch AIDS.

An unsung heroine from this grim period was a civil servant named Romola Christopherson, who died quite suddenly in 2003, at the age of sixty-four. Norman Fowler, who was appointed Secretary of State for Health at the peak of the AIDS crisis, took the humane view that the government's job was to save lives, not to lecture gay men on their sexual practices, and made the inspired decision to hire Romola as the department's director of communications.

I interviewed Romola after she retired in 1999, in her tastefully decorated home near King's Cross, where there was another woman whom I understood to be her other half. Romola was funny, as well as clever. One of her pranks was to assemble a small team of civil servants to perform a cabaret she had written, to be performed in Parliament, in front of members of the lobby. Most of the jokes were at the journalists' expense. The political editor of *The Sun*, Trevor

Kavanagh, thought that some were beyond funny. The finale was a rehashed version of the song 'There'll Always Be an England', which was a smash hit for Vera Lynn at the start of the war, which Romola turned into a mock tribute to the civil service. Marching on the spot, she and her fellow performers belted out a lusty chorus of 'There'll Always Be a Service'.

In a more serious vein, she persuaded Fowler that if they really intended to change people's sexual practices, she would need her annual budget raised from £2 million to £20 million and they were going to have to use blunt language and, despite the false belief that AIDS would be no threat to heterosexual individuals, the campaign was going to be aimed at everyone. One of the most memorable episodes of Fowler's long political career was trying to persuade Margaret Thatcher to sign off literature that referred to 'anal sex'. When he recommended placing explicit adverts in Sunday newspapers, she complained that it could cause 'immense harm' to teenagers and wanted it confined to places like public lavatories, where there was less risk of causing offence. But Fowler, to his credit, prevailed. One advertisement, aimed at drug addicts, showed an arm riddled with hypodermic needles, with the caption – 'It only takes one prick to give you AIDS.'

An early hazard was that too many MPs and peers were exercising their right to be consulted. One crowded meeting in the Commons, chaired by Fowler's deputy, Tony Newton, with an agenda as long as an arm, was enlivened by the formidable Baroness Trumpington, a former Bletchley Park codebreaker who was, briefly, a junior health minister in the Lords. She needed to leave early, so Tony Newton asked if she had anything she wanted to say. Rising to her full height, Lady Trumpington declared, 'Three things, Tony – condoms, dentists, licensed brothels!' and swept out of the room.

Licensed brothels never did become government policy, and I cannot recall whether anything was done about the worry that dentists might pass on HIV by breathing into their patients' mouths; but condoms – there is a story. Romola wanted the public to know that condoms can save lives, but the word was not in common use then. People referred to the trade name, Durex, or said 'sheath' or 'rubber johnny'. It was going to be a problem encouraging the use of potentially life-saving items which did not have an agreed name, so an agency came up with the idea of a television commercial that was to be a series of flash images of recognisable faces, who would each utter the single word – 'condom'. Romola broke the news to Norman Fowler that one of the faces had to be his. Fowler may never have had occasion to say 'condom' before, and certainly not in public, but now he was required to say it with conviction, in front of a camera, a task made harder because the producer insisted that he take off his jacket and put on a sweater, in which he was not comfortable. 'It took thirty-six takes to get it right,' said Romola. 'I reassured Norman that it also took thirty-six takes for Marilyn Monroe to deliver her line in *Some Like It Hot* about the fuzzy end of the lollipop.'

The campaign made Romola a Whitehall legend. Joe McCrea, a special adviser at the Department of Health, told me a delightful story about a meeting at which ministers and mandarins deliberated over a draft leaflet that referred to oral sex. 'What's oral sex?' a bemused Fowler was alleged to have asked, whereupon all eyes turned to the only woman in the room. After Romola had delivered her explanation, there was momentary silence, broken by an astonished exclamation from Fowler, 'Crikey!'

Sadly, that version is not quite the same as the one I heard from

Romola. She said that it was the Chief Medical Officer, Sir Donald Acheson, who explained the meaning of 'oral sex' for the benefit of anyone present who might not know, though she confirmed that Fowler did indeed react with a cry of 'Crikey!', or 'Oh Crikey!' But Lord Fowler, as he now is, told me that the exclamation was prompted by a statistic about the number of people who engaged in oral sex. He said, 'There is a wonderful and totally untrue story that I had never heard of oral sex. Curiously enough, I had.'

I did not ask Norman Fowler for his take on another story, so his recollection, if any, may not be the same as Romola's. She claimed that she was in the back of Fowler's chauffeur-driven government car, when he suddenly asked, 'Romola, what's a vibrator? What do people use it for?' Speaking in the quietly authoritative tone of a high-ranking civil servant, Romola told me, 'That was the only time in my career that I thought of telling a Cabinet minister that he could stick his question up his arse.'

● ● ●

On the day in 1967 when homosexuality was partially decriminalised in England and Wales, I was somewhere in mid-America, having crossed the Atlantic with a fellow student from Trinity College, Oxford, named Michael Page. We spent a month in New York, then separated, crossed the continent by Greyhound bus and met again in San Francisco. It shocks me now to read what I told my parents in my intermittent letters that would have arrived weeks after they were posted. In one, I boasted about the risks I was taking, such as walking through the more dangerous parts of New York alone after dark. In another, I told them I had been mugged by a youth who claimed to have a gun, who relieved me of a handful of small change.

I reached San Francisco a day early, wanting to visit Haight-Ashbury, where hippies congregated in their hundreds during what became known as the Summer of Love. I tailed a couple of them until they had unknowingly led me there. Hippies were everywhere, sitting cross-legged on the pavements, jamming the roads, leaning from the windows of multistorey nineteenth-century wooden buildings. A group of young US marines turned up in their uniforms and military haircuts, causing a chorus of amusement. One tall hippy, standing amid the seated crowd, called out in a friendly way, 'Do you realise that you guys look as weird to us as we do to you?' Later, the crowd rose to their feet and moved in great waves like a vast herd of grass-eaters setting off to new pastures. I worked my way to the front to see the cause of this disturbance. Jammed in among the middle of a moving wall of colourfully dressed and excited youngsters was an embarrassed-looking George Harrison, of The Beatles.

The next time I visited Haight-Ashbury, all the talk was about a motorcycle accident that killed a leader of the local chapter of the Hell's Angels, one 'Chocolate George'. I was with an English girl named Cassie when a stranger approached to share the exciting news that there was to be a wake for Chocolate George nearby, in Golden Gate Park, where two rock groups would be on stage. We had never heard of either of them, but he said we would never have another chance to hear two groups that good for free. One was the Grateful Dead; the other was Big Brother and the Holding Company, featuring Janis Joplin.

In the big cities, Michael Page and I were able to live most of the time off the kindness of Americans. I managed to make a few dollars as a telephone salesman in New York, and in Los Angeles found a profitable line selling a hippy newspaper called the *Berkeley Barb*. I would stand on a street corner close to the University of California campus, calling out 'Berkeley Barb!' This was the summer when every college kid in America was listening to *Sergeant Pepper's Lonely Hearts Club Band*. UCLA students would bring their friends to my pitch, exclaiming, 'Hey, you've just got to hear this guy's English accent!'

But during the trip across America, when I made no money and there was no one to treat me, I resorted to stealing. It was easily done, because the Greyhound passengers would eat together and queue to pay. I would take a position near the back of the queue but part way through the process would wander across to chat with a fellow passenger who had already paid. The ruse worked every time. However, in one American town – I cannot remember which – I was caught shoplifting. But the English accent got me out of a potential catastrophe. The man from behind the till interrogated me, took back the stolen food and told me to get lost.

When I arrived in San Francisco, in the first week of August 1967, I was thirsty, hungry, broke and the weather was scorching hot. I went to a park close to the Greyhound bus station, knowing that there would be a fountain there that dispensed drinking water. When I had quenched my thirst, I turned and discovered that a dozen or so men were now sitting in the adjoining rows of benches, watching me. I had stumbled on a popular meeting place for gay men. Though gay sex was illegal in every state of the USA, except Illinois, in my brief experience, gay Americans were bolder than their British counterparts. I had counted four approaches in a few weeks, mostly in YMCA hostels, which were not difficult to ward off. As I walked the gauntlet of hungry, timorous eyes, the boldest of the observers leant forward and asked, 'Are you gay?'

The word 'gay', in its modern sense, was part of the language by which gay individuals communicated with one another. In the UK, almost no one else was familiar with that usage until about 1972, the year of London's first Gay Pride festival. I thought that he was asking, in his American way, whether I was happy. I replied that I was quite gay.

Did I want to go back with him to his apartment?

I asked if we could go to a cafe first, because I was hungry. 'I need somebody now,' he said, firmly.

I was not so naive as to misunderstand what he was suggesting, but I believed that I knew how to keep gay men at bay, and I was very hungry. I thought I might be able to persuade him to serve up food first, after which I would ward off any advances he made. The walk to his apartment was slow, because he had a pronounced limp. He was giving me suspicious looks. He was not convinced that he had struck lucky. In his drab sitting room, he insisted that before he served up food, we would sit on his sofa and look through his pornographic photographs, repellent images of men and women, which he seemed to think would be an aphrodisiac. I announced that I was leaving.

'Why?' he demanded, petulantly. 'Is it because I limp?'

I told him that his limp was irrelevant.

'But you said you were gay!' he cried.

That was when I realised that the word 'gay' had a different meaning in San Francisco.

7

OXFORD DAYS

Some of the teenagers who go to Oxford or Cambridge University have difficulty adjusting to the discovery that they are not the cleverest in the class any more. In the 1970s, Oxford's first-year mathematics students were divided into two sets: one for the really bright, one for the so-so. I was in the so-so set. The lad next to me told me dolefully, 'I'm quite clever, you know.' I knew how he felt. I had been told that I was one of the most talented mathematicians ever to pass through Cheltenham College, plus I was the only boy in the school to have written a novel or to have had a play performed on the school stage – albeit a bad novel and a mediocre play. In Oxford, I heard about a second-year student, Michael Rosen, the future Children's Laureate, who had had a play put on at the Royal Court Theatre in Soho. Across town in St Anne's College, there was Polly Toynbee, whose first novel was on sale in Blackwell's bookshop. Even Trinity, one of the least prestigious colleges, had an American student – a contemporary and, I suspect, friend of Bill Clinton – who went back to the USA in the summer of 1968, expecting to go to jail for refusing to fight in Vietnam, whose modern take on a Greek tragedy was performed in a small Oxford theatre. The most that I dared to do was show my latest script to a few friends. I was finding out for the first time how it felt not to be special.

Alongside the precocious achievers were students who had the advantage, or carried the burden, of eminent parents. I was made aware of them through an eccentric named Linette, known to her friends as 'Lentil', who had contacts everywhere and gossiped about them with a collector's enthusiasm. She introduced me to the founder of a student society dedicated to the proposition that all power should be returned to the monarch. One day, Lentil arrived like someone guarding a state secret and showed me a letter from a bank manager addressed to an earl, a descendant of Henry VIII, concerning his son. I have no idea how she came to be in possession of it. The manager agreed that the Honourable X, who was twenty, could run up an overdraft of £300 – equivalent to more than £5,000 in today's currency – but gently insisted that he must not exceed that figure. In the room opposite mine a police officer's son from Wales was living on a grant of £20 a year. I met that earl's son years later, when he was a Cabinet minister.

On another of her visits, Lentil spotted the byline of a student journalist named Andrew Cockburn in the university newspaper *Cherwell* and announced that he was her cousin – though if they were related, they must have been distant cousins – adding abruptly, 'We don't have anything to do with him!' I could not imagine what an undergraduate might have done that was so terrible as to make close relatives disown him. All became clear when I learnt that he was the son of the journalist Claud Cockburn, who created a duplicated news sheet in the 1930s, called *The Week*, which was an inspiration in the 1960s for the founders of *Private Eye*. In the 1950s, Cockburn was eighty-fourth on Joe McCarthy's list of the 269 most dangerous communists in the world, at roughly the same time as he was denounced during the Slánský trial, in communist Czechoslovakia, as a supposed British agent. I knew Andrew's younger brother, Patrick, slightly when we were in the same Oxford college and better later when we both worked for *The Independent*. He had overcome a crippling childhood attack of polio to be one of the greatest foreign correspondents of our generation. My most vivid recollection of Patrick as a student was during a demonstration, when he was marching with the rest of us but on crutches.

There was a Cambridge student named Andrew Knox who dropped in to see me with a mutual friend during my first year and who I thought was the coolest teenager I had ever known. In Cambridge, male students were said to outnumber female students by nine to one, but those odds had not prevented Andrew from scoring with a new girlfriend in each of his first three terms. Our mutual acquaintance also told me that during one vacation, left alone in his parents' London flat, Andrew had bedded three women in a single day. These stories may have grown with the telling, but I do not doubt that he had sexual experience beyond his years. In addition to good looks, a sharp mind and a confident demeanour, there was the allure of his unusual background. He was born in Hollywood, the child of the film actors who had taken refuge in the UK during the McCarthy era and who had a second home in Bamburgh Castle, on the Northumberland coast. 'Andrew's just the sort of person whose parents would live in a castle,' our friend remarked. Yet, for his allure, he seemed confident but not boastful. In my brief acquaintance, he did not talk about himself at all. He had a way of looking directly into the face of the person he was addressing, with a gaze that suggested a capacity for decisive action. After our meeting, I tried mimicking his manner, hoping it would bring me success with the girls. But I suspect now that it was hard for him to appear so confident. I think it took willpower to suppress a hidden feeling of inadequacy. Oxford and Cambridge were well endowed with undergraduates who had very high opinions of themselves, but Andrew Knox was intriguing and quietly charismatic in a way that they were not.

About seven years after I left university, the journalist who sat next to me in the newsroom of *The Journal* returned from having interviewed Andrew Knox, who was playing the lead role in a new production in one of Newcastle's theatres. I did not take the opportunity to renew the contact. I was living alone in a rented room, a general reporter on a provincial newspaper; I could not see myself as interesting company for a star of the stage. And that would have been all I had to tell of this story, except that one day, something prompted me to google 'Andrew Knox', and I came upon a terrible story. His acting career did not work out. His father, Alexander, won acclaim in 1979, again, for his role in the BBC series, *Tinker, Tailor, Soldier, Spy*, but Andrew drifted from bit part to minor role until around the time of his fortieth birthday, when he boarded a ferry from Jersey to the mainland. As the ferry docked, a passenger was missing. No one will ever know why, but it is unlikely that a passenger would fall off a ferry in the Channel unnoticed, by mistake. I assume that he threw himself off when no one was there to see him fall, ending his life in the least selfish way that he could, leaving no traumatised witnesses and burdening no one with the responsibility of dealing with his remains. It was a terrible, lonely end.

• • •

It is rightly said that those of our generation who went to university were lucky. Our education was free. There were not very many of us, so we had no difficulty finding work and affordable accommodation. It was a privilege, but there was a drawback to the grant-funded system: our teachers did not necessarily feel under pressure to teach well. Their peer-group esteem depended on the articles and books that they published, not on their students' exam results.

Mathematics students at Trinity College were supervised by a lecturer named John Hammersley, who had been a pioneer in mind-bendingly complex fields such as percolation theory, sub-additive stochastic processes and Monte Carlo methods. To him, advanced mathematics was not art but science, that should be put to use. I suspect that he wished he could have achieved something comparable to Alan Turing's work at Bletchley, but by the late 1960s, he was a middle-aged lecturer, whose best work had been accomplished during the war, linked to a college with no tradition of turning out eminent mathematicians. He was angry, disappointed and never concealed his contempt of the students it was his misfortune to have to deal with. He never set us any work. The idea was that we would beaver away, solving mathematical problems unsupervised, and for one hour a week would visit him in the Institute of Statistics to present him with any we had tried to tackle but could not solve. He would show us how. He did once invite us to dinner at his Oxford home, because an old friend had come to stay. 'I wanted you to meet a very distinguished mathematician,' he told us as we arrived. 'And I wanted him to meet some very undistinguished mathematicians.'

My roommate in my first year had been awarded a place to read mathematics but immediately decided to switch to another course. I should have done the same, but a kind of masochistic pride told me that I could not do something someone else had thought of first, so I soldiered on, though Dr Hammersley and I had only one thing in common: he loathed me, and I loathed him. Once, when he had shown me how to solve a particular problem, I made the mistake of exclaiming, 'Of course, that's obvious!' He took that as an insult. 'Everything is obvious when you have been shown how,' he said, and he pushed back his chair, walked across the room and stood with his back to me, looking out of the window. Presently, he turned to ask, 'Are you still here?' So ended my weekly tutorial.

At the end of my first year, he showed me an assessment written by another mathematics lecturer, who forecast that I would fail the upcoming examinations, which would have meant an early end to my university days. As I read this, I looked up in alarm and saw a smile of undisguised triumph on Dr Hammersley's face. He never knew how close he was to getting what he wanted. I had been telling my then girlfriend that I might drop out of university anyway. If Dr Hammersley had been half as good at judging adolescent psychology as he was at percolation theory, he would have realised that sneering at me like that gave me all the motivation I needed to scrape through my first-year exams and come back for more. The poor man was fated to suffer my company an hour a week, twenty-four weeks a year, for two more years, in which he succeeded in killing almost any love I ever had for mathematics.

• • •

One morning at home, towards the end of the summer vacation in 1967, my mother and sister came rushing into my room and asked me, excitedly, if I knew a student at Trinity College named Simon. I knew him well, but I did not expect to see his photograph on the front of the *Daily Telegraph*. Simon's parental home had been invaded by a reporter and photographer after someone had tipped them off that a handful of Oxford students had been caught smoking cannabis. A few weeks earlier, an advertisement had appeared in *The Times*, signed by a galaxy of celebrities, calling for cannabis to be decriminalised. This was the *Telegraph*'s riposte. You see what you have done by signing your advertisement, their leader column implied: you have turned the nation's young into drug addicts. The names of the five offending students were published. Four were sent down for a year, meaning that they would be allowed to resume their studies in autumn 1968. I knew all four of them from when we used to pass the joint around in Simon's room. Another was 'struck off the rolls', because he was found to have been taking a drug more dangerous than cannabis – heroin, if I remember correctly. I had met him only once. He was a recluse; his skin was yellow and he cowered when I spoke to him. He was certainly ill and may have been an addict. The university authorities thought it appropriate to treat his illness by having him named and shamed on the front page of a national newspaper.

There was another occasion when student behaviour made the front pages. This was an incident known as the 'Storming of the Clarendon', carried by opponents of the Vietnam War. My father once said to me over the phone, 'I don't know much about you, but I know you're not one of these dreadful student revolutionaries.' The first half of this observation was true; the other, not so. On arrival at university, I was puzzled to see demonstrators holding placards referring to Vietnam, a country I could just about point to on a map. By my second year, I had read a book about the war and was convinced that the USA should pull out of Vietnam. I went on marches in London, though I did not much care for the fringe element who wanted a violent confrontation. During the pushing and heaving outside the US embassy in Grosvenor Square, a police officer was separated from the line and was surrounded by hyped-up students. His helmet had fallen off. I was so alarmed that he might get beaten up that I pushed my way to the front and was bellowing, 'Leave him alone! Leave him alone!' as the crowd calmed a little and backed off. With his arms now free, the copper clenched his fist and swung about, ready to punch the person who was shouting loudest. That was me. At that moment, looking into his flushed and furious face, I noticed that he was no older than we were. Fortunately, he heard that I was still bellowing, 'Leave him alone', lowered his arm, picked up his helmet and rejoined the thin blue line.

When the self-professed 'revolutionary students' met in Oxford, I would listen in silence, unable to match the articulate confidence of the likes of Christopher Hitchens or Michael Rosen. The association was said to have no leaders and yet, by some process of osmosis, the initial meetings were always run by a Jamaican postgraduate student named Trevor Munroe, who would go on to be one of his country's leading political scientists. Then, suddenly, he was ousted from the non-existent position of leader and relegated to the back of the room, while another student, whose name I cannot remember, stood at the front and told us that we must engage with the industrial working class. A date was set for taking the message to the

Cowley car factory. This necessitated getting out of bed abnormally early, but despite that hazard, a gaggle of us were at the factory gates handing out leaflets to the bemused employees as they turned up to work. The management at Cowley complained to the university authorities, who somehow knew the names of at least some of the offenders. Seven culprits were summoned to appear in the proctor's office in the Clarendon Building, on Broad Street. I was one of them. At a pre-meeting, it was laid down that we seven would confirm our names and colleges but like prisoners of war would refuse to answer any other questions. Six of us did just that, but Michael Rosen, who was the most recognisable student in the entire university, went one step further by refusing to confirm that he was indeed Michael Rosen. Meanwhile, the large crowd of protesters in the street outside became overexcited, shoved their way past the security and into the Clarendon Building to rescue us. That was the 'Storming of the Clarendon', which made the front-page lead of the next day's *Guardian* and *Oxford Mail*. The proctor, rather sensibly, treated it as nonsense and took no further action. Fortunately for me, the names of the seven rescued students went unreported. I dread to think how my father would have reacted if he had known that I was one of them.

• • •

Sensible people understand the value of deferred gratification, but at university I lived only for 'now' and wished that everyone else would. I did not give serious thought to how human society would function if everyone was chasing instant thrills: I just wished that they would. I wanted every day to be uniquely intense.

Consequently, most were a disappointment. Sometimes I was exhilarated; more often I was unhappy, restless and weighed down by a sense of failure. In my first year, I had a theory that you could escape the burden of being yourself by changing location, but when I saw my reflection 5,000 miles away, in a shop window in San Francisco, it was no different from what I had seen in a mirror back at Oxford. Later, I was fascinated by William Blake, and in particular the aphorism from the 'Proverbs of Hell': 'If the fool would persist in his folly he would become wise.' This seemed to give me permission to carry on behaving like an idiot, in anticipation that wisdom would come my way eventually.

A few months after I had left Oxford, I was invited back to a formal ceremony to receive my BA Hons Mathematics (Third Class) degree. I was in two minds about whether to go, but on the morning in question, I resolved that I would and walked to High Wycombe bus station to ask the time of the next bus to Oxford. To my dismay, I had already missed the only bus that would have got me there on time. I decided to try my luck hitch-hiking. A man who was only a year or two older than me offered to take me to the Headington roundabout, on the edge of Oxford, but as we drew nearer, it became obvious that time was running out, and he very kindly agreed to go out of his way to deliver me to the gate of Trinity College. There I hit upon another snag: there was a dress code for these occasions. The porter in the lodge took a hard look at me, seized the phone and exclaimed to whomever was at the other end, 'He's turned up late, in a bright yellow shirt, with no tie!' This was overheard by a student walking by, who announced that he had the correct gear in his room. I followed him gratefully, changed clothes and hurried over to the Radcliffe Camera, but I was too late. The doors were closed, the ceremony had begun. Fortunately, tradition required those who are to receive doctorates to wait outside and make a grand entrance in their magnificently colourful robes after everyone else was seated. I sneaked in behind them, in my graduate's gown, took the nearest place, on a bench all to myself, and when the other mathematics graduates were called, I joined them. Meanwhile, looking up at the gallery, I was astonished to set eyes on my mother, father, brother and two sisters. I did not remember telling them the date of this ceremony and was not expecting them to turn out for it. My mother told me later that she was sitting there thinking, 'Things I will never see – my son collecting his degree from Oxford University...' My father was seething.

Afterwards, they waited while I returned my outfit and retrieved my bright yellow shirt. The porter called out as I passed by the lodge to ask if I had made it on time. I showed him my certificate. 'That's the closest thing I've ever seen in my life,' he exclaimed, with pardonable exaggeration. That evening, my parents, siblings and I had a pleasant meal in the Radcliffe Hotel, to mark the completion of one of the least distinguished student careers in the history of Oxford University.

8

THE RICH MAN ON HEADINGTON HILL

High on Headington Hill, on the main road from Oxford to London, is a large house set back from the road. I was told that this was the family home of a left-wing student I knew by sight, named Philip Maxwell, and that his father was a millionaire Labour MP. Before I left university, everyone who watched the television news had heard of Robert Maxwell, firstly when he lost to Rupert Murdoch in a contest to buy the *News of the World*, and then because a young American entrepreneur came to the UK to buy his publishing company, Pergamon Press, but a close examination of the books showed that Maxwell had exaggerated the sales figures to pump up Pergamon's market value. In an orgy of bad publicity, Maxwell lost control of the business he had founded, lost his seat in Parliament and was judged by Board of Trade inspectors to be unfit to run a publicly quoted company. That, we could reasonably expect, would be the last we would hear of him.

But in 1984, Maxwell suddenly resurfaced as the new owner of the *Daily Mirror*, the *Sunday Mirror* and *People*. Seven years further on, he was mysteriously drowned at sea, after falling or jumping from his luxury yacht, named the *Lady Ghislaine*, after his favourite daughter. A month later, he was posthumously exposed as the greatest thief in British corporate history. His name came to the fore yet again, thirty years after his death, when Ghislaine Maxwell was convicted of procuring young women for the paedophile Jeffrey Epstein. It was Epstein who took the famous photograph of Prince Andrew with his arm around the waist of a seventeen-year-old, with Ghislaine in the background.

Robert Maxwell liked to be involved in his newspapers, despite his threadbare understanding of the industry, so as I was about to be appointed a political correspondent for the *Mirror* in the summer of 1988, Joe Haines, group political editor, told me that I would have to undergo an interview by the big man. It took place high up in an office block in Holborn, bearing the name Maxwell House, its floor covered by an aquamarine carpet into which was woven a pattern based on the repeated appearance of the letter M. Maxwell liked to be constantly reminded that he was very important. Even as he drank coffee from his favourite mug, a message would slowly emerge, embossed on its inside, telling him that he was Very Important.

Also present at this interview were Joe Haines and Julia Langdon. She was political editor of the *Daily Mirror*, at a time when it was almost unheard of to find a woman at that level in journalism. Both knew that no appointment with Maxwell ever started on time, and vanished, while I hung around alone. Maxwell had a well-known habit of collecting interesting people, adding them to his personal staff and then sacking them. Watching like a trainspotter, I identified a helicopter pilot, an admiral and someone named Humphrey, a former deputy private secretary to the Prince of Wales, but disappointingly there was no sign of Peter Jay, son-in-law of James Callaghan and former ambassador to Washington, now Maxwell's 'chief of staff', whose main job, Julia told me, was to organise parking spaces.

Across the other side of the reception area were panelled doors that reached from floor to ceiling. Suddenly, they were separated, and I experienced that shock of recognition that comes of seeing a famous face in the flesh. Maxwell was in the doorway, tall, powerfully built, with strong, chiselled, lived-in features, black hair and prominent matching eyebrows, wearing a blue suit and red bow tie and stooping slightly, as if dragged forward by the weight of his vast stomach, which was wrapped in a scarlet cummerbund, Humpty Dumpty style. In a voice that came from deep in his diaphragm, he was bidding goodbye to a visitor, whom I did not recognise.

Joe and Julia instantly reappeared, and together we were ushered into the biggest office I had ever seen. There are families living in homes with less floor space. To our left was Maxwell's monumental desk and wall of floor-to-ceiling mirrors, in which, I later learnt, there was a secret door leading to the office occupied by his youngest son, Kevin. To our right was a large round table. This being an informal meeting, Robert Maxwell steered us towards the table and bid me sit next to him, for what turned into a memorably strange job interview. In the centre of the table lay an illustrated book of folk tales. Maxwell invited me to take a look and express an opinion. I told him that it was a very fine book. He then directed my attention to a letter tucked into the inside front cover. It was from a specialist bookseller, estimating the book's value at £16,000.

'What do you think of that?' he asked.

Noting that the letter was several years old, I ventured that the book must have increased in value since. He said it had doubled. He added that he had bought a small firm somewhere in Buckingham-shire and this treasure was discovered in a safe.

'What do you think of that?' he asked, again.

I replied that it was a very good investment.

The conversation wandered through other topics of no obvious relevance. He asked where I had been for my summer holiday. The Soviet Union, I replied. He asked if I could speak Russian, so I replied in Russian. Later, due to my bragging, an improved version of this story appeared in *Private Eye*, giving the embarrassing impression that the entire interview had been conducted in fluent Russian.

I had no reason to think that I would ever meet him again, but two years later, I had a call from Roy Greenslade, editor of the *Daily Mirror*. 'This is one off the left foot,' he warned, in a tone ominous but friendly. Robert Maxwell had ordered that a *Mirror* journalist was to be seconded to his office as his press officer. Joe Haines thought it would be a valuable experience for me. I protested, but Greenslade replied that my name had already been passed on, so if I was going to refuse the assignment, I would have to say 'no' to Maxwell in person. Joe Haines once told me that saying 'no' to Robert Maxwell was like putting up your hand to stop an approaching train. It was the last week of July; Parliament was breaking up for the summer; I said that I would go, on condition that I returned when Parliament reassembled. That agreed, I was instructed to report to Robert Max-well at 3 p.m.

It is strange how often it happens in fiction that when someone needs to see the multimillionaire head of a giant corporation, they are able to walk straight in, as if such people are sitting around with time on their hands. I did not expect my encounter with Maxwell to begin punctually at 3 p.m. Nor did I anticipate that it would be delayed by twenty-six hours and thirty minutes. As Wednesday afternoon turned to evening, and I was still marooned outside the closed door of his vast office, a kindly receptionist suggested that I transfer myself down to an eighth-floor office and wait by a phone. The phone rang, soon after 9 p.m., and a deep voice boomed at me, 'McSmith, my old soul mate, how are you?' Without pausing for a reply, he moved straight to the next question, 'What are they saying about me in Aberdeen?'

He had uncovered a gap in my knowledge, because – I have to be honest here – I had no idea what they were saying about Robert Maxwell in Aberdeen.

I was saved by a Maxwell foible. He would conduct several telephone conversations at once, breaking from one to another at will. Another voice came on the line, and I was in an empty room listening to a dialling tone.

Puzzled, I rang the *Aberdeen Press & Journal,* where a helpful journalist on the night desk informed me that a helicopter belonging to one of Maxwell's companies had crashed in the North Sea, and read out the report that was to be on their next day's front page, so when the phone rang again and the voice bellowed, 'You were going to tell me what they are saying about me in Aberdeen' – I was able to reply in full.

With that, I was given leave to go home but was told to report to him at 9 a.m. the next morning. After another eight-and-a-half-hour wait, I was able, at last, at 5.30 p.m., to advance through the wood panels from Maxwell's waiting room into the office beyond. From behind his desk, he gazed upon his new press officer, rose from his seat and pronounced in that deep, growling voice, 'I'm going to introduce you to everyone who works on this floor.'

I could have objected that the hours I had spent so long waiting on this floor meant that I had had ample time to meet anyone I wanted to know, but without waiting for a response, Maxwell strode across his office, past the round table that I remembered from my first visit, and opened a door in the far wall. Three young women in the room beyond froze at the sight of him. Here, his plan to introduce me hit a snag: he was looking at his principal secretary, but he could not remember what to call her. 'What's your name?' he demanded. She gave a name. Maxwell turned to me and repeated her name. This procedure was re-enacted until both Robert Maxwell and I knew the names of all three women.

We moved on through to another office and there was another terrified employee, caught like a rabbit in the headlights, whose name was also not to be found in Maxwell's memory banks. He used what was now established procedure to effect the introduction.

Opposite the main door to Maxwell's office was a large room in which a meeting was under way around a long table. At its head sat a comparatively youthful figure who looked up with a pleasant smile. Here, at last, was a face Maxwell recognised. 'That's Ian Maxwell,' he announced.

But Robert Maxwell's success at identifying his own children was short lived, as when faced with Kevin Maxwell in a lift, the old man pointed at his youngest son and proclaimed, 'That's Ian Maxwell.' Without considering whether it was a good idea to contradict him, I blurted out, 'No, it's not, it's Kevin.' There was no further discussion; just silence, as Kevin absorbed the humiliation of having an employee remind his father who he was.

That accomplished, the old man became bored of making introductions and told me to wait in an empty office until he called me. No call came, but I was given a friendly warning by the receptionist never to go anywhere without telling her, not even the lavatory, because Maxwell expected all his staff to be available whenever he needed them. 'I don't want to alarm you,' she said, 'but we have got through a lot of press officers.'

By early evening, I reckoned that Maxwell had forgotten that I was in the building and told the receptionist that I was going down to the rotunda, where Joe Haines was hosting a reception. Maxwell was there. The sight of me reminded him that he had a new press officer, which pleased him so much that he put a fatherly arm over my shoulder. But the receptionist's warning was reinforced the next day, when my presence was required while Maxwell was interviewed by Raymond Snoddy, media correspondent of the *Financial Times*. In the background, a small crowd of executives and expert advisers waited to begin a presentation on the future of the Maxwell Communication Corporation (MCC). No one dared interrupt.

On learning that I was the new press officer, Snoddy turned to me and said, 'You're very brave. You know that he's had seventeen press officers, and he sacked them all?'

Maxwell denied it, but Snoddy laughingly challenged him to name one press officer he had not sacked. As he struggled to answer, Maxwell paced the floor, hitching up his trousers with his thumbs. I remember thinking it odd that a billionaire should be wearing trousers that did not fit. Perhaps, though, it was yet more odd that there existed a pair of trousers too large for Robert Maxwell. Having thought about it, Maxwell pointed out that Peter Jay had moved on to a prestigious job as economics editor of the BBC.

'Ah, but you sacked him,' Snoddy replied, gleefully.

Maxwell gave up and changed the subject.

• • •

I had been cast into a place of secrecy, where everyone lived in fear of the volatile temper of an overbearing boss. His life story was extraordinary. He had come from a peasants' village in Ruthenia, a place less than half the size of Wales tucked under the Carpathian Mountains, and, to all appearances, he had risen to be one of the richest men in the world, who had rebuilt a business empire in the teeth of that devastating verdict by the Board of Trade. I was curious to know how much he was actually worth. I heard Maxwell claim that the shares his family held in his public company, MCC, were worth £500 million. The *Mirror* newspaper group was worth at least as much. I concluded that Maxwell was a billionaire, which would have put him in the top thousand richest men in the world – had it been true.

But I also witnessed a crisis that cast doubt on the worth of his MCC holding. In July 1990, the author of the Lex column of the *Financial Times* took a close look at the company's newly published annual accounts and queried why anyone in their right mind would buy shares in it. Someone else giving a talk to brokers in the City that morning repeated that advice. Maxwell's tectonic temper hit the top of the Richter scale. I was ordered to change desks, moving down to the floor below his office, to make way for a financial analyst, Dr Katherine Pelly, while a long-serving employee named Bob Cole was dispatched on the first flight to Liechtenstein, Maxwell's favourite tax haven, to arrange a transfer of funds so that Maxwell could apply a tourniquet to MCC's haemorrhaging share value by buying a chunk of his company, insisting all the while that the City pundits were wrong because they had overlooked the substantial invisible assets MCC owned, as a publisher.

The ghastly truth became known eighteen months later, after Maxwell's suspiciously timely death. He had borrowed heavily to buy two huge US conglomerates, putting up MCC shares as security for the loans, on terms that required him to supply other security if the share value fell below a specified level. It was desperately important to him that shares in MCC did go into freefall. When he could not stop the descent, he started raiding pension funds under his control to keep the banks from calling in his debts. Perhaps he told himself that the crisis would pass and he would be able to put the money back before anyone noticed it had gone. That did not work either. If he had returned alive from that final sojourn on his yacht off the Canary Islands, he could expect exposure, bankruptcy and a long stretch in prison.

● ● ●

We were on our way to a board meeting of a small engineering firm in the West Midlands, where I was surprised to see the Labour MP Geoffrey Robinson, a future Paymaster General in the Blair government, in the chair. The story told was that the little firm was on the verge of collapse, until Maxwell came to its rescue. All the directors and shareholders were full of praise and gratitude for their saviour. Maxwell looked delighted, because nothing gave him greater pleasure than the hum of flattery. Eighteen months later, it emerged that he was buying firms like these for a cruel purpose. He looked for companies with healthy pension funds, from which he retained the fund and sold the rest. All the pension funds were lumped together under one management, giving Maxwell a piggy bank he could dip into at will.

He could conduct this larceny unchallenged because of the autocratic way in which he ruled his businesses. On some days, the reception area was filled with people who had appointments with Robert Maxwell, waiting like petitioners in the outer office of a tsar. One day, there must have been a dozen to twenty of them hanging around, when I also needed to be in that outer room, though I cannot remember why. Ghislaine Maxwell walked past us all on her way in to see her father. Later, he emerged, and a room full of people sat up, hoping their wait was over. Maxwell scanned the faces, saw me and asked, in a booming voice, 'Where's my friend?'

How was I to know who out of this crowd of visitors was Maxwell's 'friend'?

I could expect to be shouted at and humiliated if I said that I did not know or made a wrong guess. Fortunately, I had noticed that a few minutes earlier an elderly man was being shown up to the penthouse that was Maxwell's living quarters. I replied that he was upstairs. Maxwell marched on, ignoring the rest of the room, and since I heard nothing more, I assumed that I had got the right 'friend'.

Joe Haines could sometimes offer sound advice without detonating Maxwell's fearsome temper. Anyone else who questioned his judgement or decisions did so at their peril. It inconvenienced him that the rules that applied to other publicly quoted companies also applied to MCC. One day I was summoned because, as I recall, there was a report in the financial pages that he had sacked the company secretary, without informing the stock exchange. He also summoned Dr Katherine Pelly, who was not yet thirty but impressed me as very competent, and asked her what he ought to do. In a respectful tone, she replied, 'Chairman, it should have been done yesterday.'

Maxwell flew into a rage and shouted, 'Watch my lips and answer the question,' and again demanded to be advised on what to do. She gave him the best advice she could. Incidentally, when Kevin Maxwell's marriage ended in divorce, seventeen years later, a *Daily Mail* gossip writer identified Katherine, or Lady Katherine Innes-Ker as she then was, as his new love, so I surmise that her dealings with the Maxwells were not all bad.

Another day, the phone rang on Robert Maxwell's desk. A manager of a distribution centre somewhere outside London needed an urgent decision. His strained tone implied that it had taken him a long time to get through. After he had received his instructions, he pleaded that his job would be easier if he did not have to 'go to daddy' every time.

'You don't have to go to daddy every time.'

'But I don't have any choice,' the manager protested.

'You have got a choice. You can find another job,' said Maxwell, and he ended the call.

There was a new newspaper, the *Sunday Correspondent*, which had run into financial trouble. Maxwell so loved to see his name in the news that he announced that he was going to rescue it. Walking into his office one morning, I saw him in a towering rage, standing with a phone receiver in hand, speaking to John Nott, the former Secretary of State for Defence and now a prominent banker, who was trying to put together a rescue package for the *Correspondent*.

'That was incompetence by my staff,' Maxwell admitted.

One thing was certain: if Maxwell had been forced to apologise, someone was going to pay. I noted a change in the seating arrangements in the room next to his office. The young woman who had been seated nearest the connecting door had moved to the back of the room. That lunchtime, I saw her outside the building, deep in intense conversation with a man whom I took to be her boyfriend. The next day, her desk was empty.

The day before her disappearance, she had gone around the office, extremely tense, asking if anyone had a first-class stamp. Bob Cole provided one but mischievously insisted that he would be the one to stick it on, which gave him a chance to raise the envelope to the light for a glimpse of what was inside. He saw a cheque for several thousand pounds: if my memory is correct, it was £46,000. Even in 1990, it was possible to shift large sums of money electronically, but Maxwell preferred the old ways. I assume that he had promised John Nott that the cheque would arrive that day, but he had also previously told the young secretary that she should never order a bike messenger unless specifically instructed by him. I was sorry she had lost her job, but I suspect that nothing else she was ever paid to do was as awful as working for Maxwell.

Personally, I was not badly treated, but all I wanted was to be out of there. The chance came sooner than expected. On 2 August 1990, Saddam Hussein sent in the Iraqi Army to overrun Kuwait, and Parliament was recalled for a rare emergency session. I seized the chance to remind Maxwell that I had agreed to work for him on condition that I returned to the lobby when Parliament reassembled. Maxwell accepted without argument. With one bound, I was free – apparently.

Except that any agreement with Robert Maxwell lasted only for as long as he chose not to break it. On my first day back from a two-week summer holiday, Alastair Campbell, who had succeeded Julia Langdon as the *Mirror*'s political editor, told me that Maxwell wanted to speak to me. 'You know what that means,' he said.

Since I had not had a summons from Maxwell in person, I sat tight and hoped the threat would go away. A month passed. The Labour Party held its annual conference in Blackpool, where duty required the political staff to be at a party hosted by the *Daily Mirror*, where Maxwell held court. Catching sight of me, he summoned me to his side and announced that I was going to go back to work for him 'for a few months' and that this would be good for my future. I replied that I did not want to leave the Commons at a time when politics was about to become interesting.

'Politics will not be interesting for the next few months,' Maxwell declared, in a tone that brooked no contradiction.

This was seven weeks to the day before the fall of Margaret Thatcher. As I tried to argue, Maxwell cut me short, ordered me to see him when he was back in his office and turned to speak to a passing Labour MP, Michael Meacher. 'He seemed very friendly to us both,' a delighted Meacher told me later.

Arranging to see Maxwell in his office was a hazardous business, but I was lucky: that Sunday, I was doing a shift in the head office, and Maxwell was upstairs, bored. On the ninth floor, I was surprised that the Maxwell at the round table was not the bullying tycoon I knew so well but an elderly man with hunched shoulders, beset with cares, who expressed his disappointment at my 'lack of enthusiasm' over careful plans he had laid for my future. He warned me in a fatherly way that I had enemies in the building. Rocking back and forth from the waist up, with hands tucked into his armpits, he repeated, 'You should not assume that if you turn down my offer you will be able to continue in your present job on the *Daily Mirror*. Have you spoken to your editor recently? Then speak to your editor.'

I did not like the sound of this threat, but luck was with me that day. The senior executives took turns editing the paper on Sundays, and it happened to be Roy Greenslade's turn. I was able to walk straight into his office and repeat Maxwell's words. Greenslade looked shocked that Maxwell should say such a thing. He assured me that I was in no danger of being sacked by him and promised that if I went back to work for Maxwell and was fired by him, as so many others had been before, I would be able to return to my old job as a political correspondent, even if that meant that the *Mirror* political department was temporarily overstaffed. I did not doubt his word, but I had been at a lunch with Maxwell and Greenslade, had seen how they interreacted, and was not confident that Greenslade would be in post long enough to be held to his promise. He was, in fact, sacked five months later. On the Monday morning, I rang Maxwell and – unusually – was put straight through. I told him for the third time that I did not want to work for him. This time he accepted, with apparent good grace.

• • •

My last face-to-face encounter with the old monster was when the *Daily Mirror* held a farewell party for Joe Haines's long-serving secretary, Glo, in October 1990. Maxwell was not good at handling social occasions, unless there was business to be conducted or all attention was focused on him. At a previous party in July, he landed his helicopter one Saturday afternoon in a field close to where Joe Haines was hosting a gathering for friends, neighbours and colleagues at his home in Sevenoaks. Maxwell brought a gift for Joe's wife, a box of Bulgarian coins that he had received from the communist dictator Todor Zhivkov. Having presented it, he placed himself on a chair in their sitting room, and there he remained, silent and menacing. No one approached him. There was a child at the event, a girl aged about twelve. Suddenly, Maxwell summoned her to approach and told her in his powerful voice that he knew a good dentist who could fix her teeth. Before the child could reply, her mother hurried over, addressed a few apologetic words to Maxwell and steered her daughter out of his sight. I doubt that being told there was something wrong with her teeth did much to brighten her day.

At Glo's farewell, on 30 October, Maxwell was again to be seen sitting silently alone like a malignant wallflower. Everyone was aware of him; no one risked eye contact. Suddenly, he stood and strode across the wide floor, sending waves of uneasiness in all directions. I could see that he was unmistakably heading towards me. He had crossed the room to say that he wanted me to know that he did not hold it against me that I had turned down his job offer. A *Mirror* journalist standing next to me, Anton Antonowicz, suggested that Maxwell was still trying to make me change my mind. Maxwell retorted that he would never try to force anyone to work for him who did not want to. A diary note from that day adds, 'Captain Maxwell seized me by the hand and held on as he talked to Anton.' I had forgotten that ominous detail. For the next few days, I was expecting my notice of dismissal to arrive at any time, but Maxwell had bigger things on his mind.

I spoke to him only once more, when a phone rang in the Commons office of the *Daily Mirror* and that familiar growl ordered me, 'Tell Soames I need to speak to his mother.' It was a Friday. There was no chance of finding Nicholas Soames in the Commons, but I managed to contact another member of the Churchill family, who passed the message on. I heard the rest of the story from Nicholas Soames. His mother was surprised to receive a call from Maxwell and bemused by his opening words – 'I'm worried that you haven't been in the news much lately' – as if Winston Churchill's 68-year-old daughter might be languishing at home wondering why journalists never rang. Maxwell then declared that President Mikhail Gorbachev was coming to the UK, as his guest. He asked that she give him a tour of Churchill's former home, Chartwell.

Afterwards, Mary Soames rang the Foreign Office to ask what they knew about an impending visit by the Soviet President. Nothing, was the answer. But Maxwell had contacts in the Kremlin. In August 1990, he had invited me to a private lunch with Valentin Pavlov, who was later the last Prime Minister of the USSR, but it was a Saturday and I preferred to have a day off. The Foreign Office could not say whether he really had some private arrangement with Gorbachev, so Mary Soames cancelled a planned trip abroad to receive him, but she never heard from Maxwell again. An employee rang to say that the visit was off.

Roy Greenslade has suggested that Maxwell was losing his grip on reality as his business empire silently disintegrated, until in a moment of clarity, he decided to end it all by throwing himself into the sea. I was covering a by-election in Middlesbrough on the day he drowned, and I went out with fellow journalists to celebrate my release from this incubus but felt a bit guilty when I saw the next day's screaming headline – 'THE MAN WHO SAVED THE MIRROR' – and the sixteen pages devoted to his extraordinary life.

A month after Maxwell's death, I had a call from Joe Haines warning me that terrible news was about to break. The next day's headline was wildly different from the one that had filled the front page on 5 November. 'MAXWELL: £526 million is missing from his firms', it declared. Thousands of retired workers, most of whom had never worked for Robert Maxwell, were about to learn that he had stolen their pensions.

9

INNER DEMONS

I arrived at an exhibition of locally produced art, on my first day as a reporter for the *Wycombe Observer*, in Buckinghamshire, wandered around the room, terrified, wishing that I was invisible, until I could muster the courage to take my virgin spiral-back notebook out of its hiding place in my jacket pocket, sit and begin scribbling. Soon, I was aware of a stranger standing over me. 'Are you a journalist?' she asked. I said, 'Yes.' That was the moment that I entered the noble profession of journalism.

The *Wycombe Observer* was the struggling companion to the marginally more successful *Marlow Times*, weekly newspapers launched late in the 1960s by a businessman named John Wade, previously a substantial figure in the newspaper industry. My recollection, which I have been unable to verify, is that he had been chairman or managing director of the Pearson Group, which owned the *Financial Times*. I assume that he was ousted in a boardroom coup and sank his severance package into this new venture. He named the company Quickstavers, after a farm his family owned in West Yorkshire.

This strange little outfit was the bolthole down which I hid while I struggled with mental health issues, the likes of which I would never want to experience again. It was not an ideal journalist's training ground. Mr Wade ran it like a private fiefdom. Having previously dealt with Fleet Street's powerful print unions, he exercised zero tolerance of trade associations. Nor would he allow the National Council for the Training of Journalists to interfere in his business, which meant that I was sent out to cover law courts and other public bodies, untrained. I gathered that it was permissible to print a defendant's address and occupation, so when a lad was remanded in Marlow magistrates' court on a charge of arson, I accurately described him as an abscondee from a nearby borstal. On publication day, there was a solicitor at the door first thing in the morning, complaining that I had jeopardised his client's chance of a fair trial. Every copy of the paper had to be recalled, and the reference to the borstal blacked out.

Journalists on larger newspapers do not often meet the people who run the business side of the operation, but Quickstavers was so small that I soon knew the sales reps, accountants, photographers, vari-typists etc. as well as I knew the other writers. Job demarcation was fluid. One publication day, in autumn 1969, I was assigned to drive through the night in a hired van to the printers, to pick up the week's editions of the *Wycombe Observer* and *Marlow Times*. When I collected the van, I ticked a box to confirm that I had held a driving licence for at least two years. The question did not say 'full driving licence'. If it had been more specific, I would have had to confess that it was only two months since I had passed my driving test, at the fifth attempt, and I would not have been allowed to drive that van.

I enjoyed meeting the printers. They were hippies, whose speciality was adult comics. They also had a contract to produce a monthly parish magazine. One month, the vicar sent a note thanking them for the nice print job they had done, while asking that future deliveries should be wrapped in something more suitable than spare copies of *Little Freddy Fuckfaster*.

Mine was almost the only vehicle on the road that night, so I was having fun seeing how fast I could make it go, until I was halfway down a steep hill that led into the centre of High Wycombe, when, to my dismay, pressing the foot brake seemed to have no effect on an overloaded van which had entered the hill at sixty mph and was gathering speed. Mercifully, there was no other traffic in High Wycombe at 3 a.m., so the police did not have to spend the next morning clearing up debris and dead bodies, but as I struggled to negotiate the roundabout at the bottom of the hill, my rear offside wheel hit the curb with a very loud crack, a tyre exploded and the van veered over at a dangerous angle, causing the newspapers to slide and smack into the side, ripping it open from top to bottom, leaving a gash wide enough to insert a hand. The one thought I had was that I must switch off the engine, in case the van caught fire, but in that drastic moment, I could not remember where the ignition key was. Amazingly, the vehicle righted itself and shuddered to a halt, so I drove it carefully onwards with the rim of the rear offhand wheel clattering on the tarmac as it shed fragments of burst tyre and parked just off the road where, I judged, it would be safely out of the way. The van-hire company first learnt that something had gone wrong from an early morning call from Wycombe Urban District Council. I had unwittingly abandoned the damaged van in the mayor's private parking space.

Later, John Wade invested in a printing press and moved his operation into a small factory in the village of Marlow Bottom. The paper on which newspapers were printed was delivered in tightly packed rolls about three feet in diameter, each weighing almost half a ton. Quickstavers did not own such a thing as a forklift truck, therefore getting the huge roll off a lorry onto the ground and into the building was always a challenge. On one occasion, someone had the bright idea of placing two planks to form a ramp, down which the delivery driver would roll the newsprint, while every male Quickstavers employee under the age of thirty, including me, waited at the end of the ramp to receive it. Even now, I can remember looking up, seeing this massive white wheel start to roll and realising in a flash that to stand in its way would invite serious injury. Everyone else around me had the same thought, and jumped clear. The newsprint clattered down the planks, rolled across the yard, up a small slope, out through the main gate, across the pavement, across the main road through Marlow Bottom and came to a gentle halt against the kerb on the far side. Again, fortunately, there was no passing traffic.

John Wade was a charismatic boss, a powerfully built man in late middle age with a deep voice, who could be a fascinating conversationalist, when sober. Some middle-ranking staff were so in awe of him that they copied his mannerisms and speech patterns. For example, when he described events that happened in sequence, he would say that they went 'bang, bang, bang, all along the line', thumping the table top with each 'bang'. So others would describe things happening 'bang, bang, bang, all along the line', thumping the table three times.

He was a sharp judge of character, though he professed that I was a puzzle. 'You're the strangest one we've ever had here', he told me. Yet he had a glaring fault that he could not see, though it was in front of him and guiding him along the road to self-destruction. He drank too much. The hours that a man could spend drinking were supposedly limited by laws dating from the First World War that regulated pub opening hours, but John Wade made friends with the landlord of The Pegasus, in Marlow Bottom, who obligingly locked the pub at 2.30 p.m., with Mr Wade and his companions still inside. Thus, if he chose, Mr Wade could drink without interruption from lunchtime until late evening, before staggering to his Anglia car to drive home. But perilous were the days when he cut short a drinking bout to revisit the office. I recall him behind his desk, eyes blood-shot, elbows on the desk top, bellowing across the open-plan office, 'I'm in the mood for accepting resignations!'

Perhaps he thought someone had looked at him judgementally. It was possible. On at least one occasion one of the older secretaries walked out of the building in protest at his drunkenness.

'I'm in the mood for accepting resignations,' he bellowed, a second time. No one volunteered.

During my job interview, I was highly impressed to discover that the editor of both titles was a woman my age, just twenty-one. She must have had great drive and ability to have reached that position when so young, I thought, but I had not been at Quickstavers for very long before I learnt what everyone else knew about the young editor and Mr Wade.

He lived with his wife and three children in a large, pleasant house in a village close to Marlow, which I visited once or twice during a brief liaison with the younger of his two daughters. His son was at private school. Somehow, I knew the salary he was taking from the company; I cannot recall how I found this out, but I remember the figure – it was £60 a week, which looks like poverty pay now but was enough then to support a comfortable middle-class lifestyle in 1969. But on top of normal family expenses, Wade had to pay for his drinking habit, entertain his young editor and sustain a loss-making business. After a time, he had to move his family into a small terraced house, not much larger than a council property, where the neighbours complained about the state of the unfenced front lawn. He had a minor accident in his Anglia, and for months was driving it with one front lamp smashed and awaiting repair. Soon, he was seeking a loan to prevent the business from going under, as a condition of which, he had to put up with a sequence of consultants sent in to examine the books and improve efficiency. The first was a brash young man. Wade could barely stand the sight of him. When the youth announced proudly that he had been reading *The Economist* for two years, Wade retorted, 'Two years? Half a lifetime!' His sarcasm bounced off the younger man's impenetrable self-belief. Other consultants came and went. Savings were imposed. Staff numbers were cut. One traumatic day, Mr Wade summoned a secretary and agonised as he dictated a letter dismissing his nubile editor. I overheard him saying, 'It would be banal to pay tribute to your many services...' The young editor left the building in tears, but before long, she was back, which meant that someone else had to be sacked. That someone was me.

Wade felt so badly about dismissing me that while he was delivering the blow, he took out a fountain pen and headed notepaper and wrote a letter of recommendation to the editor of *The Economist*, Alastair Burnet, whom he knew. I went to London to be interviewed by Burnet and the business editor, Mary Goldring. She decided that I was too young.

However, I was living in a shared flat with a rare asset, a telephone, so I set myself up as a freelance journalist. Marlow and High Wycombe were on the fringe of the circulation areas of a few scattered weekly papers, particularly the newly launched *Evening Mail*, in Slough, and I was able to scrape a living by sending them titbits from local councils, coroners' inquests and magistrates' courts. I also applied to join the National Union of Journalists (NUJ) but hit a snag, because the Marlow correspondent of the long-established *Bucks Free Press* had been the only journalist in town before the launch of the *Marlow Times* and loathed the newspaper and, in particular, me. We sat side by side on the press bench in the council chamber or magistrates' court, without exchanging so much as a 'hello'. He fiercely opposed my application to join the union, on the grounds that I was not a *bona fide* journalist. He had a point. I had read and digested *Essential Law for Journalists*, after my embarrassing brush with the courts; I had paid for weekly evening classes in shorthand; and I had approached the National Council for the Training of Journalists (NCTJ) asking to be allowed to sit their examination but had been turned away because I did not work for an employer that the NCTJ recognised, so, like Dorothy's companions in *The Wizard of Oz*, I lacked a certificate to show that I could do what journalists do. The NUJ convened a tribunal in London to hear my case, at great expense. The hearing went better than I expected, because I did not know until later that one old NUJ stalwart based in the High Wycombe office of the *Bucks Free Press* had written an angry letter alleging that my membership was being held up by purely private vindictiveness. At the end of the hearing, I was welcomed into the union.

Armed with my new NUJ card, I tried to sell my wares to national newspapers, which brought me into telephone contact with the fearsome Fleet Street copytakers, a tribe now long extinct. These men – and they seemed to be all men – could type at dictation speed and reckoned they were as good as any news editor at spotting what made a story. If the piece I was dictating was too long, I would hear the scathing question, 'Is there much more of this?' Another one was 'Why are you ringing at this time of day?' But worst of all was the silence broken by the unmistakable sound of paper being pulled off the typewriter and thrown in the bin, followed by a click and a dialling tone.

My freelance career threatened to come to a sorry end when I fell out with the main tenant of our shared flat and had to move out into a single room with no telephone. I was living in a small village called Lane End. Soon residents were complaining about the youth who spent hours every day in the only phone box in the village. Sometimes, as I was dictating to copytakers, an impatient queue would form outside, loudly discussing my selfish behaviour. I was rescued when the bank that was propping up Quickstavers imposed a new chief executive, pushing Mr Wade aside. The new boss immediately sacked the editor and I was invited to come back and take over. At twenty-three, I was an editor, writing news, devising headlines, choosing the photographs and designing the pages. One week, production deadlines were looming and I did not have a story that would suffice as a front-page lead, so I improvised. For an opening sentence I wrote, 'Earlier this week, an elderly lady tripped on a broken paving stone in Marlow High Street – a small incident, perhaps, but indicative of falling standards in the town.' I have rarely had so positive a reaction to anything I have ever written. The following week's letters page was full of messages from residents praising the newspaper for raising this important matter.

Coping with all this change and upheaval was difficult for me, because I was struggling with a condition that would now, probably, be diagnosed as clinical depression. I cannot give it a name, because I never sought professional help, for fear of the stigma. In those days, it was assumed that if you needed psychiatric help, you were a nutcase, and once a nutcase, always a nutcase. The point was rammed home in 1972, when the Democratic candidate for the US vice presidency, Senator Thomas Eagleton, was struck off the ticket after it was discovered that he had undergone therapy, a full decade earlier, notwithstanding his plea that the treatment had worked and his depression was cured.

I had already seen something worse, nearer to home. During my first year at Oxford University, I shared rooms with a gentle, gifted youth named Matthew, who came from a secure, protective and well-off middle-class family but complained of having 'depressed moods' when he could not see a point in life. We were eighteen then, so this seemed to be no more than teenage angst, but in our third year, Matthew blacked out while he was walking through town and had to be helped up off the pavement. He was taken to the Warneford Hospital, where a psychiatrist informed him that he had 'cyclical depression' that would recur approximately every nine months, seemingly for the rest of his life. I thought that it was a terrible thing to tell someone in a vulnerable mental state. Perhaps unfairly, I suspected that the profession wanted to keep a permanent hold over him. Matthew was a model patient and highly creative. As soon as his mood improved, he had other patients helping him make decorative mobiles out of wire and coloured paper. He trusted the professionals and believed that he could never escape his terrible recurring attacks of despair. Five years later, I had a strange rambling telephone call from him, talking about old times. I learnt that others had similar calls. He was doing the rounds to say goodbye, before he took an overdose of sleeping pills, leaving behind a piteous message in which he wrote, 'Oh God, I've let everyone down.' His grieving father read it out at his funeral, adding, 'No, Matt, we let you down.' I thought that the psychiatric profession let him down.

That ignorance about mental illness has mostly dispelled, thanks in part to public figures who have opened up about their own experiences. During Mental Health Awareness Week in 2019, two MPs talked openly, in Parliament, about their mental health issues, and Alastair Campbell fronted a television documentary about the breakdown he suffered in the 1980s and his subsequent bouts of depression. But for me, the most interesting self-revelation came from *The Times* columnist Melanie Phillips. It took some courage for her, in particular, to write about such matters, because she must have known that she had been given the derisive nickname 'Mad Mel' by people who objected to her strident right-wing opinions, her

Zionism and her self-appointed role as the scourge of state school teachers. It offended her just to be called 'Mel' by people who did not know her well enough to be so familiar; I can only guess how much she would feel about being called 'mad'. She was volatile. The *Daily Mail* dispensed with her column after she had embarrassed the management by an appearance on BBC's *Question Time*, during which she pointed a furious finger at the studio audience and accusing them of being 'trivial'.

I knew Melanie when she was identified with the liberal left. After *The Observer* had been bought by *The Guardian*, in 1993, some of us were allocated work spaces in what had once been an attic. Melanie's desk was in front of mine. While I was basking in the experience of working for an upmarket liberal newspaper, which was an escape from a Conservative family background, she was on an intellectual odyssey in the opposite direction, so that when she left, she made a curious speech alleging that the readers, who were pleasant and reasonable when she started out, had changed and turned nasty during her time there. My reading of the situation was that the readers were the same but reacted differently to Melanie's output as she became increasingly angrily right wing.

That did not surprise me so much as her reaction to the sitcom *Absolutely Fabulous*, with its running gag about two women well into middle age still behaving like adolescents, with an exasperated daughter forced into the role of a disapproving adult. Someone suggested to Melanie that she should watch an episode. The following morning, she came to work seething. My memory is of her so angry that her face was red and her eyes were watering. 'It's not that I can't see the joke,' she exclaimed. 'The joke is that the daughter is mother to the mother. *There are women in that situation.*' It was not until twenty-five years later that I understood why she was so offended. In May 2019, at the age of sixty-seven, she opened up during Mental Health Awareness Week about the chronic anxiety disorder that had afflicted her through life, which she attributed to being the only child of a neurologically sick mother. 'Such children live to protect their parents, for whose suffering they irrationally blame themselves,' she wrote. 'These children effectively have no childhood.' Little wonder that Melanie did not enjoy *Ab Fab*.

The incubus that tormented me arrived during my school days, causing me so much distress that I wondered if I would be better off dead. This was 'privileged pain', of course. I was getting an elite education at a cut price and was popular enough not to be ever seriously bullied; but even privileged pain can be highly destructive. Two years below me at school there was another major scholar like me, seemingly bound for a place in Oxford or Cambridge, a gangly, withdrawn teenager, who in the summer of 1966 killed himself by jumping off one of the college buildings.

About two years before that suicide, I visited the school chaplain to tell him that I was suicidal. Rev. Turnbull deserved to be among the blessed in the Heaven in which he believed, but he was not so obviously suited for life on earth. He was absorbed in his vocation and floundering in agonies of doubt because of a debate raging in the Anglican Church around a book by the Bishop of Woolwich, John Robinson, entitled *Honest to God*, which criticised traditional theology. His school nickname was Fanatical Fred. One Sunday, he delivered a sermon in which he urged anyone with doubts or fears to share them with the Creator, because 'God can take it'. I had once been a deeply religious child, but my failed attempts to communicate with God had led me to the drastic conclusion that there was no such deity, which contributed to a terrible sense of isolation. I did not propose to tell Fanatical Fred that I was an atheist, which might have set off a very protracted theological discussion, but I told him that what he had said in church had made me think that there was a way out of the despair I was floundering in. Fanatical Fred was so chuffed that his words had landed on fertile ground that he talked effusively about the thought he had put into this sermon, which he considered to be one of his best, if not his very best. It was a while before the conversation turned to the reason I had come knocking on the door of his cramped quarters. Suddenly concerned, he asked if I was sleeping properly, and when I said that I had recurring insomnia, he exclaimed, 'Oh, you must get your sleep; that's very important.' That is all the advice I can remember receiving from Fanatical Fred, but the encounter was therapeutic. Some days later, looking embarrassed to see me, he asked me how I was, and I told him I was fine.

The worst came after I finished university. Healthy people experience moods but understand that they are internal and subjective, but what was happening to me did not seem to be in the mind. It was all around, like a grey, permanent joylessness. I thought I was the only person who could feel the utter senselessness of living. I was prey to an almost insane suspicion that other people were not aware of it because they did not feel anything at all, that I was trapped in a horror story like that in *Invasion of the Body Snatchers*, living among creatures who all talked like sentient beings, and gave off the outward appearance of mood changes, but internally, there was nothing. However, my BA Hons Oxon (Third Class) in mathematics had not been completely wasted. Even on the edge of madness I had faith in formal logic. For my own benefit, I wrote on a scrap of paper a reminder of why it was statistically impossible that the capacity for a range of human emotions could randomly spring up in one isolated individual. Logically, there had to be other beings capable of feeling something. That helped keep insanity at bay.

The old problem of insomnia had revisited me, more virulently than before. There were two weeks close together when my days stretched progressively further into the autumn nights, culminating on Saturday morning, when sleep evaded me until after 6.30 a.m. Living in a single room, there was nothing else to do but lie in bed for eight hours or more, trapped in a barren loop of oppressive thoughts. A proper night's sleep was like the fruit above Tantalus's head. Saturday was a working day. Having refused to use insomnia as an excuse for being late for work, I hoped that exhaustion would allow me to sleep through Sunday. On one of those Sundays, I wrote a short story about a youth who jumped out of a window for no other reason than that he knew that when he was taken to hospital, he would be given a sedative to send him to sleep.

The obverse to insomnia was occasional bouts of sleeping like a narcoleptic. On Monday 21 December 1970, when I was working as a freelance journalist, I woke up at the usual time and realised that I had no council meetings, court hearings, nor anything else to cover until after the New Year and decided to go back to bed. I slept for more than three days, waking up briefly perhaps a couple of times a day to see to bodily needs, and once when a postal worker rang the bell. Seeing me half asleep, she assured me, 'Come on, it's not that bad.' When finally I came round, it was Christmas Eve, so I dressed and drove to my parents' home.

Migraine was another hazard. In the mornings, I used to drive the four miles from Lane End to Marlow to see if the police had any news I could report. Returning one morning, I was attacked by a headache so bad that I could not see the road for the colours dancing in my eyes and had to stop the car and wait for vision to be restored. A mile or so further on, I had to stop again. Eventually, I was home, where, after an attack of vomiting, I could shut myself in a dark room until the pain subsided.

Sometimes temporary blindness came by surprise without the accompanying headache. Dark patches arose in the corners of both eyes and met in the middle, shutting out the world. I was standing in the office of the *Marlow Times* talking to an older man when I admitted that I was feeling peculiar. He urged me to sit down, but I had to tell him that I couldn't, because although there was a chair in front of me, just a few feet away, I could not see it. I was upright and able to hear, but the room was as black as a starless night.

Another time I was standing at the back of a hall during a public meeting in High Wycombe. It was crowded. I started to feel dizzy and hurried downstairs into the open air. On the pavement waiting for the High Street traffic to clear, I felt a powerful, invisible force like the undertow in the sea when the tide is going out. And then it had passed. I was standing on the pavement as before. A man approached, looking alarmed, asking if I was all right. I could not understand why he was asking. He said that I had fallen over back-wards and had banged my head loudly on the pavement. A woman with an anxious look on her face joined us and confirmed it was true. At last, there was a gap in the traffic. Without thanking them, I took flight across the road and back to the office.

Later, the uncomfortable thought came to me that the only reason that I knew that I had passed out was that two witnesses had told me so. I already suspected that I was suffering memory lapses, as if there were moments that vanished down a black hole. My mind provided confirmation one morning when I turned up as a freelance journalist to cover a meeting of Cookham Rural District Council, in Berkshire, only to be told that the start of the session was closed to the press and I must wait. This was unusual: most local authorities opened their meetings at the start and if they needed to go into closed session, left it to the end. In my fragile mental state, this small inconvenience blew up into a catastrophe. As I was waiting, agitated, I was joined by an old hand from the *Maidenhead Advertiser*, who had left school at fourteen and had lived in the area all his life, who took rather obvious satisfaction in knowing the procedure better than a young arrival out of university. With a satisfied smile, he drew my attention to a note at the bottom of the calling notice that set out this quirk in the way Cookham RDC managed its agenda. His knowing manner triggered a storm inside my head, as if two sheets of metal blades had been inserted vertically into my brain and were being pulled into a V shape, causing it to split in two. I sat tight, and with an immense effort closed that invisible gap, with my older colleague looking on in mild surprise. While the storm was in process, I remembered that this had happened before, repeatedly, and that each time, once it passed, the memory was concealed in a vault – except that this time, when the crisis passed, I remembered it all. That was cause for optimism. I was making progress.

Eventually, my demons packed up and left, without a goodbye, having made a misery of the 1970s. The lesson I would draw is this: if you were walking along a street and came upon someone crouched on the ground, clutching a leg, howling and rolling their eyes, you would observe that their leg is injured, they are in pain and you would forgive their strange behaviour. Mental illness is also painful. A person who is in pain behaves differently from one who is in good health. So be patient with people whose behaviour seems odd; they may be dealing with problems that the eye cannot see.

10

IRAQ DOSSIERS

News broke that Alastair Campbell had been expelled from the Labour Party in the week after he had laid bare his mental health history in a television documentary. After the polls closed on the elections to the European Parliament, in May 2019, he appeared on television and declared that he had voted for the Liberal Democrats, because their opposition to Brexit was clearer than Labour's. If he had encouraged anyone else to vote against Labour candidates, it would have been automatic grounds for expulsion. But he did not do that and so had not done anything that merited expulsion. However, a Corbyn-supporting official dived in and expelled him anyway, with hearty support from whoever controlled the Twitter feed for Momentum, the pressure group created to support Jeremy Corbyn, who declared, 'Alastair Campbell's "sexed up" dossier started the Iraq war and left a million dead. Being kicked out of the party is the least he deserves.'

This message has been retweeted, liked or commented on more than 7,000 times.

The notion that a spin doctor's dossier in London could cause a million deaths in Iraq is like the old canard about a butterfly flapping its wings in Brazil and setting off a tornado in Texas. Some people will believe it, come what may. Meanwhile, on this planet, the decision to invade Iraq was made in Washington, and endorsed by Tony Blair, months before the document known as 'Campbell's sexed up dossier' was written.

In the words of the then UK ambassador in Washington, Sir Christopher Meyer, Tony Blair 'signed in blood' a promise that if the US invaded Iraq, the UK would join them, when he met President George W. Bush in private on his Texan ranch on 6 April 2002. It was a day to remember. A Downing Street official who seemed to have a grudge against the travelling press pack had put us up in a town forty miles south of Waco, a name we all recognised as the site of the shoot-out in 1993 between federal agents and a religious sect that left eighty-six people dead. It was an hour's bus ride from our hotel to Bush's ranch, in Crawford, twenty miles east of Waco. Having travelled through torrential rain, we took our seats on muddy ground alongside the US press corps and waited for the President and the Prime Minister to step out and speak to us.

By the end of the question-and-answer session, we realised that our long journey had been wasted. Neither leader was telling us anything worth reporting. The only memorable moment was at the start of questions and answers, when we were given an insight into how different the relations between the President and the White House corps were from those between the Prime Minister and the lobby. As the first US journalist put his question, Bush turned to Blair and introduced him as 'Ron Fournier, a fine man who works for AP – got a couple of kids, cares deeply about the future.' Next, it was the turn of a British journalist, whom Blair introduced as 'Andy Marr, who works for the BBC… and really there's nothing else to be said.'

On the bus back to Temple, Alastair Campbell could see the risk of a mutiny by journalists who had been brought a very long way, at great expense, for very little, and he gave a nugget of information to Philip Webster, of *The Times*, to be shared around, which was enough to make the pack feel that they had a story worth writing. I cannot remember what it was, but I did not feel it was enough and rang the Washington correspondent of the *Daily Telegraph*, Toby Harnden, who suggested that I log into the website of the George and Barbara Bush Foundation. There I learnt that Blair had made a second appearance that same day. In front of the two Presidents Bush, he delivered a speech, in which he declared:

> Leaving Iraq to develop weapons of mass destruction … is not an option. The regime of Saddam is detestable, brutal, repressive, political opponents routinely tortured and executed. It is a regime without a qualm in sacrificing the lives of its citizens to preserve itself, or starting wars with neighbouring states, and it has used chemical weapons against its own people.

This speech was not meant for domestic consumption and was not distributed to the travelling press corps. The audience at home was being told that the UK's focus was on getting the United Nations to compel Iraq to abide by international law, but in front of his American audience, Blair made it plain enough that there was going to be a war whatever Saddam Hussein said or did. The 'sexed up dossier' was issued five months later, to prepare public opinion for a decision that had already been made.

The canard about the dossier attributed to Alastair Campbell is a subplot of the more pervasive and pernicious story about Tony Blair. It was impossible to count how many times it has been asserted that Blair lied when he told the public that the British were going to war to remove Iraq's weapons of mass destruction (WMDs) because he knew all along that they had none.

Even those who are convinced that Blair was dishonest enough to lie about something so important must surely contend that he was not entirely stupid. If he had been lying, he must have known that he would be caught out when Iraq was overrun and no WMDs were found there. At the very least, he would have started to prepare public opinion for that discovery from the moment the war began, on 20 March 2003. That operation would have had to start with getting friendly MPs on side. Blair did, in fact, invite selected groups of MPs to meet him in his office in Parliament, two weeks after the invasion began. They went in expecting him to talk about Iraq but learnt to their surprise that the day's chosen topic was NHS reform. 'It was surreal,' one of the participants told me the following day. 'It was the middle of a war, to be asked in by the Prime Minister – not the Health Secretary – to discuss foundation hospitals, and to be greeted with the words "Hi guys! Hey, foundation hospitals – you're concerned. Tell me."'

After the spring had turned to summer, Blair was asked about the elusive weapons when he appeared in front of the Commons Liaison Committee, and replied, 'I have absolutely no doubt at all that we will find evidence of weapons of mass destruction programmes, no doubt at all.' These were not the words of someone who was getting ready to explain away a deliberate lie. Fortified by a mix of inaccurate intelligence and wishful thinking, Blair obviously believed what he was saying.

Coincidentally, I had lunch that same day with one of his special advisers, who asked me, sounding genuinely puzzled, 'Why is the anti-war crowd making so much of the weapons of mass destruction? When they turn up, they won't have an argument left.' Again, no hint of a doubt that there were WMDs hidden away somewhere in Iraq. That was on 8 July 2003, sixteen weeks after the invasion.

Their certainty rubbed off on me. I was expecting something nasty to turn up somewhere in Iraq soon and was bracing myself for the inevitable triumphalism of those who had backed the war. That would be awkward for me, because in the small, competitive world inhabited by political editors of Sunday newspapers, my card was marked in Downing Street as a troublemaker. In the run-up to the invasion, Blair put himself through what Campbell called the 'masochism strategy', meeting people who were likely to oppose military action. The schedule included a lunch with the proprietor, executives and senior journalists from *The Independent* and *Independent on Sunday*. At the end of the meal, in Blair's absence, Campbell was invited to guess who among those present was for or against the war. The accusing finger was immediately pointed in my direction. 'He's against!'

Campbell was hoping for support from a couple of journalists at the table: Andrew Grice had been Blair's first choice to be his director of communications but turned the job down; and Don Macintyre had written a sympathetic biography of Peter Mandelson, but they were both against the war. So were the editors of both titles, while the proprietor, Tony O'Reilly, his wife, Chryss, the chief executive, Ivan Fallon, and the managing director were all in favour. After Campbell had left, O'Reilly wondered aloud whether he should emulate Rupert Murdoch and tell his papers what line to take. Fallon replied that supporting the war would not make commercial sense, whatever he and O'Reilly thought privately.

But I was not in competition with other *Independent* journalists. A political editor's single most important source of information is the Downing Street media operation, where I had to worry that others were more embedded than me. Kamal Ahmed, at *The Observer*, was so well in with Downing Street that he was almost part of their operation. When we were being briefed over a conference call with Alastair Campbell, I asked a polite question and the colleague from the *News of the World* interjected to point out that I was a 'surrender monkey' – a tribute to an old episode of *The Simpsons*, in which the French were described as 'cheese-eating surrender monkeys'.

While the Allied armies raced through Iraq, meeting minimal resistance, the war was so popular that the Blair government enjoyed what was called the 'Baghdad bounce' in opinion polls. But after the Iraqi Army had been vanquished, and the violence continued, with British soldiers being killed by an invisible enemy, public opinion turned and people wanted to know how they had come to be told that there were WMDs hidden in Iraq but none had been found. Then a story told about that dossier months earlier, while the war was popular, gained sinister significance.

It was first told on Thursday 29 May 2003. That morning, I was in the incongruous setting of Saddam Hussein's former palace by the Shatt al-Arab waterway, under the hot Iraqi sun, as part of a pack accompanying Tony Blair on his first visit to the British-occupied south of Iraq, when I was surprised to be waylaid by Alastair Campbell, who asked if *The Independent* was giving any credence to the 'bollocks' that had gone out that morning on the *Today* programme. Not knowing what he was talking about, I cranked up the cell phone to alert the news desk that something said on the radio that morning had set off a reaction in Blair's entourage.

By the end of the day, we knew that Radio 4's defence correspondent, Andrew Gilligan, had claimed that a dossier presented to Parliament the previous September, which was represented as the work of the intelligence services, had actually been 'sexed up' because Downing Street did not think the original made the case for war convincingly enough. Gilligan said that he heard this from 'one of the senior officials in charge of drawing up that dossier'. In the *Mail on Sunday*, that weekend, he specified that the person who had done this 'sexing up' was Alastair Campbell.

One confusing element of this story is that there were actually two dossiers. Travelling with Tony Blair's party just before the war began, I woke up one morning in a hotel in Washington to find that a document had been posted under my bedroom door overnight, which went into detail about the repressive apparatus Saddam Hussein had built up to keep the Iraqi people under subjection. It had been put together under Alastair Campbell's supervision so that the correspondents from Sunday newspapers would have something to write about. It later emerged that great chunks had been plagiarised from a doctoral thesis found on the internet. I was thus the owner of a very rare original copy of the so-called 'February dossier', which unfortunately I somehow lost, when I could have auctioned it. However, it was not the important dossier.

The one Gilligan was referring to was the 'September dossier', which was presented to Parliament and purported to show that Iraq had WMDs that could be activated at forty-five minutes' notice and others powerful enough to hit the British military base in Cyprus, which we now know was based on faulty or fictitious intelligence. It was issued in September 2002, six months before the Commons voted to support Blair's decision to take the UK to war. Whether the dossier had any effect on that vote is hard to tell. At least one MP, Boris Johnson, thought that it was 'probably a load of nonsense' but voted for war regardless.

If Alastair Campbell had been in London on the relevant day, he might have been able to persuade the BBC to exercise due diligence, by checking whether Gilligan really had spoken to 'one of the senior officials in charge of drawing up that dossier'. Instead, from a distance of nearly 4,000 miles, Campbell embarked on a campaign that pitched his credibility against the BBC's.

The next day, a Friday, the caravan had moved to Poland, where there was to be a referendum on whether to join the EU. Tony Blair stood side by side with the President of Poland, Aleksander Kwaśniewski, urging the Poles to vote 'yes', but the British journalists asked no questions about Poland or the EU. Instead, Blair had to bat away questions about the wretched September dossier. Saturday was taken up by a visit to Russia, for a celebration marking the 200th anniversary of the founding of St Petersburg. At that time, Blair optimistically believed that Russia's new President, Vladimir Putin, would be a reformer and an ally in the 'war on terror'. I cannot remember if it was on this visit or an earlier one when, as Blair began briefing the accompanying journalists, Campbell pointed accusingly at me and warned, 'He's going to ask about Chechnya.' So I asked about Chechnya, where the Russian Army was putting down an insurgency with the level of brutality that Ukraine would suffer in 2022. The answer was not illuminating.

Early on Monday morning, we were herded into a marquee, somewhere in southern France on the north side of Lake Geneva, so that Blair could brief us about the previous day's G8 summit of the world's richest nations. The television lights were switched on, the air conditioning was off, because the noise it made was picked up by microphones, and we waited for forty-five sweltering minutes, until at last Blair came on stage, sweating profusely, and consuming quantities of Evian water, as he was compelled, once again, to answer questions about that wretched dossier. Overhead, the roar of George Bush's helicopter told us that the President was heading for home. The Iraq War was Bush's war, but Blair was left behind to answer for it. In my diary that day I noted, 'This allegation that he misled the Cabinet, the Commons and the country over Iraq's weaponry, as an excuse to remain "shoulder to shoulder" with the US government, could be the undoing of him.'

Inadvertently, I played a small part in the terrible story that unfolded after the caravan returned to London. The Commons Foreign Affairs Committee opened an inquiry into the origin of the Iraq War and invited Alastair Campbell to give evidence. He wanted to accept, but there was a convention that ministers' special advisers did not appear before parliamentary committees, and Blair instructed him to turn the invitation down. I spoke to one of the committee members, a Labour MP named Eric Illsley, who told me, on the record, that they had enough evidence to implicate Campbell in the fiasco of the plagiarised 'February dossier' for the committee's report to 'point the finger at him'. When Campbell read this, he protested to Blair that he was being condemned without having a chance to defend himself. Blair relented. Campbell appeared before the committee in combative style, demanding that they investigate why the BBC was defending a journalist who had broadcast an allegation that was not true. 'It is a lie, it was a lie, it is a lie that is continually repeated and until we get an apology for it I will keep making sure that Parliament, people like yourselves and the public know that it was a lie,' he vowed.

At that time, no one but Andrew Gilligan knew the identity of the source on which he had based his report. But soon afterwards a weapons inspector, Dr David Kelly, came forward to admit that he recognised some of the words quoted as coming from him, though he denied that he had ever accused Alastair Campbell of tampering with the dossier. Also, although he was respected in his field, he was not 'one of the senior officials in charge of drawing up that dossier'.

Dr Kelly's confession was almost immediately leaked to Tom Baldwin, chief political correspondent of *The Times*. Tom Baldwin, who later worked for the Labour Party as Ed Miliband's director of communications, of course never revealed who leaked it, but shortly before these events, he told me a funny story about himself. He, Alastair Campbell and Peter Oborne, a right-wing commentator, were all near-neighbours in Hampstead. One day in March or April 2003, Oborne rang Campbell and offered to donate £100 to a leukaemia fund if Campbell would persuade Baldwin to stop shouting 'fuck off' at him every time their paths crossed. Campbell passed the message on, but Baldwin replied, 'There are very few things I wouldn't do for you, but anal sex and stopping swearing at Oborne are two of them.' On being told this tale, my instant response was surprise that Oborne should assume that Campbell had that sort of influence over Baldwin, because political journalists do not generally admit to being under the sway of spin doctors. Unabashed, Baldwin told me, 'That's the one thing he got right.'

That leak was helpful to Campbell, because it supported his assertion that Gilligan had lied. Gilligan's first response was to say that he talked to not one but four sources inside the intelligence services, though – as any journalist – he refused to name them unless they chose to identify themselves. Eventually, he had to admit that the source he was quoting in the disputed broadcast was Dr Kelly. In the aftermath, Gilligan resigned, though his career did not suffer: as well as thriving as a newspaper journalist, he became one of Boris Johnson's special advisers. The chairman and the director general of the BBC also resigned, as a penance for backing what turned out to be a flawed report. So did Campbell, who came close to having a psychotic episode during his relentless campaign to discredit Gilligan. But the most tragic victim of his saga by far was David Kelly. The Foreign Affairs Committee was not keen to call him as a witness but decided that they had better, after the lecture Campbell had given them. Before the hearing, Gilligan tipped off one of the committee members that Kelly had also spoken to another BBC journalist, from *Newsnight*. Asked about this, Kelly denied giving the quote attributed to him. Two days later, evidently convinced that he was finished as a weapons inspector, David Kelly committed suicide.

● ● ●

Alastair Campbell and I worked in the same confined space in the House of Commons for the three and a half years that he was political editor of the *Daily Mirror*. I have never known a more competitive colleague. He challenged me one fraught day to explain why my copy was sometimes rewritten by subeditors, when every word he wrote went into the newspaper unaltered. 'Why do you think that is?' he demanded. I could have replied that he was an aggressive office politician with a direct line to the editor, whose prose no subeditor would dare to tickle, but that is not what he meant. He was telling me that he was a better journalist than me and seemed to expect me to agree.

His work rate was phenomenal. It almost pained him to let a political story get into the *Mirror* without the words 'by Alastair Campbell' below the headline. He was also keeping a diary, and it's a little-known fact that in his earlier role as political editor of the *Sunday Mirror* he wrote a novel. It was created on an Amstrad, but when it was finished, the machine ate it. Even the IT specialist he called in could not explain where it had gone. Campbell told me that when he realised it was lost for ever, he crawled into bed and covered his head with a blanket. It was another twenty years before the canon of English literature included a published Alastair Campbell novel.

He was the only one of Blair's staff who could be heard addressing him with jocular familiarity, as if they were old mates rather than employer and adviser. When they first met, Campbell was a political editor and Blair was a middle-ranking member of the opposition front bench. It was assumed that Campbell accepted a cut in salary to work for Blair, though in Downing Street he was for a time better paid than John Prescott, the Deputy Prime Minister. The Murdoch organisation paid for a swish leaving party for Campbell, in the Reform Club on Pall Mall. Tony Blair and Neil Kinnock were there, of course. So were James Callaghan and a number of prominent

Conservatives, including Cecil Parkinson, who was once Margaret Thatcher's favourite Cabinet minister, and David Davis, who was then seen as a future Tory leader. One of the younger guests was Emma Tucker, of the *Financial Times*, later the first female editor since 1901 of the *Sunday Times*. In front of this august gathering, Campbell's editor, Richard Stott, gave a funny speech in which he pretended throughout to be under the impression that Campbell was going off to lead the Labour Party, with Blair as his assistant.

A year or two later, I was part of a pack who joined Tony Blair on a train journey to Newcastle, while he was Leader of the Opposition. Each reporter was given face time with him. I was made to wait until last, because Campbell suspected I was going to be trouble, and was made to sit across the table from Blair, with Campbell next to me, so that he could intervene if the interview went off in a direction he did not like.

Blair had done a lot of talking by now, and his mouth was dry. 'Alastair, can you arrange a cup of tea?' he asked.

'I'm not moving while he's sitting there,' said Campbell. The leader was made to wait for his cup of tea.

The satirist Rory Bremner was the first to see the comic potential here. Before Armando Iannucci picked up and ran with the same idea in the TV show *The Thick of It*, Bremner did a series of sketches in which he impersonated Tony Blair, being ordered around by an actor named Andrew Dunn, whose profile resembled Campbell's, though Campbell repeatedly objected that Dunn was too fat and unfit. When he was the visiting speaker at a press gallery lunch in the Commons, Paul Routledge, of the *Daily Mirror*, invited Dunn to be his guest. Looking in Dunn's direction, Campbell said, 'I regard this as a very unfriendly gesture – and you need to lose some weight.'

While he was gaining a prestigious range of social contacts, Campbell also made some dangerous enemies. When Mirror Group Newspapers were up for sale in 1992, he very publicly backed an unsuccessful bid by the Labour peer Clive Hollick, which meant that the new management, under David Montgomery, wanted to be rid of him. Lord Hollick later introduced me to his wife as someone else who had 'put his head above the parapet' and had been sacked as a reprisal. The truth was less heroic: the damn parapet was so low that I just could not get my head down far enough.

The new management would happily have sacked Campbell without a pay-off if they could have found a pretext, and here a Tory MP named Rupert Allason, who loathed Campbell, seemed to offer a way. Just before Robert Maxwell died, an American journalist had accused him of having links to the Israeli secret service. Allason stood up during Prime Minister's Questions to suggest that this allegation – now widely believed to be true – was worth investigating. Maxwell was furious but could not sue, because Allason was protected by parliamentary privilege, so the *Daily Mirror* retaliated with a front-page story bearing Alastair Campbell's byline, attacking Allason, who sued. Before long, Maxwell was dead and his posthumous reputation shredded, and the *Mirror* paid Allason a hefty sum in damages.

The sequel to this story would cause Alastair Campbell a great deal of grief. A day or two after the case was settled, in November 1992, a small item appeared in the *Daily Mirror* saying, 'Tory MP Rupert Allason was challenged by fifty MPs last night to demonstrate his concern for Maxwell Pensioners by giving them his estimated £250,000 libel damages. Mr Allason won the money from the *Daily Mirror* over articles concerning Robert Maxwell.'

But this brief paragraph contained a glaring error. The item referred to something called an Early Day Motion (EDM), a device that allows MPs to express opinions on matters unlikely to be debated in the Commons chamber, while still enjoying parliamentary privilege. Usually, one MP writes and signs an EDM, then passes it around so that others can add their signatures. The EDM in question had been signed not by fifty MPs but by seven.

Allason retaliated with another writ. He alleged that the EDM had not been generated by an MP at all but by Alastair Campbell as an act of revenge for the lost court case. The management at the *Mirror*, under a new proprietor, David Montgomery, took this seriously and would undoubtedly have sacked Campbell if it had been true, but he flatly denied any part in the sorry story.

Eventually, they induced Campbell to resign, by appointing one of Montgomery's acolytes, named David Seymour, over his head, as group political editor, in place of Joe Haines, who had resigned. If they thought he would go quietly, they were much mistaken. Neil Kinnock organised an EDM regretting his departure, which picked up the signatures of 184 Labour MPs. The Labour MP George Galloway, who detested Campbell with the same fervour as Allason, organised a counter EDM hailing Seymour as 'an outstanding journalist of integrity', which amassed just nine signatures. Campbell was on the rota of guest presenters of a television programme called *What the Papers Say* and immodestly devoted the whole of the next episode to what the papers had been saying about his resignation, not forgetting to correct one report which got his age wrong.

His forced departure did not deter Allason, who took the case to court, alleging 'malicious libel', which meant that the case would be heard without a jury. By the time it reached the Old Bailey, Campbell was working for Tony Blair, and it was national news, with camera crews crowding the pavement by the entrance.

At some point, Allason had added another detail to his story. He alleged that I was implicated and that I had written the disputed story because Campbell had told me to.

The *Mirror*'s HR department never asked me if that was true, but one Sunday afternoon in April 1993, shortly after Campbell's departure, I was called in and sacked, with no reason given, which set off another EDM, this time signed by 146 MPs. This must have reinforced Allason's suspicion that Campbell and I were in league, though if he had looked carefully at the two lists of signatures, he might have spotted that one was more left-leaning than the other. Peter Mandelson, for instance, signed for Campbell but not for me; Jeremy Corbyn signed for me but not for Campbell; and if the case had been delayed another couple of years, Allason might have noticed that I was the only political correspondent working for the *Daily* or *Sunday Mirror* at that time who did not go on to work for the government information service during the Blair years.

I was told that I would be called to the Old Bailey to give evidence on the Thursday, so I spent all that day in court, only to be told to come back again on Friday. I was now working for *The Observer*, and on a Sunday newspaper, Friday was usually the busiest day of the week. By the time I was on the witness stand, I was shaking with frustration. I told the judge, repeatedly, that I had not written the wretched EDM and did not know why I had been dragged into court. That evening, Alastair called me at home and said, 'You nearly lost it.' It was a friendly conversation, but I assumed he was being as competitive as usual and telling me that he had been a better witness than me.

Allason – who, by the way was described by a judge in a later trial as 'profoundly and cynically dishonest' – was right on one point: the EDM was not genuine. It had been written by a *Mirror* journalist, a friend of Campbell, who asked a friendly Labour MP to collect signatures and was under the impression he had collected fifty. But Alastair Campbell was not a party to this; nor was I.

I did not return to court to hear the verdict, but Alastair kindly sought me out in the Commons to tell me that Allason had lost and that the judge, Maurice Drake, had described me as 'an impressive witness whose evidence had a firm ring of truth'. He added that the judge had denigrated him, saying that the evidence he gave was 'not wholly convincing or satisfactory'.

I almost burst out laughing when I heard this, but something in Alastair's demeanour made me think that it was better not to make light of it. Far from being pleased that Allason had lost, he seemed shaken and hurt. I learnt just how upset he was when his diary was published. 'I felt I think for the first time in my life an instant pounding of the heart, and I was shaking with rage inside', he wrote.

I was sometimes puzzled that Campbell reacted so strongly to Andrew Gilligan's early morning broadcast, which might have been long forgotten had he ignored it. It irritated him so much that on the phone one Saturday, he said there were journalists outside his home, besieging his family, which he did not mind, he added, but why were there no journalists at Gilligan's door?

An upside to working with Alastair Campbell was that I never had to wonder what he might be saying when I was out of the room, because if he had something to say about someone, he would say it to their face, at the first opportunity. I had one particularly bad conversation in which he repeatedly told me that 'I should think

carefully about my future', implying that he wished I would go and
work somewhere else. The *Daily Mirror* had four political correspondents, all working in one overcrowded room, yet so far as I
could tell, the other two did not know that there was a problem.
Campbell was a straight talker, and in return, he expected to be
believed. But a judge called him a liar, and there was nothing he
could do about it. A journalist he despised also called him a liar,
and a large section of the public preferred to believe the journalist, who was not, in fact, telling the truth. That deeply undermined
the person he believed himself to be and drove him to the edge of
despair.

11

BUMMER NEWS DAYS

Provincial newspapers were profitable monopolies until the internet ate their advertising income. They hoovered up money because if anyone had a local business they wanted to advertise, or a flat to rent, or a secondhand car to sell, there was nowhere better than the local newspaper. They were monopolies because in most cities, a multinational company had moved in and bought one title, which gave it so much financial muscle that others could not compete.

In Victorian times, Tyneside was served by the *Newcastle Advertiser, Newcastle Daily Chronicle, Newcastle Weekly Chronicle, Newcastle Daily Courant, Newcastle Evening Courant, Newcastle Examiner, Newcastle Guardian, Newcastle Daily Journal, Newcastle Daily Leader, Newcastle Standard, Gateshead Observer, Jarrow Guardian, North Mail, Northern Weekly Leader* and *Tyne Mercury*. When I arrived in Newcastle, in the summer of 1975, all that remained were the *Evening Chronicle, The Journal* and the *Sunday Sun* – founded in 1919, with no relation to *The Sun* – all produced out of one building in Groat Market, Newcastle, and all part of Thomson Newspapers, a Canadian multinational that owned about 200 newspapers and much else.

The *Chronicle* had been one of the most radical mass-circulating newspapers in the country, served by journalists whose faultless shorthand enabled them to reproduce long speeches, word for word. The anarchist Pyotr Kropotkin was invited to Newcastle by the *Chronicle*'s radical proprietor, Joseph Cowen, to make his first public appearance since his escape from the Peter and Paul Fortress in St Petersburg. The *Chronicle*'s sales graph is an illustration of the slow destruction of local journalism. In the mid-nineteenth century, the paper sold 45,000 copies a day. That figure more than doubled during the twentieth century. By December 2022, it was below 9,000.

I was shown a map of *The Journal*'s circulation when I arrived to work there as a general reporter. There were Northumberland villages where penetration was 100 per cent, meaning that every household had its copy of *The Journal* delivered every weekday morning. By 2022, the circulation had fallen below 4,000. This catastrophic, nationwide decline means that though parish councils, magistrates' courts, coroners' courts etc. still hold 'public' sessions, which should be open to public scrutiny, the press benches are too often empty.

Politicians would often praise the objectivity and responsible reporting that they detected in the local press, so unlike the sensationalism of the nationals, but that difference was determined by the market. Having no competitors, local newspapers had no incentive to offend anyone who was in a position to complain. Before I arrived, the north-east had been home to the biggest local government corruption scandal in living memory, exposed not through local journalism but at a bankruptcy hearing. The shareholders of a failed architect's business hired lawyers to find out where their money went and learnt that much of it had lined the pockets of corrupt politicians, including T. Dan Smith, leader of Newcastle Council, and Andy Cunningham, a union organiser who controlled Durham County Council. Both went to prison. The *Chronicle* marked the fall of Smith with an opinion piece lamenting his loss to local democracy and praising him as the 'Cock o' the North'.

The majority of Britain's local newspapers belonged either to Thomson Newspapers, which also owned *The Times* and *Sunday Times*, or to Pearson, the group that owned the *Financial Times*. The editors would be shifted around from city to city, or even country to country, ensuring that their loyalty was to the company, rather than any one of the regions its newspaper covered. Their newspapers were written to a formula. News items had to include a reference to the circulation area in the headline or opening paragraph, or both. The old story that the sinking of the Titanic was reported in the *Aberdeen Journal* under the headline 'North-east man lost at sea' is untrue but accurately satirical. If a Newcastle man was in the news then the reader must be able to see at a glance that this is a local story, without being told precisely how local. The accused could not be a 'Newcastle man' in *The Journal*, because the paper circulated in other parts of the north of England. Instead, he was always a 'north man'.

At first, I was impressed by the professionalism enforced by *The Journal*. In Slough, I had been allowed to write too much, leaving it to the subeditors to cut the copy down to size. That bad habit was drilled out of me in Newcastle. Reporters on *The Journal* were required to take three sheets of paper, half A4 size, and two sheets of carbon paper, roll them into a typewriter, type a single paragraph, take them out and repeat the operation for the next paragraph. Any hack who handed in too many sheets, or a sheet with more than about twenty words on it, was sent back to try again. A week seldom went by without one of the manual typewriters giving up under the strain and being consigned to a corner of the newsroom signposted as the 'Typewriter Graveyard'.

There was a library, where every news report was cut out and filed in brown envelopes, according to the category in which the librarian judged that it belonged. There was an envelope marked 'homosexuality' in the 'crime and vice' section. 'Hovercrafts' were filed next to 'unidentified flying objects'.

It was, frankly, uninteresting, writing about 'north men' and 'north women', but the city outside the newsroom fascinated me. The Geordies are well known to be impervious to the sort of cold weather that would make a Londoner want to hug a radiator. One winter, I ventured into a pub near the river wearing an overcoat and someone shouted out, scathingly, 'Are you a southerner?' Out in the streets, you could see young men wearing string vests and women with bare shoulders, short skirts and no tights.

From Newcastle city centre, you can walk northwards for half an hour to reach comfortable, spacious middle-class suburbs, with niche shops, or, in the 1970s, you could walk a short distance west along the riverside and come upon a disgusting four-storey slum on Noble Street, which I visited to interview a family there. Climbing unlit concrete stairs that stank of urine, I stepped on something soft in the dark: it was a dead Alsatian. Newcastle Council often placed refugee families in Noble Street, including one Asian family who had been expelled from Uganda in 1972. A visiting journalist found them shell-shocked, because nothing they had seen in Kampala was as bad as this. But it was not company policy for *The Journal* to investigate housing conditions. I took one distressed telephone call from a council tenant who had water running down her sitting room wall but was sternly told by the news desk to ignore her. If the paper published one story about bad housing, the phone would never stop ringing, I was told. *The Journal* did, however, give extensive coverage to a new, well-designed estate called the Byker Wall, which was popular with tenants.

While in Newcastle I was also sent to interview a young soldier who had gone absent without leave. He was not hard to find: he was living at his parents' home, in a part of Newcastle where life's choices were few and the army was a way of avoiding the dole. The family welcomed me in, pleased that their teenager was being given a chance to explain why he had failed to report back for duty. He and his best friend from school had enlisted together and were posted to Northern Ireland, where he saw his friend being blown to pieces by an IRA booby trap. He insisted that he was no deserter but just could not face going back. To prove the point that he was not hiding, he told me he played football while he was AWOL. I asked the family to lend me his photograph, promising that I would return it that evening. I went back to the office, checked that his story about his friend was true and wrote what I hoped was a sympathetic account of a teenager who had suffered a trauma in a war zone. Back in the office for the second time, after returning the photograph, I was confronted by an unusual sight: the deputy news editor was at a typewriter, bashing out copy. As I passed, he saw me and declared, 'You really missed the angle on this story. The cheeky bastard was playing football when he should have been back on duty!' It appalled me to imagine what the family would think, after they had trustfully welcomed me to their home, but there was nothing I could do, except protest in vain.

New Year was a bigger event in the north than in the south. January was the month for covering inquests into the deaths of young people who had seen in the New Year not wisely but too well. One casualty had been standing at the top of the stairs and put out his arm to lean against the panel overhead but missed and tumbled into the hall. His fellow partygoers helped him onto a couch to sleep off the drink. There he died, quietly, from a brain haemorrhage. Another casualty fell backwards on his way home, banging his head on the pavement, got up, staggered home and put himself to bed. In the morning, his pillow was red and he was dead.

One inquest into a grim death that I covered was not attributable to drink, or wild behaviour, but to poverty and poor education. Two newlyweds from South Shields took their honeymoon on a caravan site in County Durham – not everyone's idea of a romantic destination, but it was the best that they could afford; and while they were there, they hardly left the caravan, because the wife was feeling ill. Her husband was in the kitchen area when she called out from the bedroom, 'Something's happening!' She was giving birth. She had not known that she was pregnant. The baby was either stillborn or quickly died. 'We didn't know what to do,' the tearful husband told the coroner's inquest. Bewildered and shocked, they decided to take a bus home, carrying the dead baby in a suitcase. Neither of them knew that there is the afterbirth that must be expelled. It festered inside her; she caught an infection and died. Running this story was sure to add to the distress of the affected families: the only purpose it could serve was that it might enlighten other young women who had left school without anyone having explained properly to them or their boyfriends how their bodies worked. But when I recounted the tale to the men on the news desk, they grimaced at the mention of afterbirth and told me to gloss over the cause of her death. Call it 'complications'. They wanted a headline that told how a young couple had taken a bus ride carrying a dead baby in a suitcase.

The story of the dead mother and baby was the last of any consequence that I covered for *The Journal*. A few days later, I was on the press bench in a courtroom in Durham, reflecting on how I had started to hate the job and running through the alternatives on my mind, and was shocked when an idea seemed to push itself into my head: of course, I could commit suicide. If it was that bad, there was only one sensible course. I resigned from *The Journal*, with no other job to go to. For that I was roundly told off when I next saw David Chipp. He told me you should never get off the bus until you know what your next destination is, but it seemed to me at the time that I was bound for a very dangerous destination if I stayed aboard that bus.

Freed from the woes of *The Journal*, I nurtured a faint hope that I might earn a living as a dramatist. Nikolai Bukharin, one of the leaders of the Bolshevik Revolution – who, by the way, was briefly detained by the police in Newcastle on his way to Sweden in 1915 – was put on trial in Moscow in March 1938 and shot, after being forced to confess to crimes of which he was innocent. Despite the appeals of his widow and others, the communist authorities refused to admit that the trial was rigged. So, with the fortieth anniversary of his execution approaching, I wrote a stage play, using extracts from the transcript of the trial, and handed copies around to people I knew.

A local TV producer, John Mapplebeck, liked it, and forwarded it to Trevor Griffiths, author of a highly acclaimed TV drama about a left-wing Labour MP named Bill Brand. One morning, a postcard arrived from Trevor Griffiths telling me that he wanted to direct it. The idea of Trevor as a director, unfortunately, did not catch on in the West End, but the play was given rehearsed readings for one night with the Royal Shakespeare Company, with Patrick Stewart, later of *Star Trek* fame, in the title role, and John Nettles, who later found regular employment as the fictional TV detective Jim Bergerac, among the supporting cast. It was also given a rehearsed reading for two nights at the Royal Court, in Soho Square. The best of it was that Bukharin's American biographer, Stephen Cohen, heard about it and conveyed the news to Bukharin's widow, Anna Larina, who had survived twenty years in prison, the labour camps and Siberian exile to write one of the best memoirs of the Stalin years. I half suspected that by the time the news reached her, this obscure event would have been magnified into a major West End production, but if so, all the better. Its effect on the Soviet Union's geriatric leaders was nil, of course. It took another ten years, and the advent of Gorbachev, before the Communist Party conceded that Bukharin's trial had been a frame-up.

I had also posted a copy of the script to the Nottingham Playhouse, which someone told me had a reputation for tackling new work. The assistant director, Pat Silburn, replied to say she liked it, but they could not do anything with it because Richard, their director, was leaving. I had to visit Nottingham soon afterwards and arranged to meet Pat in a pub. As we were talking, she exclaimed, 'There's Richard!' and called him over to join us. He had read the script during a train journey and made a number of incisive comments about it. When he learnt that I had worked on *The Journal*, he asked whether I had thought of writing a play about journalism. I pondered the proposition. Every relevant play I had ever seen had featured a journalist on the trail of a major story. It would be closer to reality, I suggested, to picture the newsroom of a local newspaper on a day when there was nothing going on but an increasingly frantic news editor was still expected to have a full news list ready for the afternoon conference. I added that it would be better done on television, to recreate the look of a newsroom. This produced an unexpected response. Richard said I should write to him when I was back in Newcastle, setting out what I had just said, and that he would commission the play. When he was out of earshot, I asked Pat whether he had the authority to do that. She seemed to be as surprised as I was, but she told me that he was leaving Nottingham to take up a job as a producer of *Play for Today*, a niche slot on BBC One for one-hour plays on serious themes. I had just had my first encounter with Richard Eyre, one of the finest directors of his generation.

I did as instructed and soon afterwards was startled to hear from a friend that my name had appeared in *The Guardian*, along with Václav Havel, the future leader of Czechoslovakia's Velvet Revolution, as a writer whose work was to be featured in the coming season. Through the post there came an advance of half the fee. It was £800, the largest sum I had ever had in my possession. Unfortunately, when I reached the bank, I discovered that the £800 cheque had fallen out of my pocket and was lost for ever. The BBC very kindly cancelled it and sent a replacement.

Meanwhile, I was in turmoil over the script I now had to deliver. I constructed the plot, such as it was, around a true story. The Labour government had created a number of community development projects (CDPs) in the inner cities to set young caseworkers and sociologists the task of tackling social deprivation. There was not much that a CDP could do, but they could analyse and report on the causes and effects of poverty. One such report had been sent to Whitehall from a CDP in west Newcastle. The Home Office forwarded a copy with a press release to the London office of the Press Association, who wrote it up and sent their report out on the wires. By that route, information reached the news desk of *The Journal* that a government agency was saying that there were people living in shocking conditions within its circulation area. A reporter was sent to investigate. He was a stroppy individual named David Price, who returned with graphic details of dreadful housing conditions within walking distance of the newspaper's head office, including an interview with a widow who washed herself each evening standing in a tub in front of an electric fire. Her dream was to live in a flat with a bath. This was judged not to be suitable fare for *Journal* readers. His report was spiked.

After I had delivered the script, Richard rang to say, 'I think there's a play in there,' and summoned me to London to discuss it. He approved of the main storyline but complained that too much was happening. He wanted the first half hour of the play to be written in real time, to show reporters turning up to work with nothing to do. That sounded to me like an impossible task, but I was too in awe of him to argue, so I went back to Newcastle and did as I was told. The finished play, *One Bummer News Day*, was broadcast in December 1978. The reviews acknowledged that the first half was outstanding, after which, they agreed, the play degenerated into an unfair attack on provincial journalism.

I followed it a few years later with a play set this time in a left-wing bookshop whose employees were asking for their wages to be cut because the business was likely to go bust otherwise, but they were thwarted when the shopworkers' union intervened to point out that there was minimum-wage legislation applicable to shopworkers, meaning that their self-sacrificial offer was against the law. The situation was saved by a bungled attempt to burn the shop down: the insurance payout would keep it in business. I sent the script to the BBC, who paid for it, generously, and assigned it to the same director, Michael Darlow, who had directed *One Bummer News Day*. It was to be included in a series of plays by new writers, until someone annoyingly objected that I was not 'new', because I had already had a play on television. Then it was passed to the 'series and serials' department, where a producer accepted it with enthusiasm as the first of what was to be a series of six, gave it a budget and allocated six slots in the calendar. We were in discussions about whether the spin-off novel was to be written by me or someone else when the director general of the BBC, Alasdair Milne, vetoed the project, fearing that the potential audience was too small. That was when I gave up on my ambition to be a professional dramatist.

12

DAYS OF HOPE

On the Cradlewell Road, in Jesmond, on the east side of Newcastle, there was a little bookshop, which I discovered by chance just before I left the *Journal*, where you could find titles that were not on sale in conventional shops. There were feminist novels and tracts, published between distinctive dark green covers by Virago, and other books with titles such as *Rights at Work* or *Marx for Beginners*, or magazines such as *Sappho* or *The Ecologist*. The works of Stalin, published in China in English translation, were to be found alongside the works of Trotsky, whom Stalin murdered. The shop had one worker, named Jane, who was expected to keep it open six days a week on what I have no doubt was a derisory wage. It is likely that she had to supplement it by signing on and claiming unemployment benefit. That practice – all too common in small left-wing organisations – is illegal and unfair, but there are always volunteers prepared to be exploited for a cause they believe in.

Behind the shop was a meeting room that served as the premises for an organisation called the Tyneside Socialist Centre, run by volunteers, who were mostly from the generation who had taken to the streets in opposition to the war in Vietnam a decade ago, who felt no affinity to the Labour Party and were disillusioned by the little grouplets on the outside left. The Tyneside Socialist Centre was their temporary home. At its centre was Hilary Wainwright, whom I had known from our student days, who was now employed by Durham University, in a field called 'sociology', a word that was new to me. In 1968, when the *Daily Express* set out to expose the troublemakers behind the Vietnam War demonstrations, they filled a page with mug shots and biographical notes on the likes of Tariq Ali, aged twenty-five, or Robin Blackburn, who was twenty-eight – but the reader's eye was instantly drawn to a full-length photograph of a nineteen-year-old in a mini skirt sitting on a high stool, who was identified as the daughter of Richard Wainwright, Liberal MP for Colne Valley. Hilary also caught the attention of the South African embassy, who wrote to her out of the blue to let her know that should she ever consider visiting the land of apartheid, she would not be allowed in. That revelation filled the front page of the student newspaper *Cherwell*. Her political activity did not prevent Hilary from getting a degree good enough to guarantee her future as an academic. 'Did you really only get a third?' she asked me one day, in astonishment. People who are very successful when they are young generally do not have to change as they age. Hilary never did. Apart from a slowing down in the limbs and some wrinkles and grey hair, Hilary Wainwright the Oxford student revolutionary was the same as the Hilary Wainwright whose guests at her seventieth birthday party included Ed Miliband and Jeremy Corbyn.

The most interesting of the Tyneside Socialist Centre's founders was a shop steward named Jim Murray, whom I wrote about in

Faces of Labour (1996), because of a moment when the future of the
Labour Party was in his hands. In 1980, the left turned out in force
at Labour's annual conference to change the Labour Party and won
every important vote, except one. The system for electing the party
leader remained as it was, with the vote restricted to Labour MPs,
until the left was able to regroup. The reason, it transpired, was
that the delegation from the engineering union, the Amalgamated
Union of Engineering Workers (AUEW), was evenly split, and on
this issue, one delegate switched sides to support the right. That was
Jim Murray. It was because of him that Michael Foot was the last
Labour leader chosen only by his fellow MPs, while Tony Benn was
denied the only realistic chance he ever had of being leader. Murray
was berated at the next meeting of the Tyneside Socialist Centre
but defended himself calmly by arguing that leaders are best chosen
by the 'activists' who know them, and in this context, the 'activists'
were Labour MPs.

His father, who died young, had been a shop steward; his widowed mother was an active party member; he was enrolled into the
Amalgamated Engineering Union at the age of fourteen, when he
presented himself at the Labour Exchange as a school leaver and
was sent to train as a fitter, first in Gateshead, then in the Vickers Elswick factory on the Scotswood Road, in Newcastle. Vickers
manufactured arms, as any passer-by could tell from the full-size
replica of a Chieftain tank on display outside the Vickers Scotswood
works. Jim Murray joked that it was there to draw in the 'impulse
buyer'.

He had been at Vickers Elswick for only a few years when the
regional office of the engineering union had to mediate in a ferocious row between shop stewards, in which Murray was leading

a rebellion against the works convenor, a character named Roy Hadwin, whom I knew slightly in his old age. I rather liked the old scoundrel. In 1944, the War Cabinet discussed the shocking news that apprentices on Tyneside were on strike, during a war, because of a threat that they might be sent to work in the mines. The action was condemned by politicians of every stripe, including the Communist Party, except for the tiny Trotskyist Revolutionary Communist Party. The Home Secretary, Herbert Morrison, had to explain to the Cabinet what a Trotskyist was. The *Journal* told its readers that they were 'an ill-conditioned clique with an ideological spite against Stalin, and therefore against the Russian renascence'. Actually, though there were a small number of Trotskyists on Tyneside, they were too few and insignificant to have influence over the strike, which was organised by the Junior Workers' Committee, of which Roy Hadwin was secretary. 'All this talk about Trotskyites – I never saw them,' he told me. But one ex-Trotskyist, T. Dan Smith, emerged in the 1960s as the charismatic and corrupt leader of Newcastle Council, and as Lord Mayor of Newcastle, Hadwin worked all too closely with him. Smith went to jail, and Hadwin was disgraced and heavily fined. 'They called me the bent Lord Mayor, but I don't even own my own house,' he lamented.

When Hadwin quit to work for Smith's PR company, Jim Murray, now aged thirty-two, took over as works convenor for 15,000 employees from twenty-six trade unions. In an arrangement not unusual in the 1960s, Vickers kept him on the payroll while he worked full time as a union representative. He had an office, where in quiet moments he could indulge in intellectual pursuits. By the time I knew him, he had a formidable knowledge of twentieth-century literature and was at ease in the company of university graduates.

It was from him that I first learnt that there was a political prisoner in South Africa named Nelson Mandela. If he had concentrated on career building, he could have been a Labour MP, or national president of the enlarged AUEW, which was then the UK's second most powerful union. In 1977, he was nominated to be the north-east representative on its seven-man executive, but before the final run-off, Woodrow Wyatt, who was arguably the most influential newspaper columnist of the day, urged readers of the *Sunday Mirror* not to vote for him, advice echoed by Bernard Levin, in *The Times*, and he lost. Soon after Margaret Thatcher came to power, the Vickers Elswick works were closed and thousands of workers, many of whom had worked there through the war, were thrown on the dole with no real chance that they would ever find paid work again.

• • •

After I quit *The Journal*, I decided to try out the Tyneside Socialist Centre. Wanting to know how the centre's diverse supporters would react to exiles from the lands of 'actually existing socialism', I volunteered to organise a meeting in which three guests from eastern Europe would describe the repression they had experienced under communism. Hilary Wainwright approved. She maintained that the corruption and repression east of the Iron Curtain was holding up the advance of socialism in the west.

This venture brought me into contact with two of the bravest and liveliest individuals I ever met and one of the most tedious. The most dull was Jan Kavan, who had been a student leader during Czechoslovakia's Prague Spring in 1968 and looked and sounded like a mature student heading for a career in politics, a calling he

fulfilled after the collapse of communism. He did tell me one interesting story, though. His father was arrested in the 1950s for no
particular reason and shared a prison cell with Gustáv Husák, who
would rule Czechoslovakia for twenty years after the crushing of the
Prague Spring. In prison, Pavel Kavan wondered how old comrades
could turn on one another as viciously as they did in the 1950s, but
his illustrious cellmate told him that this was how power politics
worked: if you won, you beat the other side to a pulp; and if they
lost, you should expect the same from them.

The Czechs and Slovaks who supported the Prague Spring were
caught out in terrible isolation when the tanks rolled in to crush
the experiment, in August 1968. The western powers issued stern
words condemning the invasion but did nothing; while across the
communist bloc, there was silence. The silence was almost total,
except that in Red Square, under the walls of the Kremlin, eight
unbelievably courageous men and women staged a lonely protest.
They included Viktor Fainberg, whom the police beat up on the
spot because he had the effrontery to be both a dissident and a
Ukrainian Jew. Viktor was holding his front teeth in his hand and
blood was trickling down his T-shirt as loyal Soviet citizens gathered to berate the demonstrators for their lack of patriotism. 'Look
what they did to Viktor,' one of the other demonstrators cried. The
loyal citizens looked away.

I do not know what I was expecting when I went to greet Viktor
off the London train ahead of our meeting at the Tyneside Socialist Centre, but I certainly had not pictured a short, thin, unkempt
eccentric with long, untidy hair. You could see why bullies picked
on him: he looked like a weakling. Two of the demonstrators were
sentenced to long terms in the labour camps; three were exiled to

remote parts of Russia; one was temporarily reprieved because she had recently given birth; and one convinced the police that she had stumbled into the demonstration by accident. But they reserved something worse than the gulag for Viktor. The KGB had recently, secretly, begun enlisting malleable psychiatrists, who would diagnose mental illness, so that a particularly stubborn offender could be locked away with no release date. Viktor endured five years of this, without giving in. At his lowest point, he decided that the only form of resistance left was to starve to death, but the authorities were not going to allow him even that: they force-fed him through a tube up the nose. After each painful meal, he would run around his cell, hoping to exhaust himself, so that death would come. Eventually, a sympathetic nurse passed news of his fate to western journalists, for which she lost her job, and the Nobel Peace Prize-winning physicist Andrei Sakharov issued an international appeal. In 1973, the authorities decided that Viktor was more trouble than he was worth and deported him. He recounted all this to me and an old colleague from *The Journal* semi-humorously, as if it were a black comedy.

He had travelled to Newcastle with only one objective: he had a friend named Vladimir Borisov who was still held in a psychiatric unit. He talked about nothing else during a five-minute interview that I fixed up on Tyne Tees Television and at that evening's crowded meeting. A few days later, we heard that Viktor's relentless campaigning had paid off, aided by a blast of publicity when the playwright Tom Stoppard took up the case. Viktor Fainberg and Vladimir Borisov were reunited in exile.

According to Lenin, 'Russian workers were *the first in the world to develop the strike struggle on the mass scale*' – but they were not the last. In December 1970, Polish workers suddenly rose up in protest against rising food prices with a solidarity that should have made Lenin proud. Sending in troops to restore order only stiffened the resistance. The party that ruled in Lenin's name sacked its old leaders, and the new First Secretary, the chairman of the Council of Ministers, and the Ministers for the Interior and for Defence went to the Szczecin shipyard to negotiate with the strike committee, which was led by a charismatic fitter, named Edmund Bałuka, the second brave individual I invited to Newcastle. He had tried to escape to the west once, by crossing to Czechoslovakia and jumping into the Danube, meaning to swim across, but border guards hauled him back. He decided to make another run for it after the strike had been settled, fearing he would either be killed or arrested on a bogus charge. He got himself a job aboard a ship, as an engineer, and slipped away at night, during a stopover in the Canary Islands, with fifteen dollars in his pocket. When he was on stage in Newcastle at the Tyneside Socialist Centre, it was easy to see why his fellow workers chose him as their leader. He was a true working-class hero. Lech Wałęsa, who led the next great strike wave in Poland, a decade later, was awarded a Nobel Peace Prize and became the first President of post-communist Poland, but there was no such acclaim for Edmund Bałuka. He smuggled himself back into Poland in 1981, was arrested, spent three years in prison, went back into exile, returned to post-communist Poland, where he died forgotten.

When the four of us – Edmund Bałuka, his interpreter, Viktor Fainberg and I – were alone, Edmund tapped his forehead and asked if I realised that Viktor was actually mad. You had to be a little bit crazy to defy the authorities in Poland, he said, but only a madman would step out of line in the Soviet Union and then refuse to recant for five years in an institution. Viktor laughed and replied that humans could put up with anything if they were determined enough.

Edmund did not, by the way, have much faith in the revolutionary potential of the British working class. He told me that he and his mates were fantasising about the future and imagining the workers of east Europe rising as one to throw the communist bureaucrats into history's trash can, as happened in 1989, while at the same time, in this fantasy, all over western Europe, the workers were rising to deliver the death blow to capitalism – except in Britain. In Edmund's vision, when a message came asking the British working class what they were up to, a reply came back saying, 'We're just thinking about abolishing the monarchy.'

That seemed a trifle optimistic, there being no indication whatever that working-class Britons actually wanted to abolish the monarchy, at least while Elizabeth II was on the throne. When Princess Diana came to Newcastle to open a new bridge over the Tyne, the pavements were lined by hundreds of excited teenage girls who had had their hair done in the Diana style.

Our public meeting drew a friendly crowd, including several of the younger members of the Communist Party, while the Stalinists stayed away. Afterwards, I decided to get more involved and very soon I was secretary of the Tyneside Socialist Centre, living in an unfurnished flat above the bookshop, sleeping at night on a mattress on the bare floorboards. My evenings were disturbed a couple of times by concerned citizens who objected to the existence of a left-wing bookshop, making their point first by smashing the shop window, obliging us to install wooden shutters, then by trying to push burning newspaper through the letter box. The building had no fire escape, so the thought of it being set on fire while I was asleep on the third floor inside really did not appeal to me. This precarious state of affairs lasted through most of 1977.

During that year, the Tyneside Socialist Centre attracted a formidable organiser in Bob Clay, later the MP for Sunderland North. If he had had the patience to hang around on the Labour back benches for thirty-two years, he would surely have been a prominent member of Jeremy Corbyn's shadow Cabinet, but he decided that he was wasting his time after less than a decade and stood down. At Cambridge University, Bob had got so immersed in left-wing politics that he flunked his first-year examinations and was sent down and spent several years as a full-time organiser for the group later known as the Socialist Workers Party, but he lost his job during some lilliputian power struggle. He then found work as a Sunderland bus driver and would sometimes appear at the Tyneside Socialist Centre in his bus uniform. His enemies, whom he generated in droves, sneered that he was a middle-class kid pretending to be a worker, but given the state of his CV, his job opportunities were few. During an interlude when he had no better outlet for his restless energy, Bob suggested that we uproot the bookshop and reopen it in Newcastle city centre, where there would be a chance that it could generate the sales to pay a proper wage.

My working relationship with this volcanic character was like the joke that Alan Johnson told about working with Charles Clarke, when the latter was Education Secretary in the Blair government: 'We had a charm offensive: I was charming and he was offensive.' While Bob provided the organisational drive, I raised the money we needed to set up a new business, which was somewhere over £6,000.

Feminists, who were a major presence in the Tyneside Socialist Centre, particularly objected to Bob's overbearing manner. There was one woman, named Uta, who expressed her antipathy to him so often and vehemently that one day, when we were talking privately, I suggested that perhaps she fancied him. I was braced for an outraged reaction, but there was none. She told me later that she was so shocked that she did not know what to say. On the day we cleared out the Tyneside Socialist Centre, I did my best to keep the warring factions apart by directing macho males to the top floor and feminists to ground level, while I stayed in the middle. From there, I heard the reaction when a semi-pornographic magazine was discovered, down in the bookshop. Uta announced that she was going to confront Bob with it, and she marched up two flights of stairs, magazine in hand, and demanded, 'Is this yours?' He waved the accusation away. Overhearing them each talking afterwards, one on the floor above, the other below, each seemed to think they had won the exchange. As the job was near completion, there were a few items that would have to be stored somewhere. Uta volunteered that there was room in her house, across the road. Bob agreed to help carry. They set off together and did not return. Their fortieth wedding anniversary has since been and gone.

We named the new Days of Hope bookshop after a television drama, directed by Ken Loach, but none of us noticed that swapping the initial letters turned Days of Hope into 'Haze of Dope'. For the record, it was not a hippy hang out. No one smoked anything illegal on the premises. The workers were paid £50 a week, in 1978, when the average shop assistant's weekly pay was £30. The company that owned the shop, of which I was secretary, paid employers' National Insurance, like any properly run business. Whether the shop survived or went under depended heavily on the qualities of two employees who ran the day-to-day matters. In the first year, there were constant staff problems. The first two employees did not see it as their job to publicise the new shop's existence, for instance by offering to set up bookstalls at meetings. Worse than that, when Bob Clay, the treasurer, checked the books, he found a discrepancy and started to investigate. Soon, he noticed that as he entered the shop, one of the paid employees would go pale at the sight of him. One winter's day, when snow was thick on the ground, the committee assembled, with me in the chair, to give the suspect a hearing before sacking him. We were braced for a fallout, but actually it was quite mild. Believing that the lesson had sunk in, we hired two part-time workers on a work share and again, money went missing. One of the new staff was so evasive when questioned by the committee that Jim Murray bluntly announced that he, too, had obviously had his hand in the till, and we bid goodbye to him.

The first sign that these ghastly problems were nearly over was when we had the good fortune to hire a recent graduate named Martin Spence, who identified himself as an anarchist but was the most self-disciplined and well-organised anarchist any of us had ever come across. This put him in ever-present danger of being written out of the movement. A piece he wrote for an anarchist magazine caused one reader to invoke Fats Waller's reply to those who questioned the meaning of 'jazz': 'If you got to ask, you ain't got it.' His withering verdict on Martin's take on anarchism was 'Sorry, Spency old cock, you ain't got it.' Martin later joined the Labour Party.

When another worker had quit, I took up the vacancy, intending to be there for a few months while things settled down. I stayed for three years. We intended to appoint a woman in my place after I quit, in 1982, and had a candidate in mind, a recent graduate with obvious intelligence, but she was so nervous in front of the interview panel that she could barely speak. There were hazards that came with the job. Heavy grills had to be put up every evening and taken down in the morning, and the letter box had to be sealed, to spare us the attention of the far right. I had been sent an anonymous letter, addressed to me by name, telling me that I was a 'spawn of the devil' and that the writer and his friends were coming to sort me out. Another unsigned letter called me a 'coward'. Martin Spence had a threatening call on his home telephone. It did not seem like the right milieu for a young woman with so little self-confidence.

The last person to be interviewed that day was Alan Milburn, who had no shortage of self-belief. It has often been written that he was a member then of a Trotskyist group called the International Marxist Group (IMG), known colloquially as the 'Migs'. This was not true, but when he left university, he moved into a shared house known as The Miggery because most of the occupants were IMG members. Milburn was never a Trotskyist, nor was he ever much interested in political theory, though he was present when Tony Blair first met Bill Clinton, in Washington, and they had a serious talk about the meaning of the 'third way'. When he was a Cabinet minister, Milburn was so Blairite that he unconsciously copied Blair's mannerisms and figures of speech and was tipped as the likely Blairite candidate in a future leadership contest. When he resigned, suspicious journalists thought there must be a hidden scandal. A reporter from the *Mail on Sunday* turned up on his doorstep to accuse him of being the father of the unborn child of a heavily pregnant journalist from *The Times*, which was not true. His young son overheard and started crying; but Milburn himself was not taken unawares, because I had rung him the previous day after getting a tip-off from a friendly *Mail on Sunday* journalist. He left politics because it required him to work long hours in London while his family was in the north-east. While he was Health Secretary, he had fallen out badly with Gordon Brown, and he could make much more money for less work advising private healthcare companies.

There were other serious people involved in that bookshop. Two were known as Mo – Mo Mowlam and Mo O'Toole, who later did a stint as a Labour MEP. But no other contact I ever made was as important to me personally as one that came about in 1979, after I had told one of the customers, named Peter Smith, that I was looking for a new house share and he told me that there was a spare room in his place in Elswick. There I met Sue Dearie. When we got married, we wanted to throw a party in a building called Sallyport Tower, which was part of the old city wall. Nowadays, Newcastle Council advertises it as suitable for wedding celebrations, but back then they were not permitted, so Jim Murray reserved the tower for a 'book presentation' and did, in fact, take the opportunity to return my copy of E. P. Thompson's biography of William Morris, which I had forgotten that he had borrowed. The wedding party was also our farewell to Newcastle, as we moved to London, where we raised four children. In the introduction, I mentioned that my life has been strewn with good fortune.

Other characters, whom it was difficult to take seriously, made occasional appearances at the bookshop. There was a divide between those for whom socialism was about class and those engaged in what would now be called culture wars. Once a year, during Gay Pride Week, the window of the Days of Hope bookshop would be decked in gay literature, badges and posters in a show of solidarity. After the display had come down one year, a youth stood in the centre of the shop and pedantically explained to me that socialists should not support gay rights, because homosexuality was a bourgeois vice that would be eradicated under socialism. After he had left, Martin Spence emerged from the back of the shop to say, 'I don't know how you managed to keep talking to that guy without wanting to hit him.' Another year, one man in late middle age came in, looking frightened, walked up closely to me and quietly asked whether we held meetings. I had to explain that we were not gay, we were showing solidarity. He left without another word.

Few of the many feminists involved, apart from Hilary Wainwright, had the confidence to argue in a room dominated by men, so their cause was sometimes unhelpfully taken up by a certain kind of shouty, aggressive male 'feminist'. One stood up in a packed room above a pub to denounce the Tyneside Socialist Centre for having too few women on its steering committee. He noted that one committee member was black but described him as a 'token' member, then, with dramatic sweep of the arm, he pointed to the women sitting in a row at the side of the room and declaimed, 'Here we have some OPPRESSED PEOPLE.' The oppressed people sat with folded arms, saying nothing.

That African man whom he so casually wrote off as a 'token' presence was the only one of us who belonged to a revolutionary organisation that made history, though not in a good way. He was an exile from white-ruled Rhodesia/Zimbabwe and a member of the Zimbabwe African National Union (ZANU), led by Robert Mugabe. The dozen or so members of ZANU in the area held a reception in the Tyneside Socialist Centre in honour of a leading figure who had come up from London. I was the only outsider invited. I was told that when winter turned to spring, ZANU would resume its guerrilla campaign and that the white minority would be brought down, a prediction that proved to be out by only one year. The man from London rather embarrassingly started praising me for what little I had done to help and promised that I would be an honoured guest in Harare when ZANU ruled Zimbabwe. He was so effusive that one of the others hit him on the arm and told him to stop flattering me. I never intended to take up the invitation, but I confess that I had no idea then about the monster Mugabe would prove to be. A speaker from the rival Zimbabwe African People's Union (ZAPU) movement told a Tyneside Socialist Centre meeting that Mugabe was not a true leader because he listened to others before reaching a decision, unlike Joshua Nkomo, of ZAPU. This seemed to me to be a point in Mugabe's favour. I also knew that ZANU had its political base among the Shona, who were the majority in Zimbabwe, while ZAPU's support was mainly among the minority, Ndebele. I believed at the time that it was right that Mugabe became Zimbabwe's first twentieth-century black ruler.

Disillusionment with Mugabe left me with low expectations when Nelson Mandel was released from jail, twelve years later. It is a truism now that Mandela was one of the greatest figures of his century, but we could not know for certain whether his long years in prison would leave him twisted and vindictive, like Mugabe, or would have rotted his mind. I was at Mandela's first press conference in the UK, on 4 July 1990, and saw on the podium, in that huge hall on Northumberland Avenue, a wise, alert, thoughtful old man, who took questions and gave himself ample time to think before answering, rocking back and forth in his chair. He had waited twenty-seven years to be free; he was not in any hurry to reply. Most of the questions were respectful, but the real test came when a young woman dressed in dungarees, who gesticulated as she spoke, alleged that African National Congress (ANC) fighters in camps outside South Africa had seized and tortured supporters of rival anti-apartheid groups. Mandela could have brushed her off, or replied that it was nothing to do with him because he was in prison at the time, but instead, he rocked back and forth in his usual way, addressed her as 'young lady' and told her that the allegation she had just made was true. When I heard him say that, I saw that this was a political leader in a class of his own.

It took a few weeks' involvement in the Tyneside Socialist Centre for me to grasp that nearly all the self-proclaimed 'revolutionaries' were not revolutionary at all. The organisations they joined were not there to overthrow capitalism: they were friendship groups. After a while, I reckoned I could have walked into a room full of members of the IMG and the Socialist Workers Party and deduced who belonged to which just by their physical appearance.

Those were not the strangest groups whose representatives made contact with the Days of Hope bookshop. A very shy man in his early forties would arrive once a week with copies of a newspaper called *Workers' Weekly*, which he wanted us to put on sale, though I do not recall anyone ever buying it. He was the leading light in the Tyneside branch of the Communist Party of England (Marxist–Leninist), who believed that the world's one truly socialist homeland was Albania, under the rule of that pathological dictator Enver Hoxha. Someone told me that every member of the Tyneside communist branch was male, each had a beard and they were all gay. That was certainly true of their leader. He entered into a relationship with a student at Newcastle University, who was in the painful process of coming out gay and who would come into the shop to tell us about his difficult life. Their relationship was severely strained after the youngster was invited to a meeting at which members of the CPE (M–L) reverently stood to sing a hymn to Joseph Stalin and he refused to join in.

On the opposite side of the Stalinist–Trotskyist schism was a group whom we saw only occasionally in the bookshop. The Workers Revolutionary Party (WRP) had more money than any rival Trotskyist group, because of the subsidies it was getting from Libya, but it was very short of members except in the actors' union, Equity. Vanessa Redgrave was the best known. The secretary of the north-east branch of Equity cornered me once to explain why the WRP was the true UK representative of the Fourth International, which Trotsky founded after being expelled from Russia, a title also claimed by the IMG. A man named Blair Peach had been killed by a blow to the head from a police truncheon during an anti-racist demonstration in London. The IMG gave evidence at the result-ing public inquiry, but the WRP refused to, which showed that the WRP took its internal security seriously, whereas the IMG did not. Throughout this talk, my interlocutor had one hand raised to eye level, with forefinger and thumb curled in a circle, and his hand moved to emphasise each word. At intervals, he paused, put his head to one side and looked at me intently, to check that I was taking it all in.

I can cite the exact wording he used as his peroration reached its dramatic climax: 'Trotskyism is the ideology of the working class in struggle. When the working class is called upon to fulfil its historic function, they will look around these Trotskyist groups and ask,

"Which is our leader?" – and they will choose the WRP, because the WRP has been serious about security!'

Sadly, he did not tell me how the working class would know when it had been called upon. I had a mental picture of the sky parting and an old man with a long white beard calling out, 'Working class, fulfil thy historic function!' whereupon little fellows in cloth caps and lasses with scarves around their heads would mill about in confusion, crying, 'Where are our leaders?' until over the horizon came the true Trotskyists. But that was not to be. In the mid-1980s, the WRP disintegrated after allegations arose that its founder, Gerry Healy, was a serial sexual predator.

These toytown revolutionaries did not inhabit the same mental universe as Ruth First, an intellectual whom Hilary Wainwright persuaded to come to address the Tyneside Socialist Centre. She was in her early fifties and had been the first white woman imprisoned under South Africa's Ninety-Day Detention Law. Until I heard her speak, I had naively thought that apartheid's root problem was racial prejudice, which would be overcome when the races came together in mutual respect, but Ruth First drew a vivid picture of an economic system squatting on a vast pool of black cheap labour, with black people pulled into work from their cheap homes in the Bantustans and sent back when they were not needed, while the profits they generated stayed in the areas reserved for whites. She did not declaim or wave her arms about as revolutionaries tended to do when addressing a meeting: she laid out facts and let them speak for themselves. At one point, she thought she had expressed herself badly and apologised, which I did not think was necessary, but behind me there was a contingent from the Socialist Workers Party (SWP), men less than half her age, listening impatiently. They wanted less explanation and more denunciation. They wanted to hear the heads of the South African government denounced as fascists and murderers. When she apologised, the contemptuous gasps and groans must have been loud enough for her to hear. These heroes of the SWP will have departed the meeting reassured that they were the toughest revolutionaries in the room. South Africa's notorious secret service, BOSS, took a different view. Five years later, they sent Ruth First a parcel that exploded in her hands and killed her.

13

MO

There is a house in Summerhill Terrace, further up Westgate Hill from where Days of Hope used to be, with a black plaque saying that Mo Mowlam once lived there. She threw a party in that house to introduce us to the new man in her life. He was the sociologist Laurie Taylor, who, with Stanley Cohen, had taken their academic discipline down a new path by going into the high-security wing of Durham prison to talk to the gangsters and robbers held there. Mo's affair, which lasted a couple of years, began on a day when, during a dull meal with other academics at Newcastle University, Taylor felt a stockinged foot rub his leg as an invitation.

Back then, Mo Mowlam did not look remotely like the Cabinet minister the public saw during the Blair years, as portrayed in a TV drama by Julie Walters. Just before the 1997 general election, the Labour shadow Cabinet was on parade at a press conference. Sitting not far from Tony Blair was a woman I did not recognise, who looked old, and overweight, and who moved her head slowly around to take in the room, as if half asleep. I wondered why she was there. Also, there was no sign of the slender, athletic, blonde Marjorie Mowlam, whom I had known for more than fifteen years. It took me a while to accept the disturbing conclusion that the stranger had to be Mo.

When the *Daily Mail* sets out to humiliate a woman for how she looks, a female columnist is called upon to do the deed. That day, Lynda Lee-Potter stepped boldly forth. This new, overweight Mo had all the appeal of a 'slightly effeminate Geordie trucker', she wrote. In response, Sunday newspaper correspondents were invited to a private briefing with Alastair Campbell, who told us that Mo had a brain tumour and that the shocking change in her appearance was brought about by chemotherapy. The extraordinary risks Mo took to bring about peace in Northern Ireland were the actions of a woman who knew she might not have long to live.

There was a point in the peace process when it appeared that two political parties from the Protestant side of the divide were going to boycott the talks because the gunmen held in prison intransigently opposed the prospect of power sharing. An obvious next step was to meet the gunmen, but no British Cabinet minister would deal directly with convicted terrorists – unless the Cabinet minister in question was the terminally ill Mo Mowlam. She went into Maze Prison for face-to-face talks with men who had committed murders and other acts of violence and who were proud of it. Had the visit failed, it is difficult to see what choice Blair would have had but to sack her, but she succeeded. When I saw her in the Commons soon afterwards, I asked what her civil servant advisers thought about the visit. 'They told me not to go,' she said, 'but I thought, "Fuck 'em. I'm going to do it. Fuck 'em."'

My novel *Innocent in the House*, published in 2001, included a cameo appearance by an unnamed female Secretary of State for Northern Ireland who swore profusely. As a precaution, I showed it to Mo, not wanting to offend her. That evening, the phone rang at home and I heard Mo's voice telling me, 'Andy, I have never been so insulted!'

There was a moment's awful silence as I saw a long friendship come down in flames. It was too late to apologise, because the book was with the printers. She was ill and she was offended.

The silence was broken suddenly by a peal of laughter. 'Did you really think I minded?' Mo asked, delighted that her prank had worked.

She always had a teenager's sense of humour. There is a story accurately told in Julia Langdon's biography of her, about one of her visits to the Days of Hope bookshop in the early 1980s:

Andy McSmith told her once that his partner, Sue Dearie, who worked in the reference section of the city library, had been complaining about the daft and trivial questions she got from the public. This immediately started Mo scheming. She planned to ring Sue and ask her how many sections there were to a caterpillar. At her first attempt Sue immediately recognised her voice. Mo pretended she was ringing for another reason, rang off and then grabbed some innocent customer in the bookshop. This poor sap was obliged to ring the reference library and seek information about caterpillar sections. Sue sighed and said she would need to look this up and ring him back. When he gave Sue the number on the telephone, she instantly recognised it. 'Has Mo Mowlam put you up to this?' she demanded.

Mo had other ways that were unusual in a career politician. When she arrived in Parliament in 1987, there were 609 male MPs, and just forty-one women. Mo was between lovers, which is not a comfortable position for any MP, especially a woman. There were several men in her life before she married Jon Norton, a City banker, but she never chose them with an eye to getting ahead. She did once tell me that 'power is fucking', but she did it for fun, not to advance her career. In the masculine environment of the House of Commons, men on the government front bench would think nothing of sitting back with folded arms and putting their feet up on the table, but it was expected of the women that they would sit upright with knees together. Mo had none of that. When it suited her, she would kick off her shoes and tuck one leg under her. I first had this pointed out to me by a Tory MP, who had observed her from across the aisle.

She was also unusually tactile. I rarely had a conversation with her without her touching my arm or shoulder. That aspect of her character did not appeal to some of the dour Ulster politicians she met. Seeing the Reverend Martin Smyth, Ulster Unionist MP for Belfast South and a Presbyterian minister, in the Commons lobby, I could not resist asking, 'Have you been touched by Mo Mowlam?'

'Mercifully, Satan has not brought me that experience, yet,' he snapped.

There were others who did not like her. Mo arrived in Newcastle in 1979, to a Labour Party in which the majority, who had lived in the region all their lives, supported the party's established leaders, such as Jim Callaghan, though there was a growing minority of university-educated incomers who were more likely to be part of the left-wing Bennite insurgency. Mo made a real effort to bridge the gap, which brought her friends and enemies on both sides. At a meeting of our local ward, she was replying to a fellow lecturer from Newcastle University, an angry character who had been around longer than Mo but could not match the impact she had made. Mo remarked, 'I sympathise with what John was saying...' He interrupted to say, 'I don't want your sympathy, love!'

In 1981, she put her name forward to be Tyne Bridge constituency's delegate to the annual Labour conference but narrowly lost to a supporter of the Militant Tendency. She was very annoyed, because this was a constituency party under right-wing control, but her opponent had three advantages she lacked: he was male, working-class and he had lived in the north-east all his life. Mo did eventually persuade Tyne Bridge constituency to send her to the 1983 annual conference, where she voted in favour of expelling five leaders of the Militant Tendency.

She also tried to be selected as parliamentary candidate for Newcastle Central for the 1983 general election. I was not backing her on that occasion, because she was up against my friend Nigel Todd. He won the selection, only to be swept aside in the deluge of 1983, so it was perhaps as well for Mo Mowlam that she had lost that contest. But she did not know it at the time and came out feeling very hurt, although we were still on good terms. She told me that she could not believe the animosity that such contests generated, with such feeling that I thought she might just give up the idea of being an MP.

One of the rumours put around during that time was that she was a CIA spy. I was told with great confidence, by a party member who did not know her, that Tony Benn was the source of this damaging gossip. Mo worked briefly with him in London, when she had just left university. There is a note in the published version of his diary dated on 4 April 1971 that 'she is very bright and has political ambitions'. When Benn visited Newcastle to sign copies of one of his books, he asked Bob Clay whether Mo was still based in the region. In reply, Bob Clay asked if he had heard the rumour. The three of us were in a car, so I butted in from the back seat to warn that I knew Mo, and Benn went silent. Later, when no one else was listening, he told me that the tale came about because she had gone on a trip to Turkey that seemed to be beyond her means. Years later, when questioned by Julia Langdon, Benn had completely forgotten that he had ever heard such a story and could find no record even in the unpublished parts of his copious diaries. If he had ever thought it was true, I doubt that he would have forgotten or failed to make a note of it.

In October 1985, Harry Cowans, the MP for Tyne Bridge, died suddenly, setting off a by-election in one of the safest Labour seats in the country, which drew an indecent rush of people with their eyes on this prize. On the day Harry died, I was told, phones rang in the regional offices of both the Transport and General Workers' Union (TGWU) and the National Union of Public Employees (NUPE), with callers seeking the nomination. The constituency secretary said that one hopeful turned up on his doorstep. By co-incidence, Martin Spence and Alan Milburn had organised a social event in the week after Cowans's death, in aid of the Days of Hope bookshop. Some unexpected guests turned up, including the MP for Blyth, a barrister named John Ryman, who had a very bad reputation and would eventually end up in prison. He had no empathy with the young left-wing activists who ran the bookshop, but there he was, accompanied by a county councillor from Ipswich, named Margaret, whom Ryman was sponsoring as a suitable candidate for Tyne Bridge.

Mo was another guest. She was not unwelcome or out of place. She used to come into the Days of Hope bookshop and do volunteer shifts on the till. With her extroverted manner, she made every customer feel welcome but made me nervous because of her generous habit of giving away badges or other small items for free, when I was constantly concerned about the shop's financial survival. Yet it was a surprise to see her at that social, because by then she had left Newcastle and taken a position as an administrator at Northern College, in Barnsley. I had also moved, to work for the Labour Party, but had been assigned as press officer for the impending by-election. Mo confided to me that she was on a scouting expedition to see if she had a chance of being selected. I would have been delighted to work with her as a candidate but knew that she was at a disadvantage. The north-east was more solidly Labour than anywhere else in England, but there had been no female Labour MP in the region since Ellen Wilkinson died, in 1947.

The selection took place on a Saturday afternoon. Mo was on the shortlist. Joe Mills, the regional secretary of the TGWU, had told his union's delegates that they should vote for her. Tyne Bridge was a bastard constituency, half in Newcastle, half in Gateshead, which offended sentiments on both banks of the Tyne. As the delegates assembled, an old fellow with a cloth cap on his head turned up and someone asked how he was, to which he answered, 'Fucking awful! It's the first time I've been in fucking Newcastle on a fucking Saturday, and I tell you it's the fucking last.' Hearing that, I knew Mo did not have a chance.

She was having a bad time in Barnsley. As I knew from managing the bookshop, there are people who get jobs in left-wing organisations who believe they are entitled to be paid while doing just as much work as they fancy doing. Mo thought that two of the college's staff needed to be sacked and was plunged into a losing battle with the unions. The stress had given her shingles. She was also exasperated because a lecturer at the college, Jean McCrindle, had spent the year of the miners' strike working virtually full time on the Women Against Pit Closures movement and was very close to the miners' leader, Arthur Scargill. Mo felt unable to complain, lest she be accused of taking sides against the miners.

In time, Mo decided that she could not stand working at Northern College any longer and sought me out at Labour headquarters to ask if there was any chance of a job as a researcher there. As we discussed the state of the Labour Party, she suddenly demanded, 'Why aren't you arguing with me, like you used to in Newcastle?' The reason was that she had not said anything with which I disagreed, but she may have thought I was holding fire because I was feeling sorry for her. Her prospects did not look good. The idea of her doing research for the Labour Party was a bit desperate. Researchers worked alone in their secluded offices, emerging occasionally to take a bus to the House of Commons to meet the relevant frontbench team, and were expected to defer to their head of department, to the general secretary and to the shadow ministers they served. Mo was far too sociable, and deference really was not one of her strong points.

She was still adrift when Margaret Thatcher announced on 12 May 1987 that there would be a general election in four weeks. By now, the north-east Labour Party had broken with tradition by selecting not one but two women to contest Labour seats, neither of whom was Mo Mowlam. They were Hilary Armstrong, in North West Durham, and Joyce Quin, in Gateshead East.

The campaign had hardly begun when party headquarters was lumbered with a problem they really did not need. Party organisers had gone to some trouble to support the MP for Redcar, who had been bombarding them with complaints that members of his party were trying to get him to retire, at sixty-five. With help for the centre, he was selected to run again but changed his mind when the campaign began. A replacement had to be found, urgently. The local party was told that they would have to meet the following week, when they would be presented with a shortlist drawn up by party organisers. Three local men stepped forward, but the director of organisation, Joyce Gould, refused to sign off an all-male shortlist. The only woman known to have parliamentary ambitions and a connection with the north-east was Mo Mowlam, whose name was added to the list. A few days later, she was the candidate in a seat so solidly Labour that it was hers for as long as she wanted.

In 1989, she was appointed shadow Minister for City and Corporate Affairs, which was reckoned to be the most important position outside the shadow Cabinet. So rapid a rise created resentment, inevitably. I overheard an MP who had just been dropped from the front bench assert that she was 'as thick as two planks' and had been chosen solely because she was a woman. That year, she began a passionate affair with a journalist well known in the lobby, who was also married to a well-known journalist. They had young children. I saw Mo on the day the story appeared in *Private Eye*. She judged that the best defence against gossip was to put in an appearance in Parliament and let as many people as possible see her, but she was nervous and upset. She vehemently denied being the cause of the break-up of her lover's marriage. Neither jealousy nor her messy private life prevented her from advancing quickly.

Seniority counted for a lot in those years between 1979 and 1996, when Labour's shadow Cabinet was elected annually by the MPs. Anyone who reached that level in less than ten years in Parliament was doing well. Gordon Brown set the all-time record when he was elected after only four years. The runners-up, who got there in five, were Tony Blair, David Blunkett and Mo Mowlam.

Gordon Brown had singled Mo out for rapid promotion in 1989, but it did not take many months before they had fallen out. She was the first person I ever heard suggest, in private, that Brown had a psychological problem that made him unfit to lead the Labour Party. When John Smith suddenly died, in 1994, she was the first member of the shadow Cabinet to tell Tony Blair that he ought to run for the leadership, regardless of what Brown decided to do, and that she was ready to be his campaign manager. But Blair opted for the safer choice of Jack Straw, perhaps seeing trouble ahead. And, in due course, her relations with Blair were close to breaking point. She claimed that their problems were exacerbated by opinion polls in which she was shown to be more popular than the Prime Minister – when respondents were asked whether individual Cabinet ministers were doing a good or bad job, Mo's score was plus forty, Blair's was plus one – but actually throughout her life she had a problem dealing with men in authority. On Blair's side, they blamed Mo's erratic behaviour for the rupture. She had lied to him about the seriousness of her brain tumour. When it was time for a Cabinet reshuffle, she was given the largely meaningless post of Minister for the Cabinet Office. She resented the insult, yet she must have known that she was no longer in a fit state to run a large government department.

Sue and I visited Mo and her husband, John Norton, after she had retired from politics in 2001, in a house buried along a winding country lane. She had two teenage stepchildren from John's first marriage and allowed our youngsters to run around their home freely. She was tired, and rendered old before her time, but still intellectually lively and tactile. Mo died a month before her fifty-sixth birthday.

14

THE RIVALS: BENN AND HEALEY

On 27 June 1993, Tony Benn joined a small gathering of family and friends, at which his son Stephen gave him a book as a belated sixty-eighth birthday present. That evening, as always, he dictated an entry in his voluminous diary. 'Andy McSmith, who has just written the life of John Smith, was there,' he recorded, 'and he kindly signed it "*To Tony Benn, my friend and mentor.*" It was very nice of him. He is an absolute hack Kinnockite, but a great friend of Nita's.'

There is a curious error here. Tony Benn had just received a warm message from the leader of the Labour Party, who was very likely to be Prime Minister in four years, because the handwritten inscription was not from me but from John Smith. No other Labour leader in about forty years would have written such kind words about Tony Benn, but Smith had worked with Benn when he was Secretary of State for Energy and Smith was his deputy. Benn had earned the disapproval of every Labour leader since Harold Wilson. Evidently, it did not cross his mind that there might be one in place who actually liked him.

The way it is worded also seems to imply that there was something anomalous about my being on the one hand a 'Kinnockite hack', and on the other, a 'great friend' of Benn's daughter-in-law, Nita Clarke. Nita was more 'Kinnockite' than I ever was. Her career progression took her into Downing Street, as a special adviser, and earned her an honorary mention in Tony Blair's memoirs and an OBE. Benn's second son, Hilary, would one day be Jeremy Corbyn's leading opponent within the shadow Cabinet. Emily Benn, Nita and Stephen's daughter, resigned from the Labour Party while Corbyn was leading it, in solidarity with her friend Luciana Berger, and re-joined in 2022. Politics was clearly in their blood, but Tony Benn never demanded that members of his family be 'Bennites' and never tolerated personal attacks on any of them.

That did not apply to me, of course. On that day in June, when no one else was listening, he gave me that 'disagree with me if you dare' look and declared that Tony Blair, who was then the shadow Home Secretary, was 'worse than David Owen', who had left Labour in 1981 to launch the Social Democratic Party. I did not usually see it as my role to defend Blair, but Benn was obviously expecting an argument, so I said something along the lines that Blair actually wanted Labour to defeat the Conservatives, whereas Owen's deliberate intention was to ensure that Labour was destroyed as a potential party of government. Thereby, I earned the sobriquet 'absolute hack'. I could object that calling someone who had written a friendly biography of John Smith a 'Kinnockite' suggests that Benn was not up to speed on the rivalries and tensions within the mainstream of the Labour Party.

He said another curious thing that day. He asked me how old John Smith was when he became a Cabinet minister, in 1978. I said thirty-nine. 'Yes, I was a Cabinet minister at thirty-nine,' Benn replied. I assumed that must be true, because when he was the candidate in a by-election in Chesterfield, in 1983, he wrote in his campaign literature that he had been a Cabinet minister during the entire time when Labour was in government, between 1964 and 1979. But that was not true. Benn was Postmaster General in 1964, which gave him the right to attend Cabinet meetings, which is not strictly the same thing. He was promoted to the Cabinet in 1966, aged forty-one.

No one fought harder than Tony Benn to be in the House of Commons, which he entered at the age of twenty-five, fighting two by-elections in the early 1960s to retain his right to stay after inheriting an unwanted peerage, and a third after losing his seat in 1983, and quit at the age of seventy-six. After he had retired, he often revisited the building, yet the volume of his diaries covering the years after he left the Commons were given the title *More Time for Politics*, as if his eleven years as a minister and fifty-one years in Parliament were all a bit of a distraction from the main business. He was a man of contradictions.

The first time I saw him in person was at an election rally in Slough early in 1974. He was already so popular with party activists that year after year he topped the poll in elections to the National Executive, and so reviled on the right that in 1973, the *Daily Express* published a cartoon depicting him in Nazi uniform, with a swastika armband. What I remember most about that speech was the power of his voice. He was used to speaking in public without a microphone and did not need one to make himself heard very clearly from the back of the hall.

In 1980, he discombobulated the publicity department at Penguin

Books, by telling them that he was going to Newcastle upon Tyne to sign copies of his book, *Arguments for Socialism*, at a little bookshop they had never heard of, called Days of Hope. Someone from Penguin dug out our phone number and rang to insist that we open an account with them at once, instead of ordering their titles through a distributor. Sitting at Benn's side, operating the till, I noted how, while customers were queueing to have their books signed, his face was like a mask. It came alive afterwards. He had spotted a postcard that made fun of the party leader, Michael Foot, and, with a conspiratorial look, he bought a copy. A year later, he came back to sign *Arguments for Democracy*. This time, Tyneside's small but active branch of the New National Front turned up to shout abuse and throw a stink bomb through the door.

A year and a half later, I was a new member of the Labour staff on my way to Chesterfield, as Benn battled to get back into Parliament at the first opportunity, after losing his Bristol seat in the 1983 general election. A more experienced press officer sent ahead of me loathed the candidate so heartily that she would shudder at the sound of his voice. Since Benn did not trust the head office machine, he had his own aides in town, including Nita Clarke, his future daughter-in-law, and Jon Lansman, who would resurface over thirty years later as the founder of Momentum and one of the main drivers of Corbyn's first successful leadership campaign.

There has never been another parliamentary by-election quite like the one in Chesterfield in 1984. The town was so full of party workers and journalists that every hotel was fully booked. There were days when entire coachloads of Benn supporters rolled up, giving the organisers a challenging time trying to find something useful they could all do. One polling company discovered that more than 90 per cent of Chesterfield's voters could name the Labour candidate, unprompted. In a care home that Benn visited, followed as ever by a camera crew, an elderly lady recognised him and said, in a broad East Midlands accent, 'Weren't thou t' fellow that didn't want to be a lord?' Benn was of course delighted to be reminded of his long, successful battle to renounce his hereditary peerage and confirmed that he was.

'What's thou doing in Chesterfield?' she enquired.

Hundreds stayed to hear the result on polling day, even if they had nowhere to stay the night. Photographers jostled for a good angle in front of the stage. On my way to the count, I came upon two schoolboys, aged about fourteen, who told me that they were hoping to interview Benn for their school magazine. There was no chance that they would get near him that evening. I even feared for their safety in the melee in the hall and promised them that if they called in at Labour Party headquarters the following morning, I would make sure they were able to conduct their interview, which they did. Meanwhile, I asked if there was anyone else they would like to meet, and they mentioned that they hoped to interview Screaming Lord Sutch, founder of the chimeric Monster Raving Loony Party, who had been fighting by-elections for over twenty years, losing his deposit every time but covering his costs by organising music gigs. They had spotted that Sutch had promised in his manifesto that, if elected, he would straighten out the twisted spire of the Church of St Mary and All Saints. The boys sensibly pointed out that the crooked spire was what made Chesterfield famous, so why change it?

'Politicians should be seen to be doing something. And if I straighten out the spire, I will be seen to be doing something,' Sutch replied, with mock solemnity. 'But to answer your point, I'll make all the houses crooked, then Chesterfield will be even more famous.'

Gerald Kaufman, who loathed Tony Benn, remarked that the Chesterfield by-election was an occasion when an MP's best alibi was to be at the scene of the crime. In that spirit, almost every centre-right and centre-left Labour MP put in an appearance, while half of them privately willed Benn to lose. Neil Kinnock came ten days before polling day to show support for someone he would happily have seen excluded from the House of Commons for ever. They were driven to the Market Place, where they were mobbed by shoppers. At a crowded social for party members that evening, Benn greeted Kinnock with a roaring welcome, like an old comrade. The next time they were face to face was at the next monthly meeting of the National Executive in party headquarters. They passed each other without a word of greeting. I doubt that they exchanged a courteous word ever again.

Benn's greatest opponent was Denis Healey, against whom he fought the angry contest for the deputy leadership in 1981. At a meeting of campaign staff, Benn did not hide his delight at news that his old enemy was coming to town. The visit was sure to go well, he told us, because Healey was an 'old trooper' who would know exactly what to do.

The old rivals addressed an evening rally, in which so much nearly went wrong. The biggest hall that could be booked in Chesterfield was not big enough, so as Benn arrived, there was a clamour for him to address the crowd outside, but if he had, there would have been no images of him on stage with Healey in time for the ten o'clock news. There were three chairs on stage. The general secretary, Jim Mortimer, had placed himself in the middle, but that was not the picture that Benn wanted millions of television viewers to see, so as Mortimer stood up to introduce the speakers, Benn slipped into his chair. Mortimer did not notice and very nearly sat on his lap. At the same time, someone had decided to take up a collection, and the microphones were picking up the clatter of coins being dropped into a metal bucket. None of this fazed Healey, who stood up and made a short witty speech. It was less than three years since the public enmity between these men had filled the air waves. He had to say something about Benn, because to ignore him would be a blatant snub, but if he offered faint praise, the pack of journalists in the hall would say it was a veiled attack, while fulsome praise would be denounced as hypocrisy. They reckoned without Healey's ingenuity. Chesterfield is just twenty-six miles from Nottingham, home of Jayne Torvill and Christopher Dean, whom millions of television viewers had watched only a month earlier as they won the gold medal for ice skating at the Winter Olympics. Turning to his rival, Healey said with a broad smile, 'Tony and I are inseparable. Healey without Benn would be like Torvill without Dean.' He is often misquoted as having added, 'I can't get the bugger off my back' – which he certainly did not say while the cameras were rolling, but I suspect he said something of the sort privately, afterwards.

At that exact moment, an old-fashioned banner on wooden poles at the back of the stage slid gracefully sideways to collapse in a heap, as if Healey's punchline had knocked it over. Random accidents like that can have an impact in politics. When an event is going badly, something as trivial as, for instance, a letter falling off the backdrop when Theresa May was addressing a Conservative conference, is a catastrophe. There had been much speculation that Benn might lose the Chesterfield by-election in the early days of the campaign.

The uproarious laughter that followed the collapse of the banner rang out like confirmation that he had won. That evening, a local radio station recorded the old enemies having a sing-song together. It did not matter that their singing voices were atrocious.

The by-election was Benn's last hurrah. Though he was back in Parliament, the body of political beliefs known as 'Bennism' was confined to the margins. On the day in 1985 when Neil Kinnock launched his highly publicised attack on Liverpool's left-wing councillors, Benn was notably quiet. Hovering at the back of the hall, to avoid being on stage during Kinnock's speech, he told me, 'I'm taking a rest from public disapproval.' He challenged Kinnock for the party leadership in 1988, but the result just demonstrated what a marginal figure he had become. In November 1990, he approached me in the Commons to ask if I thought Margaret Thatcher would survive that month's crisis. Minutes earlier I had been told that her time was up by Philip Webster, the political editor of *The Times*, who was far better plugged into the Tory Party than I was. I repeated this to Benn. His reaction was unusual. Other Labour MPs revelled in the prospect of her being brought down, but he replied, with a note of regret, that the pro-EU establishment was out to get her and would probably succeed. She was, like or hate her, a political giant, brought down by lesser men. I suspect in that the quiet Benn saw an echo of his life's story.

In obscurity, he at least no longer attracted the venom that was directed at him in his heyday, and when he died, in 2014, the initial reaction was as if the country was saying goodbye to a national treasure. 'Was he a teddy bear?' I was asked on television in the week that he died, to which I could only reply, 'No, he was a street fighter.'

In the days when he was not a national treasure, Benn attracted more venom than any other living British politician. During the Chesterfield by-election, *The Sun* ran a feature headed 'Benn on the Couch', which implied that he was mentally ill, though he was more often denounced for being bad, rather than mad. Curiously, one person who seemed genuinely interested in what drove Benn was his antipode, Denis Healey. 'I never could work out with him how much he really believed in what he was doing, and how much was ambition', he told me, when there was no one else listening.

It was said of Healey that he could have achieved his ambition to lead the Labour Party if only he had been less rude and more tolerant. He certainly had a temper. As Labour headed towards defeat in the 1987 general election, he knew that he would never be in government and lost his temper when questioned on breakfast television about his wife's decision to pay for private healthcare. He stormed out of the studio, live on television, and as he left, he raised an arm to push a door open, not noticing in his rage that it had already been opened by Adam Boulton, coming in the other direction, and gave Boulton a violent shove.

I was once in the enclosed space of a small car when Healey was, in his own words, 'shit tired', because he had just landed after a trip abroad that had not gone well and he had had to face journalists at the airport. As he drove, he was swearing at other drivers and cursing the foul day he had endured, until he suddenly interrupted the flow of obscenities to turn to me and say, in a silly voice, 'I'm a bad-tempered old Denis.'

I had another car journey with him in July 1986, which began with him in a foul mood because the driver who was supposed to take him back to London, from Newcastle-under-Lyme, had not turned up, and there was another delay because my car did not have a full tank of petrol. But once we were on our way, I managed somehow to inject into our conversation the fact that I had written a stage play about the Bolshevik Nikolai Bukharin. Healey was fascinated. An ex-communist, he knew all about Bukharin. From then on, if I rang him, he would greet me with an exclamation such as 'You're a lovely boy', or in a crowded room he would point at me and announce, 'There's the expert on Bukharin' – leaving his listeners to wonder who or what 'Bukharin' might be.

Healey's temper was probably anything but calm when it looked as if Benn might win the deputy leadership contest in 1981, but once it was over, he let it go. What always rankled him was that he had to settle for the deputy leadership, when he was devoutly convinced that there was no one better qualified to lead the party than him, and that included Michael Foot. When Healey arrived to campaign in a by-election in Newcastle upon Tyne, the candidate, David Clelland, greeted him with an unsolicited apology for having backed Benn in 1981. Healey shrugged that off, pointed to Kinnock, who was also in the room, and said, 'He did something much stupider: he voted for Michael Foot.'

Healey liked to play the clown. I was in a hotel room with him when he rang his wife and asked, in a voice that mimicked the camp comedian Kenneth Williams, 'Hello, is that Mrs Healey?' Edna Healey, of course, was not fooled. And no one was misled by his tomfoolery into doubting that he was a profoundly serious politician. He was also every bit as much a street fighter as Benn.

Benn, Healey and Thatcher were all of that generation who entered politics after the war of 1939–45, when huge issues were at stake. Benn and Thatcher started out by supporting the consensus known as 'Butskellism' but decided during the 1970s that it had failed, though the remedies they put forward were diametrically opposed, while Healey stayed with the old consensus. But they were all interested in how to govern and went into the political arena ready for a fight.

The day after Tony Benn died, in March 2014, I rang Healey, who was then ninety-six years old, and asked whether he had liked Benn. Healey replied, 'I disliked him intensely when we were fighting, because I felt he was raising the wrong issues and using the wrong arguments, but by the end of our careers, we got on very well and we had some very friendly conversations.'

'In those days, for politicians, politics was almost all that mattered,' he added. 'Nowadays most politicians are not much more interested in politics than the electorate.'

15

IN THE BEATING HEART
OF THE LABOUR PARTY

The press office at Labour headquarters was a place of warring factions, mutual loathing, low morale and a search for someone to blame. The party was absorbing its worst electoral defeat in fifty years. It could have been December 2019, but actually I refer to January 1984, when I reported for duty, excited by the prospect of being close to the centre of the nation's political life. At the end of the day, I joined past and present press officers in a nearby pub and heard them enviously talking about someone who had found other employment, thus escaping the awful fate of continuing to work for the Labour Party.

Apart from the party leader, Michael Foot, who said he was ashamed and resigned, no politician was accepting responsibility for the debacle in 1983. The left blamed the breakaway Social Democratic Party, for splitting the non-Tory vote, and defended Labour's manifesto, which was the most radical that any major party had ever put before the electorate. Tony Benn, its principal author, called it a 'democratic socialist bridgehead in public understanding'. But someone on the other side pithily wrote off that manifesto as 'the longest suicide note in history'. But both sides of that political chasm agreed on one point: that it had been a shockingly badly organised campaign. In the words of Ken Livingstone, it was 'the worst campaign of any major political party in a western democracy in the post-war world'. But whose fault was that?

The researchers at head office believed they were in the clear. They had done a sterling job keeping up with the policy commitments that poured forth from the National Executive while it was controlled by Benn and his allies. The party organisers and administrative staff had also done their best under difficult circumstances. By general acclaim, the fault was in the communications department.

From what I heard, it had been a happy ship until it was hit by two torpedoes. The head of the department, Max Madden, whom the staff liked, a Bennite who believed in the manifesto, resigned after securing a safe parliamentary seat. Then the left lost control of the National Executive, in October 1982, and the staff were now reporting to a committee dominated by the right, who despised Benn and abhorred the manifesto, which they saw as an incubus that it was too late to remove before the impending election. The communications department was required to sell to the public a set of policies which their employers intended to ditch as soon as the campaign was over.

When choosing a new department head, the right naturally looked for one of their own. A replacement was plucked from the quiet backwater of a press office of a medium-sized union and hurled into the whitewater rapids of a general election.

By the time I turned up, nine months after the election, most of the journalists in the building had withdrawn into a defensive cocoon. 'This party is run by fools,' one declared, during a National Union of Journalists (NUJ) chapel meeting. Another told me emphatically, 'Labour doesn't deserve to win.'

On one of my days off, the phone rang to say that I was needed on urgent NUJ business. A journalist from *Labour Weekly*, the party's official newspaper, had walked into the press office and overheard a secretary speaking on the phone. Her name was Fiona. She was one of many people for whom the Labour Party was a calling, not a career. 'When I asked for a job here, I didn't care if they told me I had to clean the lavvies, I just wanted to work for the Labour Party,' she once told me. She was still an active party member, more than thirty-five years later. Alone in the office, when all the press officers were somewhere else, she had answered a call from a journalist who wanted to know the name of the shadow Foreign Secretary, and she was pleased to be able to give an immediate answer, that it was Denis Healey. Before the day was out, the NUJ had convened in an emergency session to decide whether to invoke the disputes procedure because a secretary had answered a question that should have been answered by a journalist. I cannot remember how it was resolved.

A more obvious question was why there was a phone ringing in an empty office. That was never addressed, because the head of department was in no position to impose good timekeeping on his staff. Demoralised, friendless and out of his depth, he had developed a work pattern that involved turning up in the morning, shutting himself in his office for a short time, before crossing the room and announcing over his shoulder that he was going 'to a meeting'. Out of the building, he was out of contact, there being no mobile phones nor pagers in those days. By the time he resurfaced, it was time to go home. This happened so often that I once asked a colleague where he was, and she simply wrote the letters 'i.a.m.' on a scrap of paper, because, as ever, he was 'in a meeting'.

There was a day when Neil Kinnock came to head office to give a national television interview in the boardroom on the third floor. With the leader in the building, you might think that staff would be tripping over each other in their eagerness to get involved. Instead, they scattered to the four winds. There was no friendship between Neil Kinnock and the general secretary, Jim Mortimer, who also did not care for journalists, so he stayed away. The head of media was, as usual, in a meeting somewhere. Others had their various reasons not to be there. I discovered the previous day that I was going to be there on my own and asked a friendly colleague who worked in the publications department if he would be on hand if I needed him, to which he kindly agreed. Unfortunately, come the day, he overslept. I met him coming in, looking apologetic, as everyone was packing up. Yet, somehow, I managed to greet the camera crew, escort them upstairs, make sure they had all they needed, greet Kinnock and his entourage and so on, and the only hitch was when Kinnock asked for a cup of coffee. There was no one anywhere in sight who had the authority to tell someone to make drinks, and it would not have looked good if I had vanished to another floor for however long it took to activate the coffee machine in the press office and in my absence some other problem had blown up. As I prevaricated, Kinnock's press secretary, Patricia Hewitt, told me sternly, 'Andy, we are supposed to be the party that's going to form the next government: we can arrange a cup of coffee.' I found a helpful member of the support staff.

There is, by a way, a distinction between staff employed by a political party and advisers, such as Patricia Hewitt, who work in MPs' offices. They are paid out of public funds and are employed by the MPs to whom they report. The advisers were generally not demoralised by the defeat, for which they did not feel personally responsible, though one had a breakdown and others were on the look-out for new career opportunities. Along the corridor occupied by the shadow Cabinet, Donald Dewar and Barry Jones, shadow Secretaries of State for Scotland and Wales, had offices next to one another, and each employed an ambitious twenty-something researcher, named, respectively, Tim Luckhurst and Rod Liddle. Both soon moved on to jobs with the BBC. Fast forward to December 2021, when Luckhurst was principal of South College, Durham University, and had arranged a £10-a-head dinner for students, to which he invited his friend of thirty-five years to be the guest speaker. Liddle was by now a well-known newspaper columnist, a right-wing populist who liked to provoke, and who opened his speech by expressing disappointment that there were no sex workers in the room. The students had not been forewarned that he would be speaking. Some walked out, which annoyed Luckhurst, who called them 'pathetic'. His wife, Dorothy, a former researcher at Conservative Central Office, was filmed on social media chanting 'arse, arse, arse, arse' at a student whose opinions conflicted with hers.

There was no easy escape into an alternative job for the party's head of media. It was not a great commendation to have on his CV that he had presided over the omnifuck that was Labour's 1983 election campaign. I suspect that he knew, at heart, that he should go but could not see a way. I was briefly the NUJ father of chapel and did my best to give him a push. The chapel passed a vote of no confidence, and I spent two long meetings in Jim Mortimer's office, expounding on them of his unfitness to do the job. The head of media did not put up any defence. He sat and listened, in silence. Afterwards, he showed no resentment but would talk to me in a friendly way, as if I was the one person in the department he could trust.

The barrier to dismissal was Jim Mortimer. He was a kind man, now in his mid-sixties, a trade unionist whose life's work had been to defend employees against the sack and other hardships. Over his head was a committee dominated by trade union officials. The proposition that a party employee should be sacked for incompetence horrified him. 'This could affect his whole career,' he exclaimed, looking at me, aghast.

So far as I know, the only person who came close to being sacked during Mortimer's three years as general secretary was a young secretary assigned to a middle manager, who bullied her. She was, if my memory is correct, the only black woman employed in head office. She wanted to complain to her union, the Association of Professional, Executive, Clerical and Computer Staff (APEX), but her boss was chairman of the APEX branch. She therefore took her grievance to Andy Bevan, who ran the staff branch of the much larger Transport and General Workers' Union (TGWU). Bevan was notorious for being a member of Militant, a Trotskyist grouplet, who was given a staff job by the left-dominated National Executive Committee (NEC) against the expressed opposition of the Prime Minister, Jim Callaghan, but he was a very effective trade union representative, who agreed to take up her case if she joined the TGWU, which she was willing to do. But then APEX invoked what was known as the Bridlington Agreement, which barred unions affiliated to the Trades Union Congress (TUC) from poaching each other's members. Reluctantly, Bevan had to accept an instruction from TGWU headquarters to reject her application. She, meanwhile, refused to go back into APEX, but everybody on the Labour Party staff was required to be a union member, which meant that she was now committing the one sure sacking offence. Somehow, a compromise was struck up, under which she was moved to an office on the ground floor, away from everyone else. During 1985, coincidentally, I was working temporarily on a project which meant that I needed to move out of the press office, so I moved and took up the other half of that office. We got along well.

One evening after work I had an alarming experience in a pub, when I discovered that suddenly I could not wink or whistle. The women I was with did not think I should need to, but that was not the point. In the morning, half of my face was paralysed. If I tried to wrinkle my brow, half of it wrinkled, half did not. If I stuck out my tongue, it came out of the side of my mouth. One eye was stinging because it was permanently open. I went to the doctor, who was thrilled. He told me this was Bell's palsy, an ailment he had learnt about at medical school but had never come across in his years of practice. He asked if I would mind if he rang a colleague with the exciting news. By the end of the day, I was in a lecture theatre, being asked to do things with my face so that rows of medical students could see a genuine case of Bell's palsy. The doctors attributed this alarm to a gap under the bedroom door of our new house, which caused a draught that had affected a nerve on the back of my neck, but when I returned to work, my roommate there was convinced that I had made myself ill by working too hard. This young woman who was nearly sacked for not being in a trade union now made it her business to try to make me slow down for the good of my health.

In summer 1985, Jim Mortimer retired, to be replaced by Larry Whitty, and Robert Maxwell agreed to do Neil Kinnock a favour by offering the head of media a job in his private office, thus making way for the arrival of Peter Mandelson.

Though there was a downside to working for the Labour Party, the good days were exhilarating. Every few months, I was able to get out of the London office when there was a parliamentary by-election to be fought. The Labour Party was more working class then than it is now. Women who lacked the confidence to go out canvassing would crowd into campaign headquarters to volunteer for mundane tasks such as filling envelopes with leaflets for door-to-door delivery. Denis Healey stayed to chat with a large group after he turned up for the Greenwich by-election, early in 1987. Something reminded him of his war record as beach master during the Allied landings in Sicily in 1944.

'I had a terrible time getting back from Anzio,' he said.

'Oh, I know how you feel, Denis,' one of the ladies replied, 'It took me two buses to get here from Eltham.'

It was an amusing misunderstanding, but at least the old lady, who was likely to have left school at fourteen and spent her whole life in Eltham, felt sufficiently at home in a party office to share her travel experiences with the former Chancellor of the Exchequer.

• • •

At least one entire book has been written about 'Red Wedge', which brought musicians and comedians together in support of the miners, the Labour Party and other causes. When Tony Man-waring, a researcher at Labour's head office, first told me that he had just taken a call from Pete Jenner, who introduced himself as Billy Bragg's manager, neither name meant anything to either of us, though Jenner was well known in the industry for having managed Pink Floyd and Ian Dury, while Billy Bragg was about to make a breakthrough with the EP *Between the Wars*. Their offer to help the Labour Party deserved to be taken seriously. Manwaring arranged for the boardroom at headquarters to be used for an inaugural meeting of what came to be called Red Wedge. To make it official, it had to be chaired by a member of the NEC. Protocol said that it should be the formidable Gwyneth Dunwoody, who ran the relevant subcommittee. This could have been a problem, because when the crowded meeting began, one of the first to speak was Paul Weller, formerly of The Jam, who complained that the party had not done enough to support the miners during the 1984–85 strike. Dunwoody would not have known or cared who Paul Weller was: she would have heard a young man with left-wing opinions, would have slapped him down; but she was either unavailable or unin-terested, and her place was taken by Tom Sawyer, a union official with teenage children, who knew the contemporary music scene well. He replied tactfully, and Weller announced that his new band, Style Council, was performing for two nights at Wembley, and one night's proceeds would go to Red Wedge.

Others of us had our knowledge of the mid-1980s music scene tested to the limit. I usually turned for advice to the youngest person employed at head office. That was the eighteen-year-old Tom Watson, thirty years before he was elected deputy leader of the party. When I told John Smith that a singer named Billy Bragg was prepared to add a new dimension to the Labour Party's 'Jobs and Industry Campaign', it evoked only a blank look, until he had been home to Morningside and had consulted his daughters. He called me on Monday in a high state of excitement to say that Bragg was a tremendous catch.

It proved to be the most successful attempt to draw young people towards the Labour Party until the launch of Momentum, thirty years later. I enjoyed their company, with one memorable exception: a university student who turned up in short trousers and spoke to me and to the director of organisation, Joyce Gould, with such an air of one who is addressing his social inferiors that we sent him away without giving him any help in contacting Red Wedge. This was Toby Young, whose father wrote the manifesto on which Labour fought the 1945 election, who distilled his knowledge of human relations into a book he wrote, called *How to Lose Friends and Alienate People*.

That aside, all went well until one morning when Neil Kinnock came down to breakfast and his fifteen-year-old son, Stephen, who had been reading *New Musical Express*, told him, 'Dad, Paul Weller says you sold out the miners.'

That accusation was thrown at Kinnock time and again during the 1984–85 miners' strike – though not usually over breakfast. Coming from a mining family, he was emotionally engaged, but political realities meant that he could not support Arthur Scargill's tactic of using mass pickets to try to force workers who had never been balloted to stop work. After the defeat, the party had an annual conference in Bournemouth, at which the National Union of Mineworkers proposed a motion that would have instructed a Labour government to reinstate every sacked miner, review the cases of those arrested during the violence on picket lines and reimburse union funds sequestered by the courts. There was no doubt that this motion was going to be passed at a conference where sympathy for the miners ran high, and yet Kinnock made the unusual decision that he would go to the rostrum to argue against it, rather than leave one of his shadow Cabinet members to go down to defeat.

Kinnock was also in open conflict with Labour councillors in Liverpool and Lambeth, who had defied the law by refusing to set a rate, in protest against government cuts. Liverpool had run out of money, and since a majority of councillors refused either to set a rate that would cover their costs or to make cuts, they had resorted to histrionically sacking thousands of staff. They too were a visible presence in Bournemouth, fuelling the taunts aimed at Kinnock that he was incapable of controlling the party he supposedly led. And yet, on the opening day, a Sunday, I was surprised to see him emerge from a long meeting of the divided NEC, happily singing to himself. I noted in my diary that 'all the Kinnock camp is outwardly calm'.

On Tuesday, the day of Kinnock's speech in Bournemouth, Billy Bragg and Pete Jenner wanted to be in the hall to witness the event, but they were almost an hour late. Kinnock had meandered through topics as varied as rising unemployment and the civil war in Nicaragua by the time I heard that they had arrived. I hurried down into the garage beneath the conference hall to usher them quickly through security, warning them that they had missed almost everything the leader had to say. Just after we entered the hall, Kinnock sprung this famous passage on his unsuspecting audience:

Implausible promises don't win victories. I'll tell you what happens with impossible promises. You start with far-fetched resolutions. They are then pickled into a rigid dogma, a code, and you go through the years sticking to that, out-dated, misplaced, irrelevant to the real needs, and you end up in the grotesque chaos of a Labour council – a *Labour* council! – hiring taxis to scuttle round a city handing out redundancy notices to its own workers. *(Applause.)* I am telling you, no matter how entertaining, how fulfilling to short-term egos – *(Continuing applause)* – you can't play politics with people's jobs … *(Applause and some boos.)*

While others rose to give Kinnock a standing ovation, Derek Hatton, Liverpool Council's deputy leader, was also on his feet, waving a fist and shouting. Frances Curran, a member of Militant, who was on the platform representing the Young Socialists, walked off in protest, but almost no one noticed because of the more visible spectacle of the Liverpool MP, Eric Heffer, striding off the platform and through the hall, face red with fury. As he neared the exit, he swept between me and Billy Bragg. At that moment, I noted Billy applauding vigorously. I was surprised, because his natural sympathies were to the left, and asked him why. He said he admired how Kinnock had said where he stood.

As Kinnock had calculated, that drama drowned out the noise of the following morning's debate on a miners' amnesty. It was also a prelude to the purge of Militant. Historical examples of Trotskyists in power are rare the world over, but Liverpool was the cradle of the group that produced the weekly newspaper *Militant*, which pretended to be just a pressure group but was actually a disciplined party within the party, founded by an old trooper named Ted Grant, who had joined the movement when Trotsky was alive. Their numbers were few, but they exerted a disproportionate pressure in Liverpool. Derek Hatton, who was nominally Liverpool Council's deputy leader but was its effective leader, was Militant's most famous recruit. More colourful and attention-seeking than the average dour Trotskyist, he liked to be called Degsy and included in his memoirs a photograph of himself sprawling on the bonnet of his Jaguar, with its customised licence plate DEG 5Y. The caption read: 'Sitting on my controversial car.'

The Labour Party did not then have a constitutional committee to deal with disciplinary questions. He whose car was controversial was one of a handful of Militant supporters who were summoned to appear before the executive, while dozens of their allies demonstrated outside. The decision to expel them was ratified by the annual conference in 1986, after which it was Larry Whitty's unenviable task to go to Liverpool and tell the Labour councillors that Hatton and two others were henceforth to be excluded from the Labour group and removed from the positions they held, including the deputy leadership. I went with him and was sitting quietly at the back of the room when there was a fracas by the door, as Hatton and others pushed their way in past the bouncer. 'Who are you, pal?' Hatton demanded, looking at me. When I had introduced myself, he declared, 'They allow unelected nobodies in here and try to keep decent councillors out.'

The meeting ended in chaos, a last small victory for the Man with the Controversial Car before he and a large batch of Liverpool councillors were barred by a court order from holding public office. Afterwards, the journalists were clamouring for a briefing from the general secretary, and we were having trouble finding a suitable site, with Hatton ensconced in the only room we had booked. I was guiding a crowd up a narrow staircase towards a door that I fervently hoped was unlocked when one suspicious hack suggested that we were not going to brief them at all and that I was simply leading them on a children's crusade to stop them from talking to Hatton. A young television producer then asked an unexpected question, which made me wonder if she had fully grasped what was going on. 'Will Mr Whitty and Mr Hatton be holding a joint press conference?' she enquired.

•　•　•

After I had been hired by the *Daily Mirror*, in the summer of 1988, Patricia Hewitt asked me what I did or did not miss about working for the party. I said that what I missed least was having to put up with the rudeness of Gerald Kaufman. Kaufman was one of the cleverest men in Parliament, who was very important in the Labour Party when he was young and lingered for a very long time. Party staff who came into contact with him in the 1980s feared his acerbic tongue and readiness to complain. Much later, he cut a pathetic figure. Aged over eighty, and barely able to walk, he would hobble into Parliament alone, dressed in bizarrely tasteless colours, looking as if a by-election was about to happen. When I remarked to the Labour MP Nick Raynsford that Kaufman seemed intent on clinging to his parliamentary seat until death did them part, Nick replied, 'But without it, he would die.' There was nothing else in his life except his intellectual pursuits and his public position. When Kaufman died, after nearly forty-seven years as an MP, it was so close to the 2017 general election that no by-election was necessary, and no one seemed to notice that he was gone, except for the book-seller who bought his collection of rare books.

Kaufman did, though, have one enduring claim to fame. He was credited with that succinct witticism, that the manifesto on which Labour fought the 1983 general election was 'the longest suicide note in history'. This can be found, attributed to him, in academic publications, in his published obituaries, on Wikipedia and on about 145,000 other sources accessible via Google.

Curiously, though, I once shared a platform with Gerald Kaufman at a public meeting during which he was asked when he first uttered this famous epigram. To my surprise, he seemed uncomfortable. Leaning forward, rubbing the side of his head, he replied that he could not remember and quickly changed the subject by remarking that he wished that he had been paid a royalty for every time the phrase had been repeated.

So, when was this famous phrase first coined?

The most reliable textbook on the 1983 election, by general acclaim, was compiled by two highly respected academics, David Butler and Dennis Kavanagh, whose findings were published early in 1984. This source suggests that the phrase may have had its debut during what was called the Clause V meeting, at which the manifesto was officially signed off, and at which one member of the shadow Cabinet made a lonely last-minute attempt to persuade his colleagues to abandon what he pithily described as 'the longest suicide note in history'. But it was not Gerald Kaufman. It was a half-forgotten MP named Peter Shore.

This is most unsatisfactory, because a famous witticism ought to have come from a famous wit. Shore was an intelligent, worthy and dull Fabian intellectual, who was never funny. He probably was not trying to be funny when he uttered the phrase: he was trying to be persuasive. Once made, the joke parted company with its author and attached itself to someone better known for being acerbic and witty. Of course, Gerald Kaufman knew the phrase was not his invention but kept that knowledge to himself for the best part of forty years.

This is very similar to a story about a Labour Party supporter who mistook mushy peas for guacamole...

16

THE FIRST AMONG SPIN DOCTORS

There is a story about Peter Mandelson that he will never shake off. Jill Mortimer, the first Tory to be elected MP for Hartlepool, referred to it in her maiden speech in September 2021 when she said, 'I, as a proud northern lass, know the difference between mushy peas and guacamole,' thus implying that Mandelson didn't. By then, the story was thirty-five years old. A version of it is that after Mandelson had been selected to be the Labour candidate in Hartlepool for the 1992 general election, he spied mushy peas on sale in a local chip shop and mistook it for guacamole. The political point of this story is that the people close to Tony Blair may have been good at their jobs, but they lived a world away from the northern Labour Party voters they represented.

Like the best urban myths, this one was almost true. In November 1986, the Labour Party sent a team from London to Kirkby, in Lancashire, to help out in a parliamentary by-election. Kirkby was Liverpool overspill, with a high rate of unemployment and associated social problems. Across the road from Labour's campaign headquarters was a fish and chip shop, with iron shutters that protected the window even during opening hours and a screen to protect the staff from the customers. Jack Straw was in town, as the candidate's political minder, accompanied by an intern, named Shelley, an east-coast American who was studying British politics. Shelley visited the chip shop, with a Labour Party researcher named Julian Eccles, spotted the mushy peas on sale and exclaimed, 'That looks delicious! Is it avocado?'

I was also in Kirkby, as campaign press officer, and passed this anecdote on to a visiting journalist from the *Financial Times*, who ran it in a gossip column. There it was spotted by Peter Taaffe, leader of the Militant Tendency, who repeated it to a large crowd at a rally that same month. The story fermented for four years, before rising again as a tale about Peter Mandelson, in 1990, when he was select-ed as the candidate for Hartlepool.

All agreed that Mandelson was very good at what he did, though in the mid-1980s, what he did was only fuzzily understood. 'Ah, the Red Rose man,' Prince Charles was heard to say of him. Red was the Labour Party's colour, a red rose was the party symbol and red was the colour of the covers of party publications. When Labour poli-ticians faced the press, the backdrop behind them was red. Annual conferences ended with a badly sung rendition of *The Red Flag*.

When that song is sung in full, the words 'cowards' and 'traitors' ring out six times each. The strike breaker, or blackleg, and the fore-man who sheds his working-class background to become a tyran-nical bully, and the Labour politician who leaves behind the people who voted for him as he joins the establishment were stock villains in union culture. In Newcastle, I was told of a union official who came up north from London to settle a strike and began his address to the workers by saying, 'Brothers, I am here as your arbitrator...' Whereupon someone shouted, 'What kind of traitor?'

Middle-class socialists are also on the look-out for traitors. In the mid-1980s, a publication called *London Labour Briefing*, which Jeremy Corbyn sometimes wrote for, ran a regular feature headed 'Class Traitor of the Month'. Peter Mandelson told me that when he was awarded this title, his formidable mother, the only child of the wartime Home Secretary Herbert Morrison, asked the pertinent question, 'Which class do they think you're a traitor to?'

For the first two and a half years after the disastrous 1983 general election, full-time staff at head office were, in effect, trying to keep the Red Flag flying, running campaigns that played to Labour's strength, on issues such as the NHS or unemployment, to hold on to the core vote. Then Mandelson arrived at Walworth Road office to fill the newly created post of director of communications in October 1985, on his thirty-second birthday, bringing a very different mindset. He was indifferent to issues that set the pulses of party activists racing. Unilateral nuclear disarmament was one. It set off a sharp exchange between Joe Haines and Anna Healy, later Baroness Healy of Primrose Hill, who was then a party press officer. This was reported back to Mandelson, who seemed amused. 'Anna has *rather extreme views* on defence,' he said, in my hearing. 'She *agrees* with Labour Party policy.'

Soon after his arrival, the red rose disappeared, the backdrop at public events turned to pastel grey, the look of party publications improved. It was suggested, in jest, that come the autumn, conference delegates would be singing 'the People's Flag is deepest grey'. This was rightly assumed to be Mandelson's work. There was said to be a 'Mandelsonian' way of doing politics, and that the party was being

'Mandelsonised', which implied that his contribution amounted to much more than a change in the party colours, but there was, at that time, no word or phrase in the language to describe exactly what he did that made him so significant. The expression 'spin doctor' was not heard in the UK until after the 1988 US presidential election. As soon as it had crossed the Atlantic, it attached itself to Peter Mandelson. He was not the first on the British political scene to try to doctor spin, but he was the first to be called a 'spin doctor'.

He was a very adept spin doctor. I was with him in the Labour Party press office when the phone rang. Mandelson was on the point of leaving but picked it up, asked who was calling and why and gave the caller a rundown of the party's position. Though he was talking rapidly for several minutes without pausing, he did not give away anything that the journalist was not supposed to know or utter a sentence that could be misconstrued if ripped out of context. It was a masterclass in how to make an experienced journalist feel well briefed.

That talent made him a very valuable aide to Neil Kinnock, and Tony Blair, though after a few years, Mandelson wished that people would stop calling him a 'spin doctor'. He said he wanted to be a politician. On the eve of one annual party conference, I was asked to give an opinion on the BBC's *Newsnight* on whether he would be able to make the transition. I thought not: I said that he was like an addict trying to give up smoking; he would never be able to stop himself going back for one last cigarette. In the morning, I learnt that someone – I believe it was Tom Baldwin, of *The Times* – had wittily suggested that I was an addict who wanted to stop winding up Peter Mandelson but could not resist doing it one more time. The joke reached Peter, who said to me, 'That was your last gasp.'

One reason for his wanting not to be known as a spin doctor was that it made so many enemies. Anybody in the Labour Party who suffered bad press was likely to think that Mandelson was either behind it or could have prevented it. Tessa Jowell, a fellow Blairite, was shocked by how unpopular he was. She told me that he was sitting alone on the green bench in the debating chamber of the Commons when another Labour MP came in, sat some distance away and said loudly enough for Peter to hear, 'I don't want to sit next to the most hated man in the Labour Party.'

His unpopularity was a kind of yardstick. When Matt Hancock was looking for a safe Conservative seat, with the backing of the Chancellor George Osborne, a Tory told me that when Hancock got to Parliament, he would be 'as hated on our side as Mandelson is on theirs'. I cannot say whether Hancock achieved this level of loathing, but he certainly was not widely loved. One distinction was that though Mandelson was often ridiculed, he was not a laughing stock.

Mandelson's unpopularity rubbed off on others. The person seemingly in pole position to succeed him as director of communications in 1990 was Colin Byrne, my successor as chief press officer, whose highly successful career in public relations after he left the Labour Party included being named in *PR Week* as one of the nation's top ten PR professionals. But the National Executive was not minded to appoint anyone associated with Mandelson. Byrne was passed over in favour of an outside candidate, who did not last long. Byrne was very nearly sacked for not getting on with his new boss.

Derek Draper, who worked as Mandelson's assistant in the 1990s, did not take long to accumulate an army of ill-wishers in whose minds he was the archetypal young careerist coasting in Tony Blair's slipstream. I could not bring myself to dislike him, not least because he rang me to introduce himself soon after his appointment, at around the time when his boss told a fellow journalist on *The Observer* that I was one of 'the most biased, ill-informed, malicious and unpleasant journalists in Westminster', which impressed me as a bold show of independence. Others, though, found him easy to loathe. His weakness was that he loved to be written about or seen on television. On the night when the Labour Party celebrated its 1997 election victory, Derek Draper appeared on a spoof BBC Two show about the election, in which he showed off his quick wit as an accomplished spin doctor, and went from there to the celebration, where he was to be seen in the front row, alongside Neil Kinnock. He was still only in his twenties and had monetarised his political connections by starting a lucrative new career as a lobbyist.

But his world crashed around him when an investigative journalist, Anthony Barnett, working for *The Observer*, had the smart idea of hiring an American journalist to pose as a businessman wanting access to the Labour government, and to approach Draper, who was now working as a commercial lobbyist. Draper could not help boasting that 'there are seventeen people who count in this government ... to say that I am intimate with every one of them is the understatement of the century' and 'I just want to stuff my bank account at £250 an hour.' When the scandal broke, I was greeted in the Commons by a middle-ranking government minister, who told me cheerfully, 'I've never seen the lads in the tea room looking so happy.' Meanwhile, Draper lost his job, had a breakdown and sought professional help.

When John Smith was party leader, he was heard to say, 'What has that little bastard Draper been up to now?' I quoted that comment when I wrote *Faces of Labour* in 1996. At the time, Derek brushed it off, telling me he had been called much worse, but when he was at his most vulnerable, it did not help his mental state when he looked at the bookshelf in his therapist's office and saw a copy of *Faces of Labour*. When he told me this one evening, I thought nothing of it, because he seemed robust to deal with it, but I was sorry later, when Draper was hit by a life-changing catastrophe that he in no way deserved.

Despite all that, Derek Draper came back and tried to instil in the Labour Party apparatus an understanding of the importance of online communication. He founded the LabourList website and was an early user of Twitter, but someone who worked with him took against him and passed his indiscreet, private emails to the Guido Fawkes website, causing another scandal that ended his involvement with the Labour Party. The third time he made national news was in horrible circumstances, when he was struck down by Covid in March 2020 and was trapped in hospital for an entire year. His plight was told in a television documentary and a book by his wife, Kate Garraway. It was pitiful to see this man, who had been so full of noise and bombast, lying on a hospital bed, barely able to speak – but in a career of many disasters, he did one outstandingly sensible thing when he married Kate Garraway.

• • •

While Peter Mandelson was making enemies, he was also acquiring very valuable allies. During the 1987 general election, protocol laid down that there had to be members of the shadow Cabinet at the morning press conferences held every Monday to Friday. At weekends, however, there were still journalists hungry to be briefed, so that was a time to promote two more junior figures, whom Mandelson nicknamed the BYTs, or Bright Young Things. They were Gordon Brown and Tony Blair. He saw Brown as the future Prime Minister and no doubt envisaged himself and Blair at his side.

In the immediate aftermath of John Smith's sudden death in 1994, I was surprised to learn that Mandelson was still saying that he backed Brown. It was out of character for him to pick the losing side. That is not said with hindsight: I had predicted on the BBC and Sky that it would be Blair. Brown's team were also surprised to hear that Mandelson was on their side. Nigel Griffiths, a genuine Brown acolyte, went around telling journalists that it was a dirty trick intended to make Mandelson's unpopularity rub off on Brown instead of Blair. The people officially running the Blair leadership campaign were no keener to have him on side. I was assigned by *The Observer* to find out who was supporting the declared candidates and was emphatically told by Blair's official campaign manager, Jack Straw, that Mandelson was not a member of team Blair. That was another surprise, because I knew of three television journalists who had had unsolicited calls from Peter Mandelson about a speech that Blair was about to deliver, which, Mandelson avowed, would go 'beyond spin'. As a courtesy, I rang Jack Straw to say that I was going to report that Mandelson was back in action. Very soon, an emotional Peter Mandelson was on the line, telling me that it would cause all kinds of trouble if his activities became public knowledge.

'I shall have to ring Tony,' he warned.

'Peter, I'm not suggesting anything that would damage you in the minds of right-thinking people,' I said. There was an exasperated sigh at the other end.

'We are not talking about right-thinking people,' he replied. 'We are talking about my parliamentary colleagues!'

After he had been elected the new party leader, Blair hosted a party for all who had helped the campaign and made a speech thanking them, which included a mysterious tribute to 'Bobby, who worked so hard.' Almost no one in the audience knew who 'Bobby' was. In the following Sunday's *Observer*, I repeated something that had been written in a diary column in the *Daily Telegraph*, that 'Bobby' was Blair's nickname for Peter Mandelson. (I don't know why he was 'Bobby'. I assumed it was a reference to Jack and Bobby Kennedy.) That week, a junior member of Blair's staff told me that it was wrong of me to report what was said at an event to which the press had not been invited.

'My project will be complete when the Labour Party learns to love Peter Mandelson,' Tony Blair declared in 1996. Nine years and three general elections later, those words were quoted back at him by the outgoing Conservative leader, Michael Howard, who asked, at Prime Minister's Questions, for a 'progress report'. Blair replied with one of his favourite clichés, 'I may have to say on that one: a lot done, a lot left to do.'

● ● ●

My working relationship with the mercurial character of Peter Mandelson did not start well and did not improve over time. A general rule about bosses is that the fussier they are about the symbols of their status, such as the size of their office or the quality of their swivel chair, the worse they are at the job. That did not apply to Mandelson. He was brilliant at doing what he did and endlessly pernickety about visible symbols of his important status. The office that his predecessor had occupied would not do. At the far end of the open-plan pressroom were two other offices, allocated to long-serving but relatively unimportant employees. They were dislodged, the connecting wall between their offices was taken down so that Peter had an office of a satisfactory size. Each time I entered that grand space, he would be busy reading or writing a document, and I would have to wait in silence, sometimes for several minutes, until he looked up and I was invited to speak. It was to remind me that he was important, and I was not.

This preoccupation with the size of the room or building allocated to him was almost his undoing. The first time he was forced to resign from the government, in 1998, was because he was secretly in debt to the wealthy MP Geoffrey Robinson, who was being investigated by the department Mandelson headed. He had borrowed the money to buy a house he could not afford, which would reflect his status as a confidant of the Prime Minister, but had failed to declare the loan. I was later told by a mischievous member of the team that ran Labour's 1997 campaign that as they were moving into new headquarters, in Millbank, Peter's assistant, Ben Wegg-Prosser, produced a plan of how Peter wanted his office laid out, which was to include a sofa costing thousands of pounds. When someone queried the expense, Wegg-Prosser replied that it was not negotiable. Once purchased, the expensive sofa proved to be too big to fit through the door.

Mandelson's second Cabinet position, as a Secretary of State for Northern Ireland, came with a satisfactorily grand grace-and-favour residence, in Hillsborough Castle, a magnificent eighteenth-century mansion fourteen miles south of Belfast. At last, Mandelson had a place as big as he was important. David Trimble, who was then Northern Ireland's First Minister, told me that he had a fraught meeting with Mandelson in the castle, which culminated in the Secretary of State rising to his feet and exclaiming, 'Get out of my house!'

A hazard of working for a political party is that ordinary office politics, of a kind found in any large organisation, is overlaid by real politics. I think it was from our first meeting, when we talked freely in a pub just before his appointment, that Mandelson decided that I was an 'unreconstructed Old Labour leftie'. It had been agreed that in his enhanced department, he would have a deputy with the title of chief press officer, and he heartily intended to ensure that person was not me. The title was first awarded to an outside candidate, a subeditor from *The Guardian* named John Booth.

Head office had recently been restructured to cut what had been an unwieldly sized management team down to just four directors. They were: Larry Whitty, the general secretary; Geoff Bish, the head of research; Joyce Gould, the director of organisation; and Peter Mandelson. One meeting began unexpectedly, with Larry Whitty demanding to know what role I was going to play in this new structure. Caught by surprise, Mandelson replied, 'So far as I am concerned, Andrew will sit in the press office and he will answer the phone.' When this comment was passed on to me, by all three of those who had heard it, I was reminded of how I had returned from spending a few weeks handling the Newcastle Central by-election to find that the furniture in the press office had been rearranged and I had been allocated the only desk that had no telephone on it. I also learnt that Mandelson had put a memo out to all the staff asking that they suggest ways to improve the work of the press office. I replied with a single sentence, saying, 'Can I have a telephone?' My working days would have been very dull if, as Mandelson had wanted, I was to spend them waiting for the phone to ring at a desk where there was no phone.

The appointment of John Booth worked out so badly that after a few months Mandelson wanted him to leave, but he refused to resign. He went after about twelve unhappy months. Fifteen years later, when Mandelson was running for re-election as MP for Hartlepool, who should turn up to challenge him but Booth, standing as an independent. He harvested 424 votes to Mandelson's 22,506.

After Booth's departure, I reapplied for the post but was then absent from London for the duration of the Knowsley North by-election. One evening, I thought it necessary to ring Peter Mandelson at home. He was out, but his then partner, also named Peter, answered the phone and talked to me like an old friend, though we had never met, telling me how Mandelson was very stressed but would be able to ease off when I took over as chief press officer. This came as a pleasant surprise, until it dawned on me that it was a case of mistaken identity: there was another press officer named Andrew, who was ten years younger than me, who was not marked down as 'an unrestricted Old Labour leftie'.

There was still the formality of an interview process, involving members of the National Executive. Before it began, I was handed a written job description that was all about running a press office during an election. After it was over, I learnt to my surprise that we had been interviewed for something entirely different. There was to be a 'key campaigners' unit', which had not existed in previous elections, whose task would be to maintain constant contact with Labour politicians when they were out on the stump, to make sure they were not suddenly ambushed by journalists over some new development in the campaign about which they had not been forewarned. The other Andrew and I were being interviewed to see which of us would run this unit. I was told afterwards that he seemed to have given it more thought than I had.

I was so irritated by this manoeuvre that I tried to get out, by applying for a job as a lobby journalist. That failed, but a by-election in Greenwich took me out of the office for several weeks. When it was over, the entire head office staff was assembled for a talk to prepare them for a general election, which was now less than three months away. We were handed a diagram of how the campaign was to be structured. Looking at it, I spotted that with the title of chief press officer there were two names. Larry Whitty announced to the staff that he had unilaterally decided that there would be two chief press officers, for the duration of the campaign.

When it was over, and the key campaigners' unit had been disbanded, I was relegated back to the ranks with the younger Andrew as my line manager, but he soon left for a job in regional television, and for the third time in eighteen months, I submitted my application for the post of chief press officer, but Mandelson told me that, notwithstanding his John Booth experience, he was looking to recruit someone from outside. Then, one morning, Larry Whitty called me in to say that much to his surprise, Mandelson had executed an about-turn. The job was mine.

The previous evening, the lobby had held a reception in the Commons for selected guests, hosted by Julia Langdon. Towards the end of the evening, she started talking about me, loudly enough for me to hear her across the room, when Neil Kinnock was standing near her. She claimed that I was a 'brilliant journalist', and that the *Daily Mirror* should have hired me a long time ago. I related this story to Larry Whitty.

But for all the grief I had working with Mandelson, I owed him a debt. One of the main reasons I was able to make the extremely rare career move from a party press office into the lobby was the very high reputation of Labour's communications department. There was a general view among journalists who covered the 1987 election that Labour won the campaign but lost the election, for broader political reasons. Some of the glory of that startlingly good campaign rubbed off on me, but it was not my achievement – it was Peter Mandelson's.

He had star quality, of a kind. He was someone people loved to talk about, no matter how much they disliked him, because he had a way of walking around Parliament's precinct at speed, with an air of mystery, like a man on a mission. People constantly wondered what he was up to. This made him fun to write about. That he reacted with such thin-skinned fury to any hint of bad publicity was part of the fun. Covering his career was like poking a wasp's nest.

● ● ●

After the Iraq War, when Tony Blair had led Labour through two election victories and would soon have completed ten years as party leader, there was an effort to force him out of office, by some people who thought their career prospects would improve under Gordon Brown. While I was political editor of the *Independent on Sunday*, I was trying to keep in regular contact with both sides of this hidden power struggle. One day, I was told that there had been a private retirement party for a long-serving party official and that when Blair and a couple of aides put in an appearance, they noticeably kept a distance between themselves and Peter Mandelson, as if they did not want to be too closely associated with him. I checked this with someone else who was at that party, who told me that it seemed to be true, and I wrote about it. This sent Peter into a cold rage. He asserted that it was blatantly untrue that there was friction in his relationship with Blair. He had even arrived at the party later than he intended because he had had to hover outside while he talked to Blair on the phone.

In this instance, he was unusually well placed to retaliate. Tony O'Reilly, proprietor of *The Independent* and the *Independent on Sunday*, thought it useful to have a politician from each of the main parties as non-executive directors of the parent company and had invited Peter to join the board. It was therefore as a company director that he demanded a meeting at which he could give voice to his many complaints about me. It was held in the boardroom, with the editors of both *The Independent* and the *Independent on Sunday*, and the chief executive present. At the last minute, Peter said that he was too busy to make a personal appearance and made his contribution by phone, so we heard his disembodied voice as he read from one newspaper cutting after another to back his claim that I was conducting a malicious campaign to damage his reputation. A common hazard of journalism is that its practitioners churn out so much that they can barely remember what they have written from one day to the next. As Peter read out my words, I was continually visited by the illusion that I was hearing them for the first time. It was disorientating. I had intended to be calm and conciliatory throughout, but when Peter angrily announced that one item had caused him 'embarrassment', I blurted out, 'Why shouldn't I cause you embarrassment?' That was a mistake. It made it all sound personal. He, on the other hand, did not help his case when the editor of the *Independent on Sunday*, Tristan Davies, intervened to try to calm the atmosphere, and Peter, who was by now thoroughly worked up, snapped, 'Oh, well wriggled, Tristan!' By that point, he seemed to realise that he was getting nowhere. Tony O'Reilly had ruled in advance of the meeting that the *Independent on Sunday* was not going to retract anything, I was not going to be instructed to lay off and if Peter wanted to resign from the board, another Labour politician would take his place.

A sunny patch in this stormy relationship was during my time on the *Daily Telegraph*. Ben Wegg-Prosser told me then that Peter regretted that we had not got on well, and I had friendly messages from the man himself, whose extensive range of contacts had not previously included anyone on the *Telegraph*. In those days, he wrote a blog. One day, I saw myself described as a 'reputable journalist', which was so unlike the things Mandelson had said about me in the past that I sent him a jovial text saying that there appeared to be an error, that 'highly dis-' was missing before the word 'reputable'. A text came back saying, 'It's never too late to repent.' For a wild moment, I thought he was telling me that he was repenting. He meant, of course, that he was offering me the chance to repent the wrongs I had done him.

There was a side to this contradictory character that the public never saw. In 1987, I took my seven-year-old nephew into the Labour Party press office for a day. He did a drawing and marched uninvited into Peter's office to show it off. For the remainder of the day, he was in and out of that office, chatting away happily to the infamous spin doctor. Later, my mother rang asking about this 'Peter' about whom she was hearing so much from her small grandson. 'Oh yes, I've heard of him,' she said. Ten years later, after she had read that Peter had run for a place on Labour's National Executive and lost, she told me that she was going to send him a letter of condolence, saying, 'I don't care what my son writes about you: you were very kind to my grandson.' That message was never sent, mercifully, so I will never know what use Peter Mandelson would have made of it.

17

THE LOBBY

I am tempted to call it Her Majesty's lobby, that institution steeped in the awareness of its importance, with rules and rituals, officers and members, sometimes operating in full view and sometimes out of sight. I did not know that it existed until after I had moved south to work for the Labour Party. When a journalist suggested that we talk 'on lobby terms', I had to pretend that I knew what he was talking about.

Anyone who has been on a guided tour of the House of Commons will remember a large room adjoining the debating chamber, with walls of stone, a high ceiling and tiled floor, dominated by life-size statues of Lloyd George, Winston Churchill, Clement Attlee and Margaret Thatcher. That is the Members' Lobby, from which the collective of political journalists known as the lobby take their name. Parties of visitors are taken there on guided tours when Parliament is not sitting, but when the MPs are back, no one is allowed to dally or chat in the Members' Lobby, apart from MPs, members of the House of Lords, authorised members of staff and lobby journalists. Others may pass through, including members of the public who have tickets to watch the debates, but the officials, known as Badge Messengers, will guide them quickly through, making sure they do not linger.

Access to the Members' Lobby was a vital privilege when I was given my first lobby pass as a political correspondent for the *Daily Mirror*, in 1988. When email did not exist and mobile phones were as big as bricks, there were only two ways to contact MPs: you could ring their offices and wait at your desk, hoping that they rang back, or you could linger in the Members' Lobby and catch them as they walked by. Diligent lobby journalists spent hours standing in that room, so that MPs would notice them and hopefully stop to talk.

But you had to know the rules. First, and most important, everything said in the Members' Lobby was confidential. You could quote someone but not by name, unless you had specifically asked, and the person you were speaking to had agreed to go 'on the record'. You were not allowed to butt in on another lobby journalist's conversation. You could not sit on any of the benches in the room, except one by the door to the corridor that led to the library. You could enter the Members' Lobby if its doors were closed, but if they were propped open, it meant that there was a vote in progress, in which case you were barred from entering. However, a vote would draw MPs towards the debating chamber in large numbers, so it was a good time to catch a word with them, and lobby journalists would line the walls of that corridor between the Members' Lobby and the library like prostitutes on a meat rack, hoping to catch some passing trade.

Another privilege accorded only to lobby journalists was the daily briefings by the Prime Minister's press secretary – one at 11 a.m., in 10 Downing Street, the other at 4 p.m., in the lobby room high up in the Parliament building. Lobby briefings are not secret any more; anyone can read a summary of them on the web, but they are numbingly dull. Back then, they were more interesting and very hush-hush. The general public was not supposed to know why a little procession of journalists could be seen every morning heading up Whitehall and into Downing Street, nor why a group of three civil servants made the journey in the opposite direction just before 4 p.m. What was said at these secret sojourns might be all over the mass media that day and the next, but the words were attributed to a mysterious anonymous 'source'. When a 'source' contemptuously described one Cabinet minister, John Biffen, as a 'semi-detached' member, or likened another, Francis Pym, to a character called Mona Lott from a 1940s radio comedy, only those on the inside track knew that the person bandying these insults was Thatcher's loyal press secretary, Bernard Ingham.

There are lobby journalists working in Parliament still, and it has a committee, office holders and a bank account, but almost everything else about the institution as it was in the 1980s has gone. The first breach in the wall resulted from the launch of *The Independent*, in 1986. The new paper's political editor, Tony Bevins, decided that they would forego the privilege of being briefed by Bernard Ingham, but if they could find out what he was saying, without having been in the room, they would quote him by name.

I was there, in Downing Street, in July 1989, when Ingham gave what was arguably his most portentous briefing, after Margaret Thatcher had shunted the Foreign Secretary, Sir Geoffrey Howe, whom she despised and with whom she had clashed over relations with the EU, into the less important job of Leader of the House of

Commons but as a sop had awarded him the title of Deputy Prime Minister. I listened to the questions and answers without immediately understanding the impact of what I was hearing. Someone asked Ingham about the 'constitutional significance' of the title 'Deputy Prime Minister'.

'No, no constitutional significance whatsoever,' Ingham replied, shaking his head.

He was asked about Chevening, the grace-and-favour residence usually occupied by the Foreign Secretary. That was to be given to John Major, Howe's replacement, and the other residence, Dorneywood, would continue to be used by the Chancellor of the Exchequer.

Back in the Commons, I was waylaid by Tony Bevins, who was on a mission to find out what Ingham had said. It was at that moment of being asked that I suddenly took in what I had been hearing. Howe's new courtesy title did not mean a thing; he had been downgraded; he was no longer important enough to be entitled to a grace-and-favour home; and Thatcher did not mind how public was his humiliation. The front page of the next day's *Sun* reported that Sir Geoffrey and Lady Howe had had to move their stuff into a flat on the Old Kent Road.

It was not long before Howe had had a read-out of what Thatcher's press secretary had said. His parliamentary aide, David Harris, was soon stationed in the Members' Lobby, counter-briefing every journalist who passed by. That evening, a Tory MP named Ken Warren, who had a reputation as a Thatcher loyalist, told me that the way she had treated her most senior colleague had been 'very cruel' and would probably be the cause of her downfall – which proved to be true. I was in the public gallery sixteen months later, when Howe mumbled his way through an inflammatory speech urging his fellow Tory MPs to put an end to Thatcher's eleven-year premiership, which they did before the month was out. He spoke so quietly that Thatcher sat with her ear pressed against the microphone in the back of the bench.

Bit by bit, the privileged secluded world of the lobby correspondent was chipped away. There was a restaurant for journalists only, with its own kitchen, served by waiters in white jackets. Journalists could bring guests to this restaurant but could not sit them at the long table nearest the entrance, which was the 'lobby table'. It was at this table that the political editor of *The Times* held court during the 1930s, making sure that lesser journalists understood how wise Stanley Baldwin and Neville Chamberlain were being in avoiding unnecessary conflict with Nazi Germany. Unusually, I was allowed to eat at this table once while I was only a Labour Party press officer, but first my host had to check with everyone else at the table that they did not object. Michael Jones, political editor of the *Sunday Times*, replied in a loud voice, 'It's so long since I've spoken to anyone from the Labour Party that I've forgotten what they look like,' and invited me to take the seat next to his.

Adjoining this restaurant there was an exclusive cafe, which is still there, though its hours are shorter and it is open to anyone with a Commons pass. Nearby, there was a bar where journalists could drink late into the night, and alongside that, a small library, in which there were books donated and signed by Winston Churchill. Not much research took place in that library, but in the afternoons, its deep leather chairs were handy for those who needed to sleep off the effects of lunchtime booze. Nearby there were also dozens of phone booths for those who did not want their calls to be overheard. The phone booths, the bar and the deep leather armchairs have gone, and all that remains of the library is shelves against a wall. After the Labour Party had gained control of Parliament, the Commons authorities decided that they could not justify the cost of a subsidised bar and a restaurant for journalists. They also decided that health and safety regulations should apply in Parliament, which had been exempt from regulations that Parliament imposed on other workplaces. There were six of us employed by the *Daily Mirror*, *Sunday Mirror* and *People*, crammed into a room that is now an office for one person only. Also, in the 2000s, for the first time, journalists employed by websites such as the Huffington Post were judged to be eligible for lobby passes, increasing the demand for workspaces.

In the 1980s, and before, the lobby was exclusively white and mostly male. When I arrived, there were two female political editors – Elinor Goodman at Channel 4 and Julia Langdon at the *Daily Mirror* – plus a scattering of women in less prominent positions. The only non-white face in any of the offices occupied by journalists was that of John Pienaar, who joined *The Independent* when it was founded. He was not then a lobby journalist but belonged to another category, called the gallery reporters, who did not have the freedom to linger in the Members' Lobby. In those pre-internet days, the upmarket daily newspapers would set aside a whole page for straightforward reporting of MPs' speeches. It was the gallery reporters' task to fill those pages. When Pienaar first sat in the gallery, he was looking down at a sea of white faces: at that time, there were no black or Asian MPs present, until 1987 when Diane Abbott, Paul Boateng, Bernie Grant and Keith Vaz were elected.

There was a hierarchy in the lobby, which is less strict now. When the political editors took lunch in the cafe, they would sit together at one table, like the Village Elders, and generally no one below the rank of political editor would be so presumptuous as to join them. The irascible Tony Bevins usually preferred to be with his colleagues on *The Independent*, but I was told of one occasion when he joined the Village Elders. The centre of attention was Mike Brunson, the newly appointed political editor of ITN, who told me that while he was introducing himself and chatting to his peers, he was aware of someone staring 'malignantly' at him, saying nothing, until Bevins suddenly broke into the conversation to announce, 'You'll never be any good as a political journalist. Do you know why?'

Taken aback, Brunson asked why.

'Because you're too fucking smooth!'

Brunson would try to get to know more junior journalists, but his memory for names was not faultless. There were two BBC correspondents, one named Mike and the other named Huw, whom he had trouble telling apart. He told me that he walked past one of them one day and greeted him with a cheery 'Hello Mike, how are you?' – to which he received the very grumpy retort from Huw, 'I'll feel a lot better when you get my name right, Brunson.' Huw Edwards was later known to millions as the leading anchor on BBC One's nightly news.

Though highly competitive at times, the lobby looked after its own. The first time I worked a Sunday shift was during a summer break, when there were no MPs in the building, nothing seemed to be happening and I was on my own in the *Mirror*'s little office. On days such as these, experienced political journalists can mould a news story out of virtually nothing, but I was new and did not know what to do, until John Deans, from the *Daily Mail*, walked in and presented me with a complete run-down of what he and colleagues from *The Sun* and the *Daily Express* were writing. I copied the list and submitted it all to the news desk, naturally without telling them that it was not all my own work, and head office was given the misleading impression that I was on top of the job.

I also witnessed another drama highlighting the comradery among lobby journalists. During one of Margaret Thatcher's trips abroad, a member of the accompanying press party arrived at the VIP departure lounge at Heathrow and realised, to his horror, that he had forgotten his passport. He rang his wife, who gathered up the passport and got herself to Heathrow as fast as the traffic allowed but was too late. The Prime Minister and her entourage had flown away, leaving him stranded. But all was not yet lost. He knew that Thatcher was due to stop over and deliver a brief speech in Glasgow before leaving the UK, so he rushed to get aboard the first flight to Glasgow, which promised to get him there in good time. But the plane did not take off when it should have. There was a union dispute involving ground staff, who had blocked the runway. Finally, the runway was cleared and the plane took to the sky, but now his chances of catching up with Thatcher's party had almost vanished. He shared his problem with the cabin crew, who sympathetically arranged that he would be the first off the plane, with a car waiting to reunite him with the Prime Minister's entourage. He arrived with minutes to spare, but still his problems were not over. He was supposed to file a report on Thatcher's speech but had no idea what she had said. This was when the solidarity between lobby hacks came into play. We were all equipped with a new invention: the laptop. The correspondents from two rival tabloids sat one on either side of him and called up the copy they had filed. He looked first to one side and rewrote the opening paragraph he saw there, and then to the other side for a second paragraph, and was able to press 'send' just before we were told to return to the plane. His employers never knew how close he came to spaffing the thousands of pounds they had paid to have someone aboard that plane, and he is still so embarrassed by the episode that he would rather I did not identify him.

But the career of journalism was often precarious, and team solidarity amounted to little against the whims of the higher-ups. After the death of Robert Maxwell, the *Daily Mirror* went through a short, golden period when, in effect, it had no proprietor. The editor, Richard Stott, was in full control. It was too good to last. One day, in spring 1993, we learnt that the board had handed control to David Montgomery and that Joe Haines had resigned in disgust. Montgomery had been a subeditor on the *Mirror* and acted like someone with a long-held grudge against his old workmates. I turned up to do a Sunday shift at head office and was surprised to see a crowd of journalists on the pavement, looking shell-shocked. Montgomery had ordered that every casual worker was to be sacked without notice. Some had been working shifts consistently for years, hoping to secure a staff job. Now, there were men in uniform in reception, who had installed a barrier to prevent them from entering the building. I had to prove my identity so I could be checked against a printed list of staff journalists. Upstairs, those of us who were not locked out were called into the editor's office, to be addressed by a large man with a small brain, who told us that he had flown in from Australia overnight to be the new editor. Richard Stott had been summoned that morning to a meeting in a hotel with David Montgomery, who told him that he was sacked, with immediate effect, and would not be allowed back in the building.

After wiping out the casual staff, management's next priority was to pick off selected staff journalists and sack them. Once my turn came, in April 1993, I had a few grim months, out of work, with two children under four and another on the way. We had moved house five months earlier and I feared we would have to move again, to somewhere we could afford. But at least I never felt friendless. Alan Milburn, who was a newly elected MP, organised that Early Day Motion deploring the decision to sack me, and Tessa Jowell, another new MP, insisted that I have dinner with her one evening when the Commons was crowded and demanded a table in the middle of the room, so that people would see that while I was out of work, I was not out of action.

When *The Guardian* bought *The Observer*, and Tony Bevins was appointed its political editor, he insisted I be taken on as a correspondent. But there was a hitch. My predecessor had left, taking his lobby pass with him, and was refusing to hand it back until his new employers at the *Independent on Sunday* had arranged for him to be fixed up with a replacement. Unfortunately for me, someone at the *Mirror* had been sharp enough to see that I might want to pull a similar stunt and had instructed the finance department to withhold my severance pay until I had surrendered my pass. With a young family to feed, I needed the money too badly to argue. I did not yet have a staff job on *The Observer* but was being paid a daily rate, and to earn that precious cash I had to get myself into the Parliament building without a pass. These days, every entrance to Parliament is controlled electronically, so that no one can bluff their way in, but in 1993, all I needed to do was walk past police officers with the casual air of someone so sure of his right to enter the building that there was no need for me to present a pass. I was loitering in the normal way in the Members' Lobby when I was taken aside by Robin Fell, one of the doorkeepers, who had worked in Parliament for decades and knew every lobby correspondent by sight.

'Me and the lads have been talking about you,' he said. 'You haven't got a pass, have you?'

I confessed that it was true and explained how I had been landed in this situation.

'Well,' he said, 'we've decided to turn a blind eye – but if the Serjeant at Arms catches you, don't drop us in it!'

Robin was an imposing figure, with a face that exuded amusement and kindness. He was bald but with whiskers florid enough to compensate for the hair he lacked on top. I once saw him deal with an ageing member of the House of Lords, who was in the early stages of dementia. The old fellow had been an MP for decades and thought he still was. He shuffled into the Members' Lobby, heading for the Commons debating chamber, until Robin intervened with a cheery cry of, 'Wrong way, my lord!' The peer of the realm looked confused, then laughed at his mistake and headed towards the Lords. Minutes later, he was back, and once again, Robin called out, 'Wrong way, my lord!' I witnessed this three times, in the space of an hour. Robin never showed impatience with or contempt for the bewildered old man, but after the third intervention, he remarked, 'The House of Lords is the place for the terminally confused.'

Terminally confused but still entitled to speak and vote on the whole range of issues that affected the nation, he could claim his daily attendance allowance if he could just remember where he was supposed to be.

Robin Fell worked in Parliament for forty-six years, rising to be principal doorkeeper. In that role, he was stationed in a sentry box by the door that separated the Members' Lobby from the debating chamber and one of his duties was to ensure that there was snuff available in his sentry box to be given free to any passing MP who asked for it. Presumably, at a date lost in history, MPs agreed to ban smoking in the debating chamber but insisted that snuff be always available for those who needed to feed their nicotine addiction on their way in or out. They also ruled that if the snuff ran out, it was incumbent on the principal doorkeeper to replace it, at his own expense. This did not bother Robin, because when he took up his new position, there was already a box, made of wood taken from the chamber door that was splintered by a German bomb in 1941, which was full of snuff. No MP asked for a snort – there cannot have been many who knew they were entitled to – but he invited me to try some. My first snort almost had me toppling over. When I wrote about this in *The Independent*, it transpired that there was a company somewhere in the UK who manufactured snuff. They sent Robin a gift of a large consignment of snuff, which I presume is still available, if any MP reading this feels the need.

18

PLAIN JOHN MAJOR

There was a time when I almost lured John Major into saying something interesting. He was the blandest of Prime Ministers. Though his six-and-a-half-year premiership never ran smoothly, it was not because he was deliberately making waves, as Margaret Thatcher did, but because the right wing of the Tory Party could not forgive him for not being Thatcher. He entered the leadership contest that followed the fall of Thatcher as her chosen successor. In office, he immediately assigned her old enemy, Michael Heseltine, to abolish the Poll Tax, and over time he filled all the most sensitive Cabinet positions with the big names from the pro-EU wing of the party, such as Heseltine, Douglas Hurd, Ken Clarke and Chris Patten. He was also different from Thatcher in another way: he willingly delegated. One minister told me how odd it was to consult Downing Street about a decision that needed to be made, only to be told to do what they thought best. The right despised Major. Woodrow Wyatt, a *News of the World* columnist who was infatuated by Thatcher, told a cruel and dubious story that Major was challenged over a rumour that he was controlled by his civil servants, to which Major reputedly replied that he had only recently overruled advice given by the mandarins, and then turned to one of them and said, 'Wiggins, what did I overrule you on?'

The ridicule hurt Major. During the 1992 general election campaign, his life story as a boy from Brixton who left school with three O levels worked to the party's advantage, but in office, surrounded by graduates from elite universities, he struggled to throw off a feeling of inferiority. I was at a rare private briefing that he gave inside Downing Street. We journalists sat in a circle, with Major in the centre. Speaking without notes or prompting by the civil servants standing to one side, he gave us a detailed run-down of the conflict in the Balkans, where Serbs and Croats were fighting over the spoils as the former state of Yugoslavia fell apart. I noticed how Major never made eye contact with any of the listening journalists. He used his hands to emphasise his main points and talked like someone facing a board of examiners. Frankly, he was wasting our time. We were not foreign correspondents, but if we had wanted to be briefed on the disintegration of Yugoslavia, we would have gone to the relevant Foreign Office expert. This briefing was not for our benefit but his, so that he could prove to himself and to us that he had mastered a complicated subject.

That was not the day when he nearly said something interesting. The near miss occurred in Moscow, in April 1996, when Major met President Boris Yeltsin in the Kremlin and spoke afterwards to a mix of foreign correspondents based in Moscow and lobby journalists who had travelled on the Prime Minister's plane. It went well. The questions were not provocative, and he answered them all easily. When it was over, he was steered to an adjoining room by his civil servants but was so pleased with his success that he came back, to socialise, but was confronted by a group of journalists with their heads down, writing copy – except for me. I was the only Sunday newspaper journalist in the room, so, suddenly, I was having a friendly one-to-one conversation with the Prime Minister.

All I wanted was for him to say something that I could quote in that week's *Observer* under a tagline 'exclusive', but first I had to put him at ease, so I told him about a bad experience I had had that morning. Walking through Moscow, taking in the unusual sight of western goods on sale in shops with familiar western names, I was approached by a young woman and stopped to find out what she wanted. That was a mistake. The next I knew, I was surrounded by women, all colourfully dressed, crowding so closely that I could not move my arms. I felt my wallet slip out of an inside jacket pocket and shouted in alarm, whereupon the crowd scattered, running in all directions. I set off in pursuit of a woman with long, black hair, who I believed was in possession of my wallet. She was holding her sandals, which she threw aside as she hurtled barefoot down the street. We rounded a corner, and there I spotted a uniformed policeman and made my second error. I slowed down, to shout to the officer that I had been robbed. He stared in astonishment at this foreigner exclaiming in broken Russia about something that did not concern him. His job was directing traffic; street crime, which had been almost unknown under communism, was someone else's department. My quarry had kept on running. There was no hope of catching her now. As I threw up my arms in exasperation, a taxi halted and the driver asked me, in English, if something was the matter. I explained that all my money had been stolen. But if my money had been stolen, I could not pay his fare. He drove off.

I relayed this story to John Major, who listened attentively. 'You say you were surrounded by young women, who held on to you?' he asked.

I confirmed that it was so.

He remarked, 'Hmm, some men would think that rather agreeable.'

'Rather agreeable' was one of his stock phrases. It was not one I would have chosen to describe a mugging in a foreign capital that left me bereft of money, credit cards, driving licence and other essentials – but, no matter, I had his attention. Now was the moment to generate a story. Knowing how irritated he was by sections of the mass media, particularly right-wing columnists such as Woodrow Wyatt, I told him that *The Observer* was putting together a piece about journalists who doubled up as political activists. It was not true – it was something I invented to test his reaction, which was exactly what I hoped it would be.

'Oh,' Major exclaimed, 'I could tell you some stories about that.'

Everything was falling into place. That evening, I would be able to phone through a potential front-page splash, with an opening paragraph along the lines of 'A furious John Major lashed out yesterday...' followed by 'Speaking exclusively to *The Observer*...'

But no sooner had this vista opened than it was closed down. A civil servant named Jonathan Haslam, Downing Street's director of communications, was behind me. He was tall enough to talk directly to Major over my head.

'Yes, but you're not going to, are you, Prime Minister?' he said, and Major obediently shut up.

It hardly needs saying that no one – not even her long-serving press aide, Bernard Ingham – would have presumed to speak to Margaret Thatcher like that.

There was an appealingly ordinary quality to John Major. When he handled Prime Minister's Questions for the first time, Thatcher made a point of being there to show support. Even three rows back sitting bolt upright, never moving unless it was necessary, she looked every inch a Prime Minister. Her main challenger, Michael Heseltine, was among the last to arrive. Tall and leonine, he too looked every inch a Prime Minister. Then the actual Prime Minister scuttled in, head bowed, clutching a folder under one arm, seemingly embarrassed to be in this position. It was as if when faced with a choice between two credible Prime Ministers, the Conservative Party rejected both and chose a garden gnome instead.

During the 1992 general election, I saw Major outside Conservative Party headquarters talking to the party chairman, Chris Patten. He was standing by his chauffeur-driven car. The passenger door was open, waiting for him to get in. When a car took Thatcher away, it took her to an elevated world, closed to the rest of us. But Major lacked any sign of awareness of his own importance, so it was as if the door to that chauffeur-driven car was open for anyone who wanted to be Prime Minister.

Tristan Garel-Jones, a heavy smoker, who was then the Foreign Office minister handling relations with the EU, told me that he had an emergency meeting with Major in a hotel room. As it ended, the Prime Minister started emptying the ashtray, not wanting to make work for the hotel staff.

A female civil servant once told me that he had the cleanest glasses she had ever seen on a man, though no one that I know has ever said that they saw him cleaning them. Perhaps in rare moments when he was alone, he whipped off his glasses to give them another wipe.

Alastair Campbell was to blame for the motif that was a recurrent feature of Steve Bell cartoons, which showed Major wearing his underpants outside his trousers. The first few weeks of Major's premiership were great fun for the political crew of the *Daily Mirror*. Each new Prime Minister has what is known as a 'honeymoon', when the media go easy on them, but the *Mirror* was not giving Major a honeymoon, so the Thatcherite diehards came to us with tales of how disappointed she was in him. Major read this, and with rather touching naivety, asked Margaret Thatcher whether it was true, and on what may have been his first foreign trip as Prime Minister, foolishly approached Campbell to say that the *Mirror* had got it wrong: she had no complaints about the way he ran his government. During this conversation, Campbell spotted that the Prime Minister had his shirt tucked into his underpants and duly shared this observation with the readership of the *Daily Mirror*. This was not an uncommon habit among men who had grown up in post-war austerity, when homes were not well heated, yet somehow this trivial detail spoke eloquently about the ordinariness of John Major.

Yet even ordinary Prime Ministers can be prone to scandal. During Major's time in Downing Street, there was a rumour that refused to go away that, though he seemed happily married, there was another woman in his life. Soon, the rumour became more precise: it featured a Downing Street caterer, named Clare Latimer. She was a near neighbour of Alastair Campbell, in Hampstead. He tipped off the news desk that she had put her house up for sale. The *Mirror* treated this as a major item of national news. A reporter went in, posing as a buyer, and reported at length on the interior of the house, including the detail that there was a framed photograph of John Major on display. The average reader could not know that the piece was coming as close as the lawyers dared allow to hinting that Latimer was Major's mystery ex-lover. Other newspapers dropped knowing hints, until the *New Statesman* rashly decided to explain what was being implied. They declared that the rumour was false, but that did not save them from receiving a writ from the Prime Minister which nearly bankrupted the magazine. John Major and Clare Latimer were never more than acquaintances.

It took nearly ten more years before the truth emerged that the other woman in John Major's life was the flamboyant Conservative MP Edwina Currie, who was not popular with her fellow Tories. It was said that the only cheer heard in Tory central office on the night of the 1997 general election was when the news came through that Currie had lost her seat. She was a compulsive attention-seeker, with a flare for publicity, who was never more than a very junior minister in the mid-1980s but was more famous than most of the men in Margaret Thatcher's Cabinet. I knew her slightly and quite liked her. I thought that the hostility she attracted was misogynist, with possibly an added touch of antisemitism. She was observant and not a bad judge of character. She was attracted to Major when she spotted what others missed, that he was not as grey as he appeared but quietly, deeply ambitious. It was unkind of her to tell the world about her old affair with Major when she wanted to boost sales of her memoirs, in 2002, but she had kept silent about it throughout his time as Prime Minister, when it might have done him irreparable damage.

A fun fact about Edwina Currie. Female students arriving at Oxford University for the first time in the 1960s were assigned a second-year student as a mentor. When Hilary Wainwright arrived, in 1967, she was mentored by eighteen-year-old Edwina Cohen, as she then was. One went on to be a right-wing Conservative, the other a Trotskyist.

• • •

John Major seemed more at ease with himself as a former Prime Minister afterwards than he was while in office. After a decent interval, he accepted an invitation to be the guest speaker at a lunch hosted by the lobby, in Parliament, and spoke so freely about the EU and other contentious issues that a journalist was heard to say, 'He gave us more stories in one lunch that he did in seven years!'

I encountered him at another lunch, hosted by the *Oldie* magazine, about fifteen years after the end of his premiership, and told him, 'I don't know if you remember me, but I was a lobby journalist during your time.'

'Yes, you were,' Major replied, and for some reason, started chuckling. He did not explain why it was funny.

19

ARCHIE

My children lost the grandfather they adored thirty-two hours into the New Year in 1997. I wish I could remember Archie Dearie growing old disgracefully, but his life came to a violent end in a place he detested, doing a job he did not enjoy. When I wrote about it in *The Observer*, as the Tony Blair era was just beginning, the headline writer called his an 'Old Labour death' – and not just because Archie's political sentiments were broadly 'Old Labour' but because of where and how he died. A junior minister addressing Parliament in 1997, with his head full of optimistic modernity, claimed that the UK was in a 'post-post-industrial era', but Archie's was an industrial-era death. It could have happened in Charles Dickens's time. In a dark, dirty, noisy foundry, he was buried alive under three and a half tons of sand.

Archie would never have entered that foundry if he had had a choice. He would have preferred to be back working for his old employer, Rolls-Royce, in Derby, but they would not have him back. It is likely that he had been blacklisted for his trade union activity, but he could not prove it. Unable to find an engineering firm that would employ him, he spent eight unfulfilling years as a maintenance fitter in a factory called QDF Components, in Sinfin, near Derby, which supplied moulding for the motor industry.

Foundries are terrible places, to those of us used to more comfortable surroundings – dark, dirty, airless and unbelievably noisy. On the day after my father-in-law's death, the management of QDF were kind enough to let his son and two daughters see where he had died. Sue said she felt as if she was walking back into Ceauşescu's Romania.

The factory had closed for twelve days over Christmas, so it was always likely that there would be problems when the machinery started up again at 6 a.m. on 2 January. Patrick Kennedy, a foundry worker, told the coroner's inquest in Derby, six months later, 'Start-up day is chaos. Belts are slipping, sand blockages, spillages – it's a regular curse after an 'oliday.' The burden falls heaviest on the maintenance staff.

One of the foundries at the QDF factory, known as Diva 1, had six hoppers, or chimneys, down which tons of heavy, fine-grained black sand tumbled on to a conveyor belt. Two of the hoppers, 19E and 19F, could each hold forty tons of sand. The process was fully automated. The person watching over it, Arthur Bodey, who had been with the factory for thirty-one years, stayed up in the control tower. He could see some of the machinery from there, and there was a panel of lights to tell him whether what he could not see was working properly.

Within quarter of an hour of the foundry starting up, those lights were warning him of problems in hoppers 19B and 19E. Neither was emptying its load of sand, though the conveyor was apparently moving. When left undisturbed for days, the sand forms layers, with the wet sand on the outside creating a kind of skin that prevents the dry sand from moving. He rang maintenance to let them sort it.

Maintenance, predictably, had their hands full. Another foundry, Diva 2, had gone into operation only the previous September, and for the first time ever, it too had developed problems. Patrick Kennedy, whose job was to sweep and tidy up after the maintenance men, was called to three separate jobs in the space of fifteen minutes. By his own account, he was 'ranting and raving'. Around 6.45 a.m., Archie set to work alone on the two errant hoppers.

By the time Arthur Bodey took a break, at 8.15 a.m., the problem with 19B had been fixed. Around that time, Archie went into the maintenance workshop and took a torch and a spanner from his locker. A little while later, he was seen about eight feet above the ground, standing with one foot on each of two steel girders astride the conveyor belt, reaching up to remove a hatch from the side of hopper 19E. Patrick Kennedy, who was rushing from one job to another, saw him again a few minutes later, now standing with his back to the hopper, his feet still astride the conveyor belt. The hatch was off and sand was starting to flow out of the side of the hopper onto the belt. 'He didn't look distressed or bothered about the situation at all,' Kennedy told the coroner. 'I assumed he was in full control. The only thing I can say is that he didn't look distressed, because if he had I would have been up there with him.'

As it was, he shouted to Archie to take care not to make a mess, because he had already had enough sweeping to do for one day. In front of a coroner's jury of four men and four women, he preferred not to repeat the exact words he used, which he described as 'industrial language'. Those obscenities shouted by a workmate may have been the last words Archie ever heard. He may have replied in kind, but if he did, his words were drowned in the foundry din.

At the inquest, we learnt that there is a correct way to unblock a hopper full of sand, which is slow, and there is a quick way, which is dangerous. The maintenance staff were under pressure that day to get everything up and running as soon as possible, and Archie chose to clear hopper 19E by a quick but dangerous method. That allowed the management to imply afterwards that what happened was his own fault, which begs the question: how pleased would they have been if he had pedantically insisted on doing everything by the book, no matter how long it took?

The method Archie used was to remove the hatch from the side of the hopper, whack the sand, then turn around and hold the hatch against his back, like a shield. The idea was that the sand would flow from the hopper and he would use the hatch to channel it onto the conveyor belt, to avoid creating another mess for Patrick Kennedy to sweep up. He was counting, of course, on the sand coming out in a gentle, manageable flow. That did not happen.

At some point – alone, unseen, eight feet above the ground in that hellish workplace – Archie must have felt a terrific blow in the back, as if a giant hand had pushed him, sending him tumbling face first on to the moving conveyor. If he shouted in fear or pain, no one would have heard above the racket of the machines. As he struggled to get up, sand poured down remorselessly, creating a pyramid about four feet high and weighing around three and a half tons. Black grains were in his eyes, his ears, his mouth, his lungs. Sometime within twenty minutes of being knocked forward, he died, helpless but fully aware of what was happening. Technically, the cause of death was 'mechanical asphyxia'.

Andrew Neal, the young production foreman who had supervised the foundry for two of the eleven years he had worked at QDF, was in Diva 2 when he heard a shout. It was not obvious what it signified, nor whence it came, but when he heard another, he decided to investigate. He spotted the edifice of black sand alongside hopper 19E, whose weight had brought the conveyor belt to a halt. He suspected at once that this was something worse than a technical hold-up. Clambering up for a closer look, he saw a glove protruding from the pyramid. When he touched it, he realised to his horror that there was a hand within it.

At some risk to his own life, with sand still pouring from the hopper, Neal began digging, afraid that he might cause unnecessary injury if he tried to drag the buried workman out using brute force. There were other men across the foundry floor, but it was useless trying to shout to them above the din, and they took a frustratingly long time coming to help. He carried on digging alone and managed to get an arm around Archie's head and shoulders. He struggled to lift the blackened head, but at that terrifying moment, the conveyor belt lurched into action again. Archie's legs were dragged around the drum and his head forced up against it.

Others now joined the scramble, smashing at the cover of the drum with an iron bar and eventually wrenching it off. A nurse arrived with an oxygen mask and tank but too late. The advice from the paramedics was to leave the body where it was and let the fire brigade extricate it.

• • •

Archie was the youngest of ten children of a Scottish miner who moved to Derby in the 1930s to work on the railways. A month before his fifteenth birthday, Archie left school to work at British Rail's Derby Carriage and Wagon Works as a fitter and, apart from two years' national service between 1952 and 1954, it was as a fitter he spent the rest of his working life.

In 1980, ITV screened six episodes of a sitcom called *Sounding Brass*, which used as its model Ilkeston Brass, which claims to be Derbyshire's finest brass band, in which Archie played trombone. A dog-eared photograph of the cast, and some of the band members on whom their characters were based, turned up among his effects. Along the front row were faces that would have been recognisable at the time to viewers of *Coronation Street* or *The Bill*, including Brian Glover's. At the photograph's edge was Archie, holding his trombone. It was the closest he came to fame and prompted him to decide, in middle age, that he might like to be an actor. He had a series of character photographs taken. They show Archie displaying rage, Archie wildly happy, Archie undergoing a full repertoire of thespian passions – but when we found the pictures, he was no longer around to tell us which was which. Two brass bands turned out in full dress uniform to line the church path at his funeral.

Becoming a grandfather forced him to admit that he was not as young as he pretended to be. He was sixty-two when he was killed, three years from retirement. Once he had come to terms with having moved up a generation, he proved to be perfectly suited to all the standard grandfatherly tasks of chucking children in the air, of having his hair pulled and his dignity assaulted and of coming up with delightful gifts on birthdays and at Christmas. And not just for children. One year, I mentioned casually that I had seen a television clip of a New Orleans jazz musician calling himself Dr John – who was not well known in the UK – but could not find any records by him. That Christmas, there came a double LP (we are talking vinyl here: if you don't understand the terminology, ask an old person), a compilation of New Orleans jazz, with a note saying that this was all he could find by Dr John.

When Sue and I bought our first house in London, it came without a kitchen. Archie took a week off to come and build a kitchen for us, while we lived off McDonald's takeaways. Some years later, when I lost my job at the *Daily Mirror*, without being asked, he posted a cheque for £100. There was a company car that had come with my job, which had to be returned. All of a sudden, Archie had a second car that he did not need and insisted that we take it.

These are private reflections, important only to those who knew and loved him. In the larger world, what mattered were the implications of his horrible death. If a soldier, or a police officer, or a firefighter, or even a journalist is killed in the course of their work, death brings praise and recognition, even if the deceased has taken risks in order to do the job well, but being buried alive under a mountain of filthy black sand in a noisy foundry is not recognised as a heroic way to die. Public opinion, of course, demands that such things do not happen, so after a death such as Archie's, an inspector calls. It is in the interests of the management and shareholders that the inspector's conclusions do not find fault with the health and safety regime. It is less trouble all round if the inspector finds that the victim died because they foolishly disregarded correct procedure.

Her Majesty's Inspector of Health and Safety Clifford Seymour, who knew this factory from previous accidents, was quick to conclude that what Archie had been doing was unacceptably dangerous. He should not have been standing astride a moving conveyor belt; nor should he have removed a hatch from a full hopper when there was no one else watching, in case of an accident. 'There is a duty for employees', he said, sharply, 'to look after their own health and safety.'

But after listening to the evidence of some of Archie's former work-mates, the coroner concluded that there was a 'conflict of evidence'. Patrick Kennedy, who had worked in the factory for twenty-four years, said he had seen this method of unblocking a hopper used several times. Andrew Neal said that there was no written proce-dure, but the only method he had ever used, which had never failed, was to whack the outside with a sledgehammer until the skin of wet sand fell off. A multitude of dents around the sides of the hopper backed up his story.

Management's strongest witness was Archie's fellow fitter Graham Hodson, whose answers to the coroner's questions were long, care-fully prepared and full of detail. He was adamant that what Archie did had contravened a comprehensive list of dos and don'ts passed on to maintenance fitters by word of mouth. Asked why someone should deviate from normal practice, Hodson answered that it was a matter of 'personality'. He added, without prompting, that though he meant 'no disrespect to anyone', what he called a 'weak charac-ter' would cut corners under pressure, whereas a 'strong character' would have had the conveyor shut down and locked before opening that fatal hatch.

There had evidently been some friction between Graham Hodson and my father-in-law. Hodson was in the workshop when Archie went to collect his torch and spanner, but they did not exchange a word. Hodson was the brother of one of the managers. Relations between Archie and management were never good. Respect for au-thority and loyalty to his employers were not prominent within his skill set. His working hours were time given over to the bosses in return for money. Life began when his shift ended.

Of course, he should have done what Hodson suggested. He should have refused to attend to the problem on hopper 19E until after the conveyor belt had switched off and allowed management to fume in silence about the obstreperous worker who placed his own safety above the need to get machinery up and running after the Christmas break. There was no gain for him in carrying out his assignment in a dangerous manner, except the personal satisfaction from a job done well, for which the thanks he got was to be maligned as a 'weak' character.

A dead worker cannot speak for themselves. Management can hire lawyers to defend the firm's reputation, and maybe call on a loyal employee to do the same free of charge, but there is not much the dead person's family or friends can do to spare them being posthumously traduced. Fortunately, Archie was a union man, and the much-maligned Transport and General Workers' Union looked after the family and made sure that they too were represented at the inquest.

Anyone who has been in left-wing politics long enough will have come across the middle-class activist who thinks it would be cool to have been working class. I had a full blast of this at a party in Kennington, in south London, when a lad who had the pitiful misfortune to be well educated and in a well-paid office job had too much to drink and declaimed at boring length about how he wished he had been working class. He stared at me and demanded, 'Don't you wish you were working class?'

I did once take a casual job in a factory, when I was twenty-three and short of cash. I pulped eggs into powder and packaged the product into huge sacks. I found the work so mind-numbingly dull and the smell so unpleasant that after a few days I rang in pleading that I was ill, and I never went back. No, I do not wish I had had to leave school at fourteen, or that in my fifties I had ended up in a workplace I hated, in constant conflict with management, only to die horribly in an accident that officialdom would announce was my fault.

But Archie never had any choice, though part of him longed to escape a life of monotonous labour. Once, when talking to me about his prospects, he shook his head, spread out his powerful hands, and said with wistful regret, 'I've got nothing to sell but these.'

20

THE BROTHERS BROWN AND BLAIR

Early in 1984, a BBC producer rang asking for Labour's youngest current MP, whoever they might be, to appear on a children's television programme – John Craven's *Newsround*, if memory serves. I was a very new press officer, but by a happy chance, I already knew the name of the youngest Labour MP. He was thirty-year-old Anthony Blair. I also knew which constituency he represented and that he was a lawyer, from London, but I would have been embarrassed if the caller had asked me for anything more than these rudimentary details.

On my desk there was a photocopy of an A4 document with biographical information of 632 of the 633 candidates the Labour Party had fielded in the 1983 general election. A small white slip of paper attached to its front page explained the one omission. The local Labour Party in Sedgefield, in County Durham, had been so late choosing a candidate that they missed the final deadline for inclusion in the volume. In the press office, we could answer detailed questions about any Labour MP, or anyone who had run as a

Labour candidate in 1983 and been defeated, except one – the elusive Anthony Blair.

Blair would never have been the MP for Sedgefield, and probably would never have been Prime Minister, if a plan devised by the northern regional office of the Labour Party had not gone belly up at the eleventh hour.

The Boundary Commission had redrawn the constituency map of north-east England to reflect the movement of people out of Newcastle and Gateshead city centres into the countryside, so that Tyneside lost one constituency and County Durham gained one. The new map, which included Tyne Bridge, half in Newcastle, half in Gateshead, reducing the number, offended local opinion. The Labour Party decided to fight it in court, and while the case was pending, refused to select candidates to fight the new constituencies.

Disaster struck when Thatcher called a general election a year earlier than the law required, the courts ruled in favour of the Boundary Commission and Labour was caught with no candidates in place. Fortunately, the party could invoke a procedure under which any candidate who had been selected on the old boundaries would have an automatic right to be shortlisted for any new overlapping seat. Labour had twenty-seven properly selected candidates and twenty-seven seats to fill, so there should have been a straightforward solution, but the incumbent MP who was offered Sedgefield did not want it and fought a selection battle to secure his preferred option of North West Durham. Suddenly, there was a solid Labour seat going spare. Men poured in from all over England, hoping to grab this – the last remaining safe Labour seat. It was something of an anti-climax when we heard that the eventual winner was an unknown young barrister from London, Tony Blair.

I did not know how this lawyer would react to being invited to go on a kids' television programme, but there was no harm in asking, so I rang his office. His reaction surprised me: he bubbled with enthusiasm. Proudly, he confirmed that he was the youngest Labour MP, and he was delighted to be invited to go on television and was not at all daunted by the format or the age profile of the audience.

I heard very little more about Tony Blair for the next couple of years. Other Labour MPs who had arrived in Parliament in 1983 were quicker to make the national news. Jeremy Corbyn got arrested; Dave Nellist and Terry Fields were declared supporters of Militant; Clare Short created a sensation by accusing a minister, Alan Clark, of being drunk when addressing the Commons; while Blair quietly went about building a reputation for competence. Roy Hattersley told me that he was 'doing very well in the House' – meaning that he was a good parliamentary performer – and that his 'happy temperament' was working in his favour.

Blair was a strict believer in discipline and loyalty to the party leader, which made him a rarity in the troubled Labour Party of the early 1980s. In one of our first conversations, he gleefully related how in 1982 he had turned up at party headquarters, in Smith Square, introduced himself as a candidate in an unwinnable by-election and asked for a complete run-down of party policies, so that he could defend them all. He said that the researchers were astonished to be confronted with a candidate who actually wanted to stick to agreed lines.

That by-election was in Beaconsfield, previously the seat of Ronald Bell QC, who died of the side effects of rumpy-pumpy in the office. It was the only by-election during the 1979–83 parliament in which Labour's share of the vote fell. That setback was not a reflection on the candidate – he was excellent, no doubt – but on the timing: it was held in the midst of the Falklands War. Blair will have noted how fighting and winning a short, sharp war greatly enhanced the government's chances of a second full term in office. Hearing him tell that story about how he had demanded to be briefed on party policy made me almost regret that I left my job on the *Evening Mail* in Slough: if I had stayed, I might have witnessed the young Blair going from door to door telling the good people of Beaconsfield why a Labour government would nationalise the commanding heights of industry, unilaterally abolish the UK's nuclear weapons and withdraw from the EU without a second referendum.

Every week while Parliament is in session, Labour MPs and peers gather for a meeting which is otherwise closed to outsiders, including journalists, who nonetheless usually lurk in the corridor outside hoping to find out what has been said within. As a member of staff, I was at one of these events when the Bristol South MP Dawn Primarolo was on her feet, pointing an accusing finger as she berated Neil Kinnock over something or other. She was known in those days as 'Red Dawn', though later she was a long-serving and loyal Treasury minister. As she ranted, I became aware of tuts and mutterings of disapproval at my side, looked around and found that the person next to me was Blair. 'This is the sort of thing that drives Neil to despair,' he declared.

Note the word 'Neil'. Using the leader's first name was a signal of support.

The general public started to notice Blair in the 1990s, when his boyish looks and happy grin served him well. MPs nicknamed him 'Bambi' or 'The Pixie'. Barbara Follett, who was Labour MP for Stevenage for several years, told me that he was the kind of man women wished they were married to, whereas Kinnock was the sort they were married to but wished they weren't. My experience was that there was cold, hard ambition below the friendly surface. Years later, I heard Alastair Campbell say how he admired Blair's ruthlessness.

I was not alone in feeling his disdain. After the 1987 election, I sat in on meetings of Labour's shadow Treasury team, where John Smith presided with Gordon Brown as his deputy. These meetings were tightly disciplined, with no idle chatter, but they were friendly and very different from the atmosphere when the trade and industry team gathered under the chairmanship of Bryan Gould, with Blair as his second in command. I did not know then about the fierce dispute that had not yet broken into the open over whether the UK should co-operate with the plan to stabilise currencies across the EU, in which Gould was pitched against the formidable combination of John Smith, Gordon Brown and Neil Kinnock's principal economic adviser, John Eatwell. Blair will have known exactly what was brewing, which might explain his off-hand manner towards Bryan Gould.

Gould was not a strict chairman. Instead of aiming for quick agreement, he liked to talk through an issue, as if thinking aloud. 'What's the principle behind this?' he once asked, speaking to no one in particular. His special adviser pretended to be deeply shocked. 'Ooh Bryan – principle! – how could you say that word!' he exclaimed in mock horror. Blair had no time for this sort of banter. His demeanour was so detached as to be almost rude. Thinking that it was time that the meeting was over, he stood up to leave, but Gould detained him to discuss a detail of a copyright bill going through Parliament. With Blair standing and Gould sitting, questions and answers flashed back and forth about the potential impact of cheap cassette tapes and recorders on musicians' livelihoods. During those few minutes, more real business was conducted than in all of the long preceding meeting.

I also felt the cold wind of Blair's disdain. When we were walking along Millbank towards the BBC studio, I remarked that I had met a Treasury civil servant named Adam Sharples, who had been a member of the Ugly Rumours rock group at Oxford University when Blair was its front man. The response was a look which told me that his days of singing Rolling Stones songs were not a fit subject of conversation.

Part of my job as a party press officer was to devise ways to get MPs mentioned in the news. I went to the Commons to discuss one such scheme with Blair, when he was a middle-ranking shadow minister, but at the appointed time, I found myself alone in a Commons lobby, waiting, until the clack of metal heels on a tiled floor told me that Blair was walking briskly in my direction. He did not apologise for being late. There was no small talk of any kind. He asked me to repeat the explanation I had given over the phone, curtly agreed to the proposal, turned about and walked away. In my suspicious mind, I wondered if he had been advised by Peter Mandelson that I was someone he should avoid.

In the summer of 1990, when I was a political correspondent for the *Daily Mirror*, I treated Tony Blair to lunch at my employer's expense, in a French restaurant in Covent Garden, at a time when there was a lively rumour circulating in Westminster that Peter Mandelson was looking for a safe Labour seat. The sitting MP for Hartlepool had indicated that he was going to retire, and it was rumoured that Tom Burlison, the regional boss of the GMB and a major figure in the north-east Labour Party, was fixing up the seat for Mandelson.

If anyone was going to know whether this was true it was surely Blair, given his friendship with Mandelson, and that Sedgefield and Hartlepool share a common border, but, looking me directly in the eye, he maintained that he had not heard and did not know. That was odd, because it was rumoured that the Blairs had moved their daughter out of her bedroom in their Sedgefield home so that Mandelson could use it as his campaign office. You might think that Blair would have asked why his friend and ally suddenly needed an office in that part of England, but apparently not.

However, I saw Blair again after it was public knowledge that Mandelson was the Labour candidate in Hartlepool, and he went into an unprompted eulogy about what an asset his friend would be to Parliament and in particular to the north-east group of Labour MPs.

On the day after I was sacked by the *Daily Mirror* in 1993, when a fellow journalist suggested that I should talk to Blair, there did not seem to me to be any point, but this was no time to ignore advice, so I rang him. To my surprise, he seemed shocked that I had been dismissed. He said that I should ring his wife, whom he referred to by her professional name, Cherie Booth, but asked me to wait until he had spoken to her first. In all, he used probably fewer than forty words.

I had met Cherie Booth's father, Tony, famous for playing the left-wing son-in-law in the BBC sitcom *Till Death Us Do Part*. In real life, he was, if anything, further to the left than his fictional character. In March 1984, he and his partner, Pat Phoenix, a star of *Coronation Street*, came to support Tony Benn in the Chesterfield by-election. They caught up with Benn in the streets, when it was still daylight but not too early in the day for Booth to have fortified himself with alcohol. A BBC radio journalist named John Harrison had also spotted Benn and had put a microphone in front of him and was asking questions, which Benn answered calmly but with a touch of impatience. Suddenly, Tony Booth started bellowing at the journalist, accusing him of bias and suggesting that he go bother some other candidate.

I did not know until that day I spoke to Blair that Booth had a daughter, who was a barrister specialising in employment law. The following day, I visited Lincoln's Inn and was immediately admitted to a book-lined office, to be plied with questions. Cherie was as committed as her husband to the Labour Party. She wanted to know whether the mass sackings at the *Daily Mirror* meant that its new owners were reneging on the papers' long-standing support for the Labour Party. She also let slip how well the Blair family knew Alastair Campbell, which was news to me. As to my situation, Cherie could not offer any advice until she knew the terms of my dismissal, so told me to come back when I had something in writing. On my next visit, she advised that I had to choose – either I could take the *Mirror* to an employment tribunal, which, she said, would undoubtedly find that I had been unfairly dismissed, but the compensation they awarded would be no greater than the pay-off I had already been offered; or I could let it go and focus on finding another job. With two very young children, and another on the way, that choice was a no-brainer.

The next time I saw Cherie was at the Labour Party annual conference in Blackpool in 1994, three months after Tony Blair had been elected leader. He saw me in a crowded room and said, 'Hello, Andy, are you here to make trouble?'

It was not the first time he had said something of the sort, and I did not mind at all. If anything, I thought it rather flattering that he cared, but Cherie seemed to fear that I would take offence and, to my great surprise, in front of numerous witnesses, roundly told her husband, 'Of course he's not here to make trouble!'

There was a fleeting moment in his life when Blair was pleased to see me. He became so used to being flanked by advisers that he lost the habit of taking his pass with him when he walked around Parliament. One day, he left the committee corridor intending to return to his office through Speaker's Yard but was confronted by a closed door. He was standing forlornly in front of it when I turned the corner. Unusually, I was greeted by a look of relief. I was about to break into a brisk walk to come to his rescue when a voice in my head told me not to be a toady. Blair's smile turned to a frown. After I had opened the door for me, he gave me a nod and went on his way.

● ● ●

Office space was at a premium on the parliamentary estate in the 1980s. New MPs were lucky if they were given half an office. Some had to manage on a quarter of a shared table in the basement. When Ken Livingstone was elected, in 1987, the Labour whips refused to give him even that. It would be interesting to know what went through the mind of the whip in charge of accommodation in 1983 when he decided that this unknown new MP for Sedgefield would be the right person to share an office with Dave Nellist, MP for Coventry South East, a well-known member of Militant who would, in time, be expelled from the Labour Party.

After a year of loyal service, Blair had enough credit in the whips' office to be allowed to part company with Nellist and team up with Gordon Brown. I occasionally visited their shared office. It was like a pad for students who worked hard and played hard. Their desks were so close together that their elbows must have been in constant danger of colliding. Everywhere there were documents, books and more documents. Shelves groaned under the weight of political information. Hanging from hooks there were tennis rackets and sports clothes. There were trainers on the floor. In this crowded windowless space, they worked together like brothers. The bond between them was so close that party staff named them 'Pushmi Pullyu', after Doctor Doolittle's two-headed llama. Brown was the older and more experienced of the pair. Blair was like his kid brother.

My first encounter with 'Pushmi' was in 1986, when a call came through to the Labour press office to say that someone named Gordon Brown wanted to hold a press conference. Generally, journalists are not going to turn out to listen to a junior opposition spokesman whose parliamentary career has barely begun, but Brown had uncovered an interesting titbit that could make a news story. I agreed to go to Parliament to help out. When I informed Peter Mandelson, he told me, 'You are going to meet a future Prime Minister.' He was proved right, twenty-one years later.

Any fears I had that Brown would be talking to an empty room were dispersed when a handful of journalists turned up, including Andrew Marr, representing *The Scotsman*, whom Brown recognised and addressed by his first name. The questions the hacks asked showed that they were interested. In all, I thought it had gone well, but Brown was distraught. 'Why was there no television?' he exclaimed.

If hard work and unquenchable ambition were the qualities that make a Prime Minister, there would have been none greater than Brown. Nobody else in the Labour Party put in the hours that he did. It helped that, unlike Blair, he had no family life to distract him. On Sunday mornings, between 1992 and 1997, when the political correspondents would be fretting because they had to fill column space the next day but nothing was happening, the phone would ring. It would be Brown, the shadow Chancellor, on the line, with some nugget of information about the nation's finances that he had turned into a press statement, opening with the words 'Shadow Chancellor Gordon Brown will today demand...' New Labour MPs arriving in Parliament for the first time in 1992 were surprised that Brown would wait on the front bench all afternoon to hear them make their maiden speeches, and they would be flattered afterwards to receive a handwritten note saying how well they had spoken.

He took more trouble than Blair did to build a political base. A solid group of Labour MPs from constituencies in Scotland and the north-east of England invested their futures in Brown, staying loyal to him through the Blair years. The Brown gang would gather for an evening in an Indian restaurant in Kennington, in south London. The most prominent was his near namesake, Nick Brown, who later served as Chief Whip over a period of twenty-five years, under Tony Blair, Gordon Brown, Ed Miliband, Jeremy Corbyn and Keir Starmer. Tony Blair would have been welcome to join them but preferred to be at home during the children's bath time. Brown also attracted the personal loyalty of those who worked for him for years, including Ed Balls, Sue Nye – now Baroness Nye of Lambeth – and Charlie Whelan, who was his spin doctor for seven years until the feud with Peter Mandelson got out of hand.

Charlie Whelan was almost never heard to utter a word of criticism of Brown, but a year after his forced resignation, I was in a bar in the Commons with Andrew Marr, the recently appointed political editor of the BBC, when Whelan joined us. With unusual frankness, he admitted that Brown had a difficult personality, which he summed up with the cliché that 'he doesn't suffer fools gladly'.

It was true that Brown could be brutal with people he considered to be incompetent or inefficient. When Chris Smith, whose politics were soft left, was shadow Minister for Social Security, he made some generous promises which he had not cleared with the Treasury team. Away from the public eye, there was a long meeting in which Brown tore the offending minister apart. One of the witnesses told me it was painful to watch.

But Mo Mowlam, who rejected the invitation to join the Brown gang, thought that he had the opposite problem, that he suffered fools all too gladly, if they looked up to him and soothed his insecure ego. Many of the people Brown could not suffer – Robin Cook, Peter Mandelson, David Blunkett, Alan Milburn, Patricia Hewitt, Charles Clarke etc. and ultimately Tony Blair – were not fools. Mo Mowlam was the first person I heard suggest that Brown was not psychologically fit to lead the Labour Party. She was the first to approach Tony Blair on the day John Smith died to urge him to run for the leadership, against Brown if necessary.

Women, in particular, complained about Brown's apparent inability to treat them as sentient beings. This, and the fact that he was unmarried until a few months before his fiftieth birthday, set off a false rumour that he was gay, which someone sought to squash on his behalf by leaking to a friendly journalist a list of names of women who had featured in Brown's love life. They included a BBC journalist, whom I met by chance in a bookshop soon after she had been included on the list. She was furious. She told me that she had rung Brown to tell him that he was like a schoolboy boasting about his success with the girls. This, of course, was before he married Sarah Macaulay.

During the last party conference over which Tony Blair presided as leader, in September 2006, Tessa Jowell told me, with feeling, that the party was disposing of a leader with a high degree of emotional intelligence for someone who had none. There was a comic example during the 2001 general election. The Labour Party held morning press conferences throughout the campaign, in a hired hall on Millbank, which nominally featured three government ministers of varying seniority. The party took meticulous care to make sure that there was always a woman on the platform, but her role was normally to go to the rostrum when her turn came, read her prepared statement and sit quietly while men answered questions. This inspired the lobby to enter into a mischievous conspiracy. Secretly, they agreed among themselves that on a particular day – Friday 25 May, to be precise – all the questions would be asked by female journalists, while the male journalists listened in silence. There were actually two women on the platform that day, on either side of Gordon Brown. Jackie Ashley, from *The Guardian*, pointedly announced that she had a question which she wanted Estelle Morris, an education minister, to answer. Why were women never allowed to answer questions at Labour press conferences, she asked. Before Morris could utter a word, Brown intervened to say, 'I don't think you're accurate... sorry, Estelle...' Whatever else he had to say was drowned in laughter. The lobby's prank had worked better than anyone could have hoped.

Brown was too obsessive and single-minded to relate well to

others. His elephantine memory and attention to detail made him a very effective Chancellor, but it was a weakness in other respects. In November 1995, I reported on the front page of *The Observer* on a revolt in the shadow Cabinet against 'out of control' Brown, who seemed to want to get his hands on every detail of every party policy. The editor of *The Observer* had a long angry call from Brown that evening, and the Labour Party's director of communications, Joy Johnson, was instructed to get up early on Sunday morning, to ring around the broadcasters and national newspapers, giving out a new detail of Labour's tax policy, to draw journalists away from what was in *The Observer*. According to Alastair Campbell's diary, the report threw Gordon Brown into 'a real state', and Tony Blair warned the shadow Cabinet that if he ever found out who leaked the information, he would sack them, and they would never work in his shadow Cabinet or in his Cabinet. To make peace, the editor invited Brown to a private lunch, to which I was not supposed to be invited but fate intervened. The editor was sacked. His replacement, Will Hutton, found the lunch in the diary, decided that it should go ahead and innocently added me to the guest list. The conversation was of the highest quality. At one point, Brown, Hutton and *The Observer*'s veteran economics editor Bill Keegan exchanged well-informed views on the likely impact of a recent flutter in the value of the Japanese yen. During a pause, Hutton sat back and asked whether the lunch was in aid of anything in particular. There was a moment's awkward silence. Brown looked at me out of the corner of his eye and told Hutton how I had written that he was 'out of control'. His spin doctor, Charlie Whelan, joined in to say, 'When I read it, I was out of control.' But none of the journalists around the table was shocked. Brown quickly caught the mood, turned to me and said, 'Actually, it was a good story.'

But that did not mean that all was forgotten or forgiven. Approximately sixteen years later, I wrote in *The Independent* about the huge fees Brown commanded on the international lecture circuit after leaving office, which pushed his income way above what he had been paid as Prime Minister. At that time, he cut a tragic figure: no one was giving him credit for his long mastery of the economy, or his adept handling of the 2008 financial crisis, nor for the way he was avoiding the temptation to get rich quickly. Instead of trousering his vast fees, he was putting them into a charitable trust he had set up with his wife, Sarah. I mentioned this, not in the first paragraph, where Brown thought it should have been, but further down. During an irate call to Chris Blackhurst, editor of *The Independent*, Brown complained that this was my second offence. The first, still fresh in his memory, was back in 1995.

There was a time, though, when I saw him looking happy. It was a freezing December day in Brussels, during a European summit, when I was allowed to interview him one to one. After we had covered EU budgetary and other such matters, I said I had one more question. I told him that it was well known that he liked to be organised and on top of things – how therefore, I asked, would he cope with the chaos of living with a newborn child? Sarah Brown was nine months pregnant. Brown's demeanour suddenly changed: all that seriousness, that look that said he had the world's burden to carry, dropped away, and his broad and haggard face lit up. He told me how much he was looking forward to fatherhood. Unfortunately, the little girl born that same month died after just ten days.

• • •

The brothers Brown and Blair advanced in tandem through the Labour Party but always with Brown in front. From 1979 to 1996, the shadow Cabinet was elected annually by Labour MPs. Seniority counted. As a general rule, a Labour MP needed to have served for at least a decade before their peers were ready to elect them to the top team. Brown reached the shadow Cabinet in 1987, just four years after his arrival in Parliament, a record that no one matched, and in 1988, he topped the poll, beating John Smith into second place. Blair also did well: he reached the shadow Cabinet in 1988. Later, they both ran for seats on the National Executive Committee, a test of their popularity among the party membership. Both were elected, but Brown won more votes. In 1992, John Smith knew that he must give each of them a major job, shadowing the so-called great offices of state, but to no one's surprise, Brown was awarded the more important role, as shadow Chancellor, while Blair was shadow Home Secretary.

One day in 1993, when I was in the lobby of the House of Commons, where MPs would stop to chat to journalists, Blair was having a conversation on the far side of the room. I heard the journalist he was talking to suggest that one day soon, Brown would run for the party leadership and Blair would be his campaign manager. The comment did not surprise me, it was the accepted wisdom in those days, but I was struck by Blair's reaction. Standing with hands in pockets, feet apart, he winced and frowned and seemed to be on the point of saying something, but changed his mind and let it pass. His body language was the first hint I ever picked up that Blair had higher ambitions than to be Brown's loyal second in command.

Writing in the *Sunday Mirror* soon afterwards, Alastair Campbell commented in passing that Neil Kinnock had once thought of Brown as his obvious successor, but he was 'not sure' that it was still how Kinnock thought. That was disingenuous: Campbell knew Kinnock too well to be 'not sure'. It was a sign that Brown's support was slipping.

On the day John Smith died, I was in the library at the offices of *The Guardian* speed writing a 3,000-word obituary, when the BBC rang to ask if I would do a pre-recorded interview for the *Six O'Clock News*. I said that I did not have time to go to a studio, so they offered to bring the camera crew to me. I had answered a few questions about Smith, then, without warning, with the camera still rolling, the interviewer asked who would be the next Labour leader. I had not given the question any thought, it being only a few hours after Smith's death, but as soon as it was asked, the answer was obvious. I said that it would be Tony Blair. My reply went out on that evening's six o'clock, making me the first to predict in public the coming of Tony Blair. I was asked the same question by Adam Boulton on Sky News's seven o'clock bulletin and gave the same answer. So did Alastair Campbell later that evening, on *Newsnight*.

Sixteen years later, the political world was treated to the psycho drama of Ed Miliband running against his older brother for the party leadership and beating him. The chagrin that David Miliband felt will not have been very different from what Gordon Brown went through in 1994, when he realised that he would give way to the junior member of the decade-long Brown–Blair partnership. When Blair stood down, thirteen years later, Brown looked like a man who had wanted to be Prime Minister so much for so long that he had forgotten what he planned to do when he got there.

21

HOW I WAS ROGERED

The glory days of printed newspapers are gone for ever. Back in the 1980s, I used to amuse myself from time to time by listening in to conversations on public transport and guessing which daily newspaper people read from their appearance and the sentiments they expressed. During the miners' strike, a youth on the train to Newcastle could be heard declaring in a Geordie accent that members of the National Union of Mineworkers had no choice but to obey their leader, Arthur Scargill, because, in that union, 'he's like Hitler'. A *Sun* reader, patently. On another train, a woman with a tight, rising hairdo and an outfit that probably came from Marks & Spencer was expressing her disgust that traffic in London had been disrupted by marchers who wanted to 'ban the bomb'. 'That's what they should do,' she declared, 'Drop a bomb on them while they're protesting – pouf!' A *Daily Mail* reader, then. There was a comment I set about recording in longhand, but I gave up before it found its way to a main verb, so all I can offer is this fragment: 'What I am really kind of lumbering towards is saying that the traditional mode of militancy...' A *Guardian* reader, of course.

There were some people I could not place. When the pubs closed in Newcastle, the buses came alive. Commonly, one passenger would talk loud enough for everyone on the crowded deck to hear and another would reply. Alternatively, someone would sing to the crowd. One evening, the conversation turned to a well-known local character who would stand out in the streets, singing her heart out. The bus passenger talking about her was likely to have left school at fourteen and lived his whole life in west Newcastle, doing manual jobs. These were his alcohol-fuelled thoughts, spoken in pure Geordie:

I'll say one thing for her, though – she's happy. There are millionaires who would give a lot of money to be what she is – happy. Millionaires! Am I right, or am I wrong?

It's Darwin's theory, which happens also to be mine, if I may say so, that it's the fate of circumstances that occur which makes people what they are and what they're not. It's phenomena. And it's the circumvention of certain devious circumstances – if that's the right word – which lead to other circumstances, which makes the world go on as it is.

Take the ancient Briton. One of them could invent the flint, just like that, and he'd be better off than all the others around. It's the fate of circumstances that occur.

He had not read that in any newspaper.

For me, there was no greater newspaper than *The Observer*, which I loved from when I first came across it at university. Nora Beloff, its mercurial political correspondent, the first woman ever to cover politics for a national paper, seemed to be forever in court suing *Private Eye*, while the newspaper's mega-rich owner-editor David Astor was visiting the serial child-killer Myra Hindley in prison and calling for her to be given a release date. I was in awe of people so unafraid of making complete arses of themselves in public.

Later, there was the political columnist Alan Watkins, a provocative writer who took such care over his craft that he would refer to the 'architecture' of what he wanted to say. I knew readers who turned to his column just to be annoyed on a Sunday morning. When David Hill was being interviewed by Labour's National Executive in 1990 for the post of director of communications, he was asked what he thought of Watkins's most recent column, and he replied, 'Alan Watkins is an idiot.' As soon as the words were out of his mouth, he heard Neil Kinnock say, 'He's just got the job.'

But when *The Observer* was bought by *The Guardian* in 1993, somebody decided that it was time to put Watkins out to grass and replace him with Andrew Rawnsley, who would spend decades not annoying the readers by reinforcing what they already believed. Watkins was taken on by the *Independent on Sunday*, and in 2003, he set out to provoke a reaction by repeatedly describing Tony Blair as 'the young war criminal'. I believe he was the first to accuse Blair of war crimes; but he meant it as a wind-up, a joke, unlike the thousands who have repeated the mantra.

The creativity Watkins invested in his weekly column also shone in his expenses claims. At a private dinner in his honour, when he had won another award some time after his seventieth birthday, a former managing editor told the diners that week after week he wondered whether he should challenge Watkins's expenses claims, until one came in that was so obviously dodgy that he summoned up the courage to ask the great man to explain. He had put in a receipt for a lunch he claimed to have had with a political contact, from which it was obvious that only one starter and one main course had been consumed, although with ample alcohol. Watkins's written riposte was four words long – 'He ate, I drank.'

I first visited *The Observer* offices as a kind of hanger-on while working for the Labour Party. It seemed then that I would never be anything more than a visitor, but I was lucky. In the same month that I was sacked by the *Daily Mirror*, *The Observer* was bought by *The Guardian*, creating churn that enabled me to get shifts as a part-time political correspondent. In June 1993, I joined my new colleagues for the first time. It was the day after the opening night of *Jurassic Park*, which I had watched in one of London's suburban cinemas, but before I could boast about this, the arts correspondent, Richard Brooks, started quietly talking about how he had been at the opening night in Leicester Square, where he had met Steven Spielberg.

There was a talented social affairs editor at *The Observer* named Heather Mills, which was also the name of a model and media personality who had a short unhappy marriage with Paul McCartney. Heather Mills the model was a liar. One of her lies was to pretend that she was Heather Mills the journalist. She turned up at an interview for a job in television, with an armful of press cuttings of stories the other Heather Mills had written when she was home affairs editor of *The Independent*. As it happened, the producer, Steve Hayward, was married to a friend of Heather Mills the journalist, and went home and said, 'You never told me that Heather Mills had only one leg.' Heather Mills the model had lost part of a leg when she was hit by a police motorcycle. To make quite sure that there was no mistake, he rang a mate on *The Guardian* and asked how many legs Heather Mills had. 'Three', he was told.

In one of her television appearances, when she was basking in the fame of being Mrs McCartney, Heather Mills claimed, with bare-faced insouciance, 'There was a journalist going round pretending to be me.'

There were also sharp elbows and egos in the *Observer* news-room, of course. There was an instance when two journalists cov-ered a street disturbance, one on location, the other keeping an eye on agency reports coming in over the wires. They were awarded a joint byline, but when the man on the spot returned to the office, he learnt that his name came after the word 'and', not before. This caused such a ruction that the two journalists fought it out with clenched fists and flailing arms on the newsroom floor.

There was just one person on the staff whom I actively loathed. He knew that he was not liked, so was constantly trying to enlist allies in a vendetta against someone or other. Robin McKie, the science editor, remarked that he was like the monster in the film *Alien*, so toxic and malicious that if he dribbled, his spit would burn a hole in every floor on its way down to the ground. The man took me aside on my first day to say that he had noticed how shoddily I was treated by Tony Bevins, the political editor. Actually, I had no complaint against Bevins; I was very grateful to him for helping to get me on the paper.

There was worse. In the pub one lunchtime, my nemesis began talking about under-age prostitutes in Thailand, in a tone that implied that to be a real man you needed to have had sex with a twelve-year-old in Bangkok. He pestered the news desk to assign him to go to Thailand to write about this vile trade. Permission was refused. During a slack period on a Saturday afternoon, he moved to a quiet corner to use a computer where no one could look over his shoulder, but he forgot how rapidly computer technology was advancing. On a new system, someone on the news desk was able to check what he was watching. It was child pornography. When called upon to explain himself, he claimed that it was research, for the piece that he had been refused permission to write. This was before it had been established in law that viewing child pornography is a criminal offence. The management told him – too leniently, I thought – to take a week's gardening leave and seek therapy. He was sacked later.

In my time at *The Observer*, the newspaper got through four editors. The first, Jonathan Fenby, was an outstanding authority on Chinese history but seriously lacking in the kind of skills that make a good boss. His successor, Andrew Jaspan, was in constant conflict with the management of *The Guardian*. When he was sacked, a whole battalion of middle-management was taken out with him.

His successor, Will Hutton, came with exceptional qualifications. His recently published book *The State We're In* was reckoned to be the best left-wing analysis of British society since Anthony Crosland's *The Future of Socialism*, published forty years earlier. He was, as it were, the Stephen Hawking of left-wing political thought. On his first day in the editor's chair, one of the reporters remarked, facetiously, 'Bugger! I spent the whole weekend reading *A Brief History of Time*, then realised I'd got the wrong book.' But sales of *The Observer* fell under Hutton, as they had under each of his predecessors, so in 1998, he was given the honorary title of 'editor-in-chief', and Roger Alton arrived, on a mission to be the first editor in decades to push the circulation figures up.

Roger Alton brought a lifetime's experience in putting together news and feature pages. Sometimes he reacted as if it reflected on his worth as a human being if something badly written somehow crept in. Tall, balding, exceptionally fit and strong for a man of his age, bursting with nervous energy, his voice was loud and he had a manner of self-expression that was distinctly his own. He used the word 'fucking' more often than anyone else I ever knew. One Saturday, he burst forth from his office, sweating with horror, strode across the editorial floor and exclaimed something like, 'Babs, Babs, we can't have the fucking gulls circling mournfully over Lake Geneva.' Barbara Gunnell, aka 'Babs', was at a computer screen, subediting a story for the front page. She showed him the changes she had made, which had an instant calming effect. 'Fucking better, fucking better!' Alton declared, as he turned about and returned to his office.

When Ian McEwan was researching for his novel *Amsterdam*, he spent time in the offices of *The Guardian*, watching senior journalists at work. I have no doubt that Alton was the model for the frustrated editor 'Vernon Halliday'. The resemblance is too great to be coincidence. His mannerisms were also caught with delightful accuracy in the 2019 film *Official Secrets*, starring Keira Knightley as Katharine Gun, an employee of GCHQ who lost her job and risked imprisonment by leaking a communiqué to *The Observer*. I watched that film at a special showing for past and present *Observer* staff. When Conleth Hill, playing Roger, uttered his first line, the audience burst out laughing in recognition. They also greatly enjoyed an in-joke, when Matt Smith, playing Martin Bright, the journalist who broke the story, is told by a fellow journalist that there is a call for him. We all recognised the person playing the unidentified colleague. He was the real-life Martin Bright.

When Alton first took on the editorship of *The Observer*, he was so afraid of failing that he seemed to want to run the paper by remote control, without speaking to members of the staff, let alone the readers, some of whom held positions of importance. When he heard that Tony Blair wanted to meet him, he went into a flat spin and cried, 'I can't meet the Prime Minister! I'm only a fucking sub.' He made Patrick Wintour, who was then political editor, accompany him on this ordeal. Outside the great man's study, they encountered David Miliband, head of the Downing Street Policy Unit, who had had many differences of opinion with Will Hutton over the finer points of stakeholder socialism. What changes, if any, might Roger be thinking of making, Miliband asked. Talking rapidly, his nerves on edge, the new editor replied that he might put a bit of sport on the front page – and 'more sex!'

On a Saturday, Roger would abandon his office to sit in the middle of the newsroom reading copy as it came in and thinking about how to make the pages look good; and yet, though they could see him, the staff were visibly discouraged from approaching him by a protective wall of three middle managers with two-word job titles, who surrounded him at all times. Sometimes, to relieve stress, Roger would stand up and wander over to the notice board to read the notices, with his hands in his pockets, whereupon three middle managers would also stand up and go over to read the notices, with their hands in their pockets. Roger would return to his seat, usually without a word said, and they would return to theirs. John

Sweeney, then one of the less respectful members of the *Observer* staff, nicknamed this quartet 'the Pod'.

Later, as sales figures crawled upwards, Roger gained in confidence and progressed from remoteness to all-round mateyness. While other editors might fuss for hours over the leader columns and left whole pages unread, Roger read everything, even including the business pages, and got to know everyone who wrote them and who subbed them. If he found out that someone was known to their friends by a nickname, such as 'Babs', he would use it.

Sometimes, his matey manner jarred. When he was editor of *The Independent*, he was told by the company board that he had to sack a couple of journalists, one news reporter and one from the features, which of course he did not want to do. If someone is to be sacked, it is always cheaper to choose someone new. One morning, Amol Rajan, who was one of the youngest and newest reporters, if not the youngest and newest, and whose desk was near to mine, was called away and came back with face like thunder. After a few minutes' broody silence, he announced that he had been sacked. The way Amol described it, Roger's opening words were, 'Hi Amol, how are you?' Amol had already guessed why he was there and replied, 'That depends on what you're about to say.'

There was an immediate reaction. The health editor, Jeremy Laurance, who had no track record as a troublemaker, went in and politely warned Alton on behalf of the senior writers that this sacking was a bad idea. The decision was rescinded. Later, Amol Rajan was taken on as an adviser to Evgeny Lebedev, *The Independent*'s spoilt, young, social-climbing proprietor, and handled him so skilfully that before he was thirty years old, Amol was editor of *The Independent*. After he had moved to the BBC, I told Amol that I was trying to write a thriller based in a newspaper office, which was never published. He told me, 'You should include a Russian proprietor who wants to own a newspaper for no good reason.'

Early in 2000, Patrick Wintour returned to his old job on *The Guardian*, creating a vacancy for a political editor. I put in an application, urging that the newspaper should rely less on the Blairite spin machine and give more room to the likes of Blair's internal critics, such as Robin Cook, the Foreign Secretary, and to pro-EU Tories such as Ken Clarke. Roger Alton told me this was very interesting. He did not say that putting daylight between Blair and the editorial stance of *The Observer* was the last thing he wanted, and he spent a long time looking for someone else to appoint. Eventually, he called me at home to say that he had appointed someone named Kamal Ahmed, the media editor of *The Guardian*. The resulting conversation was written up in a book published eight years later, by the *Guardian* journalist Nick Davies:

McSmith was so furious that he could barely speak and slammed down the phone on Alton. The next day he went to see him – insulted at losing the job; baffled that it had gone to a man who had no real experience at all of Westminster; aghast at the idea that he would have to take orders from somebody whom he was simultaneously teaching. He asked his editor why he should accept this. 'Well, you'll be a better human being,' replied Alton in what may have been intended as a joke.

In the Commons the following morning, I was greeted by a journalist from a rival newspaper with the words, 'Hi Andy, I hear you've been stitched up.' I also had a call from Derek Draper, who told me that he had been in the Groucho Club the evening before Alton rang me and had been introduced to Kamal Ahmed as the new political editor. Derek asked where that left me. It was kind of him to ring, but I was none too pleased to know that frequenters of the Groucho Club had been informed of the appointment before I had. When I went over to head office, I discovered that the staff there had not been told either, though as I arrived, a one-line announcement was pinned to the notice board. When the science editor, Robin McKie, greeted me with a cheery 'How are you?', I am afraid he received a bad-tempered reply. 'Go read the fucking notice board before you ask me how I am,' I suggested.

I had another talk with the editor, who suggested that I work alongside Kamal Ahmed for six months, and if it did not work out, then I would be assigned another job. It reminded me of a scene in David Hare's play *Plenty*, in which a diplomat's wife who fears that her husband's career is on a downward slope sounds out a senior official at the Foreign Office on whether his being offered a posting in Monrovia was a deliberate insult. The mandarin replies, 'Monrovia is not an insult. Monrovia is more in the nature of a test. A test of nerves, it is true. If a man is stupid enough to accept Monrovia, then he probably deserves Monrovia.'

Luckily for me, I was rescued by the grapevine. Before the week was over, I had approaches from five newspapers. An executive from the *Mail on Sunday* asked if I would be interested in being their 'foreign fireman' – i.e. the person on call to cover the week's biggest story from abroad. I would have taken it, had the *Daily Telegraph* not come in with a better offer, that I could stay in Parliament as their chief political correspondent. Fifteen days after Kamal Ahmed's appointment, I was able to hand in my notice. But then I made the mistake of walking into Roger Alton's office with a book in my hand. Sensing that I might have come in to say something he did not want to hear, he seized on this wretched book and started questioning me about it in such detail that I feared that at any moment a phone would ring, or someone else would walk in, and he would have an excuse to break off the conversation. I interrupted abruptly to say that I was leaving.

'I so don't want you to do that,' he exclaimed.

In the year 2000, it was a fashion among the young to put 'so' before a negative, as in 'I'm so not going there' – but it sounded oddly inappropriate in the mouth of a man aged over fifty.

I wanted to leave immediately but was perversely held to my notice period, so Kamal Ahmed and I were colleagues for a fortnight. In that brief period, a civil servant rang me from the Treasury to say that Gordon Brown had invited the new political editor in to meet him and had been shocked that someone of so little relevant experience should hold such a senior job. Then a woman who worked with Harriet Harman rang me to say that when Harriet agreed to meet him, Kamal had suggested a rendezvous at noon on Wednesday, apparently unaware that he had picked the exact time when the Prime Minister answers questions in Parliament. None of this mattered to Roger Alton. Journalists who brought strongly held beliefs to work exasperated him. I once heard him complain with feeling about what a pain it was working with Martin Bright, and with the columnist, Nick Cohen, of whom Tony Blair once said, 'If I listened to Nick Cohen I would never win an election'. Seemingly, he preferred colleagues for whom journalism was a job. He was certainly comfortable with Kamal Ahmed. It also suited Alastair Campbell that there was a reliable outlet for whatever Downing Street wanted said. They got on so well that Kamal was accused of co-authoring the so-called February dossier that helped put the case for the Iraq War, a claim which he strongly denies. In *Official Secrets*, he was portrayed as wanting the paper to suppress the story brought to it at considerable risk by a GCHQ whistleblower because running it would conflict with the editorial line, which supported Blair's decision to send British troops into Iraq. But he was a fast learner, who, fourteen years later, proved himself as an effective business editor of the BBC and moved up into those heights inhabited by BBC executives with huge salaries, only to be made redundant.

I was not expecting to come upon Roger Alton in a professional capacity after I left *The Observer* – until one day in 2008, when it was announced that he was to be the new editor of *The Independent*. This was just two months after Nick Davies's book *Flat Earth News* had come out, with that account of my dealings with Roger of which I was obviously the source. On the day of the announcement, the *Standard* ran a diary item naming three journalists at *The Independent* who were said to be angry about the appointment of an editor who had so uncritically supported the Iraq War. I was named as one of them. Patrick Cockburn was another.

This did not bode well for a smooth working relationship. During my first conversation one on one with the new editor, in his office, Alton stood with hands in pockets, looking out of the window, as I addressed the back of his head. I wrote a political diary for the paper and received an email from him, copied to others, suggesting that I needed advice on how to do it properly and that there was a clever young reporter in his twenties working on the same floor who could show me. In those days when screen savers were a novelty, I thought I had been quite clever to upload a family photograph. I did not expect many people to see it, since my computer was usually either in use or asleep, but I left it on once while I was away from the desk. When I returned, I was told by other reporters that Alton had walked by, seen it and then delivered a tirade about people who flaunted images of their children in the workplace.

For all his sound and fury, Roger Alton was not vindictive. His attitude to me changed suddenly after I had written a fly-on-the-wall description of a confrontation between Gordon Brown and the Speaker, Michael Martin, over the MPs' expenses scandal. He announced at an editorial meeting that I should be asked to write more of the same. Soon afterwards, out of nowhere, he suddenly told me how much he loathed Nick Davies, both as a journalist and as a human being, then abruptly switched tack to say that generally he liked almost everybody and did not hold grudges. 'You may have called me a complete cunt: I don't remember,' he said. It was his way of saying let's be friends.

22

THE *TELEGRAPH*

In my teens, I was trying to form my own ideas about how the world worked, but all around me were adults who already knew the answers. There was no dissent on any major question; everything that needed to be known was known. I searched for a different point of view by scouring the pages of the *Daily Telegraph*, the only newspaper I knew of read by anyone in our Hertfordshire village, but it was a shuddering disappointment, because every word on its printed pages told me that the adults were right: there was no other way of seeing the world. It took me a while to work out that this was a circular phenomenon. The *Telegraph* understood its readers well. We hear about how social media acts as an echo chamber; but back when households took all their news from the same daily newspaper every day, they too functioned like echo chambers. I remember looking through the window of my parents' home and seeing a paperboy doing his round on a bicycle, delivering the *Daily Telegraph*, and thinking, despairingly, that I was up against something too powerful to be gainsaid by a schoolboy.

The memory of that disappointment rose up and brought out a childish act of protest as we marched through London on Sunday 27 October 1968, in protest against the Vietnam War. It was the second such event in that exciting year. The first, in March, had deteriorated into a heaving confrontation between protesters and police in front of the US embassy in Grosvenor Square, during which hundreds were arrested, a few were hurt, though not badly, and my female companion fainted in the crush. Luckily, there was no room for her to fall over. She was held upright by the bodies pressing against her while I pulled her out.

The organisers of the second march had agreed to stay away from Grosvenor Square, though a minority broke away to have another set-to with the police. It annoyed me when the next day's *Daily Telegraph* reported that Grosvenor Square was the protesters' 'main objective', when even by the official count, three quarters of the marchers respected the request to stay away. In addition to the usual slogans – 'Hey, hey, LBJ, how many kids did you kill today?', 'Ho, Ho, Ho Chi Minh' etc. – a chant of 'Sundays off for policemen' rang out as a goodwill message to the uniformed coppers working overtime to make sure that we behaved. The march was directed along Fleet Street, homeland to the newspaper industry. On the balcony of the head office of the *Daily Telegraph*, high overhead, a few journalists working the Sunday shift watched us go by. From below, I had the impression that they were sneering, and in childish fury, raised my arm in a mock Nazi salute and bellowed 'Sieg Heil! Sieg Heil!' I was with a new girlfriend – not the Fainter – whose eyes widened with shock. She pulled my arm down. So far as I can honestly remember, it was the only time in my life that I ever sank to both likening someone to a Nazi and doing the Nazi salute.

Whoever wrote the following day's Peterborough column in the *Daily Telegraph* had been on that balcony watching the marchers. 'Some of their faces were jolly enough,' their diarist recorded. 'Others were strangely twisted with hate.' They added that it was odd for someone from the generation that had fought a war against fascism to be the target of Nazi taunts from youngsters who had only ever known peace. I read that and felt ashamed of myself.

Thirty-one and a half years later, I was in the head office of the *Daily Telegraph*, on Canary Wharf, to meet the editor, Charles Moore, who wanted to know if I would like to take over as their chief political correspondent. I did not mention that I had once flashed a Nazi salute at *Telegraph* journalists, but, by way of disclosure, I did say that I had worked for the Labour Party. He already knew. There had been a Labour government for almost three years, and would be for ten more, and the *Telegraph* was woefully short of writers with good contacts within the ruling party. 'We are looking for somebody who knows the Labour Party but is not part of the Blair gang,' Charles Moore explained.

There had been pieces in *The Spectator* and the *Daily Mail* that had accusingly named political journalists who were said to be too close to Downing Street's media operation.

The person who most vehemently advised me not to join the *Telegraph* was Ken Clarke, whose many claims to distinction included being the only MP to hold office under five Tory Prime Ministers, from Edward Heath to David Cameron. I wrote a biography of him in 1993, when he was Chancellor of the Exchequer. He seemed then to be in pole position to follow John Major as the next Tory leader; but each time he ran, he was beaten by someone younger and less well qualified, until, after nearly half a century in Parliament, he had the Conservative whip taken away from him, because all his life he believed that membership of the EU was good for Britain.

He refused to have his Nottinghamshire home sullied by the *Daily Telegraph* or any other publication owned by its proprietor, Conrad Black, nor any paper owned by Rupert Murdoch. Every journalist on the *Daily Telegraph* was 'weird – physically weird', Clarke told me, emphatically. This was not strictly true. Some *Telegraph* journalists had unusual physical mannerisms, but by no means all.

Being the *Daily Telegraph*'s in-house Somebody-Who-Knows-the-Labour-Party was fun. One of many differences with *The Observer* was that almost everyone in the *Observer* newsroom, including the receptionist and the news desk secretary, believed in what they thought the paper stood for, except for the editor, political editor, news editor and a few others, for whom it was all about how to sell more copies. The *Telegraph*, by contrast, was made ready for the printers every day by a squad of jobbing journalists who could comfortably have worked anywhere in the industry, overseen by a phalanx of section heads and leader writers, who watched over the paper's ideological content. Apart from Charles Moore, most members of this college of cardinals were not well known outside the profession, though one, Daniel Hannan, now Lord Hannan of Kingsclere, was very much in the public eye later, as a member of the European Parliament, a guru of the 2016 Brexit campaign.

Highly committed activists are prone to overestimating public support for the causes they support. In 2001, Hannan was convinced that the Conservatives could win the upcoming election and that William Hague would be Prime Minister. I know this, because the morning after Tony Blair announced that the election would be put back from May to June, while farmers were grappling with a catastrophic outbreak of foot-and-mouth disease, I was called to a morning conference and Charles Moore opened a discussion by asking me what I thought of this decision. I replied that it was sensible, because it showed that Blair was concerned about the farmers and because a month's delay would not change the outcome. To my surprise, Hannan broke in to say that during that extra month, people's eyes would be opened to the faltering state of the economy and Labour's support would evaporate. Another Daniel – Daniel Johnson – agreed, but Charles Moore replied that the public's mind had been made up two years earlier and that Labour would win. A couple of days later, I was walking into Parliament with Daniel Hannan and he again expounded his view that the Conservatives could win if they ran an effective campaign, though he was no longer predicting that they would.

Boris Johnson was not one of the keepers of the creed – not serious enough – but he was looked upon as the newspaper's wittiest commentator. I did not think he was. I did not think he was even the sharpest writer on the paper named Johnson. As an observer of the absurdities of political life he was outclassed by the late Frank Johnson, who was the son of a pastry cook, educated at a secondary modern after failing the eleven-plus, who left school at sixteen to become a messenger boy on the *Sunday Express*. Frank Johnson was long established as one of the finest writers of his generation by the time I knew him, but he was free of vanity. He did not want to be a star. He just enjoyed writing, which he did so well. He had preceded Boris Johnson as editor of *The Spectator* but was not at home there. The *Spectator* subeditors were all 'rather well-bred generals' daughters', he told me. When the magazine's publisher, Kimberly Quinn, was all over the news, because she had conceived two children by

different lovers while married to a man who had once had a vasec-
tomy, and her seduction of the blind, sexually naive Home Secretary, David Blunkett, had been turned into a TV drama, I asked
Frank Johnson what he thought of her. He did not usually speak
badly of people, but of Kimberly Quinn, he said, 'Oh, she's awful. To
know her is to hate her. Her whole life is dominated by sucking up
to anybody who appears to be in charge of anything, sucking up on
a colossal scale.'

On the day I was appointed the *Telegraph's* chief political correspondent, Charles Moore said that he expected that my arrival
would cause trouble but promised that so long as I did the job
properly, it would not land in my lap. The people at the top end of
the Conservative Party had my number. When I was invited to a
reception in William Hague's office, his press secretary, Nick Wood,
helpfully introduced me to other staff as 'the *Telegraph's* resident
Trot troublemaker'.

I had been in the job for a few months when a former employee
from Conservative Central Office told me that relations between
William Hague and his shadow Chancellor, Michael Portillo, were
so bad that Hague had resolved that if the result of the next general
election was good enough to allow him to continue as leader, he
would relegate Portillo to a lesser position and purge the shadow
Cabinet of his main ally, Francis Maude. My informant knew very
well that, for William Hague, the worst possible place for this story
to appear was on the front page of the *Daily Telegraph*. George
Jones, the political editor, advised me to talk to Charles Moore
before I wrote it. I spoke to him over the phone. He knew enough
about strained relationships at the top end of the Tory Party to believe what I was telling him. The antagonism between Hague and

Portillo would burst into the open after Hague resigned, after the 2001 general election, when Hague's former spin doctor Amanda Platell broadcast a 'video diary' in which she accused Portillo of being vain, opportunist, ambitious and treacherous, not forgetting to say how much she despised his coiffed hair. While Portillo took great care of his hair, Hague had no hair to take care of. When he was standing for the leadership, in 1997, that louche diarist Alan Clark remarked scathingly that he looked like a golf ball.

Charles Moore said I should write the story but that I must only write what I knew and nothing more. 'Don't do a Tom Baldwin,' he warned.

Tom Baldwin, deputy political editor of *The Times*, was a good story getter, often the first in a competitive field to break a story, but in his eagerness to stay ahead, he would sometimes take a flyer that crash landed. He came to me once to give vent to his exasperation because the political editor, Philip Webster, had just written a front-page lead in *The Times* which was no different from a story that Baldwin had written days earlier. Webster had told him, 'But I've found out that it's true!'

As soon as the first edition of the *Daily Telegraph* hit the streets that evening, William Hague's chief adviser, the former track athlete Sebastian Coe, was on the line to the night news desk, with Hague standing by, to say that the story I had filed was false and demanding that it be removed from all subsequent editions. The night editor passed the message on to Charles Moore, who ordered that no word of what I had written was to be changed, though if Hague wanted to issue a statement, it should be added at the end. He was saying, in effect, that he was prepared to trust the word of a journalist with a known link to the Labour Party over that of the leader of the Conservatives. For several days afterwards, George Jones would vanish from his desk for an unexplained purpose and come back looking mildly harassed. After one of these absences, he turned to me and said with feeling, 'You have no idea how much trouble you caused.' But that trouble never landed in my lap, just as Charles Moore had promised.

In July 2000, I was told to report to a hotel in Westminster, where Senator Phil Gramm, from Texas, was due to speak. The senator was in London to promote his idea that Britain should leave the EU and join the USA, Canada and Mexico in the North American Free Trade Agreement (NAFTA), across 3,000 miles of Atlantic Ocean. His audience was seated at round tables, each accommodating a dozen guests. I struck up a friendly conversation with a woman sitting next to me, who seemed so pleasant and sensible that I made a point of asking if she agreed with me that the senator's proposal was bonkers, when I spotted her place name. She was Wendy Lee Gramm, the senator's wife.

At another table, there sat the towering, unmistakable figure of Conrad Black, the Canadian owner of the *Daily Telegraph*, *Sunday Telegraph* and *The Spectator*. Senator Gramm ladled him with flattery. 'Never argue with a man who buys ink by the barrel,' he declared. Lord Black responded by announcing that he too had concluded that Britain's future was as part of the North American trade zone.

I could not leave without introducing myself to my proprietor. He asked what I thought of joining NAFTA, and I reached for the only reply I could think of that was honest without being too obviously confrontational. I said I thought that the Labour Party was hoping that the Conservatives would make it their policy. Black was so used to flunkeys agreeing with him that he did not listen properly but dived into an account of divisions in the shadow Cabinet. Some were for NAFTA, he said, William Hague was yet to be persuaded, while the main enemy was the shadow Foreign Secretary, Francis Maude. Suddenly, he stopped mid-sentence, when it struck him that what I said was not an endorsement of his cherished scheme.

He took a half step back, stared at me and asked where I was working before I joined 'his' newspaper. I told him that I came from *The Observer*.

There was a snort. 'I don't want any of your *Observer* attitudes in my paper,' he declared. I was rather heartened by the thought that even with Roger Alton and Kamal Ahmed in control, *The Observer* might yet have attitudes that could offend Lord Black. 'I shall look for them now,' he added. 'If I find them in my paper, I'll ring your editor at three o'clock in the morning. I do that, you know.' So saying, he marched away.

He did not ring Charles Moore at 3 a.m., but he did read what I wrote in the following day's *Telegraph*. I could not write up Senator Gramm's speech unchallenged, so I sought out Ken Clarke, who declared, 'Nobody believes that Senator Gramm is typical of American opinion, because he ain't.' Robin Cook, the Foreign Secretary, described the idea of joining NAFTA as 'pretty barmy', while Chris Huhne, who was then a Liberal Democrat member of the European Parliament, said it was a 'mad, bad and dangerous idea'. I bundled all these comments together and sent in a report. Standing on the platform on Lewisham Station that evening, I received a call from a leader writer who asked if I understood that the idea described in my copy as barmy, mad, bad and dangerous was championed by the man who owned the newspaper. I said that I was well aware of that.

The next day, the prime slot on the readers' letters page was occupied by a reader who angrily defended Senator Gramm and attacked Ken Clarke. It was signed by Lord Black of Crossharbour. But his rage never reached my corner of the office because, as before, Charles Moore kept his promise. It is no small thing to know that you have a boss who can be trusted to keep his word.

Conrad Black was the second most bombastic, egocentric proprietor I ever met. He was Godzilla to Robert Maxwell's King Kong. Maxwell should have gone to prison but avoided it by propitiously drowning at sea. Black emerged from two years in a Florida jail over fraud charges no humbler nor more self-critical than when he went in. But, curiously, journalists who worked for either of them had reason to miss them when they were gone. In the old, pre-internet newspaper trade, it was usually better to have a self-aggrandising megalomaniac as a proprietor than the cold-eyed money man who only wanted to generate a profit. When the Barclay family took over the *Telegraph*, there was a forced exodus of good hacks, just as there was when David Montgomery captured the *Mirror*.

Charles Moore had already left before the Barclay twins arrived. He had been commissioned to write the authorised biography of Margaret Thatcher, which, by agreement, would not be published while she was alive. In June 2003, he was at Denis Thatcher's funeral, took a close look at the newly widowed ex-Prime Minister and decided that he had better get seriously to work on the biography. In the event, the task was not as urgent as he feared. She lived for another ten years. Volume One was published, punctually, in 2013.

Though he was mocked by *The Guardian* as 'the last of the 80s power fogeys', Charles Moore was not born with his beliefs. His parents were eminent Liberals. He was brought up in the Church of England. He converted to the Conservative Party as a young adult and later to the Catholic Church. Though he is deeply serious, and rarely joked, I sometimes thought I detected a hint of self-parody in his high church conservatism. In one of the columns he wrote for the *Telegraph*, in August 2019, he suggested that Olivia Colman was the wrong person to play the Queen in the Netflix series *The Crown* because of her 'left-wing face'. Was he really being serious? Who knows?

During a morning conference at the *Telegraph*, the features editor submitted the usual day list of pieces they had commissioned, including one with the catchline 'He works, she works, who does the housework?' Charles asked what this was about. The features editor explained that it was very much a 1980s phenomenon that husbands and wives both had demanding full-time professions, which gave rise to his question of who would do the housework. 'The staff, surely', said Moore. A room full of journalists was left wondering whether he was joking.

Another list on another day included a reference to 'posh wives'. Just as the meeting reached that item, a phone rang on the editor's desk. The caller evidently knew his direct line, because his secretary knew better than to put calls through during the morning conference. He spoke in a very low voice, and when the call ended, he announced, in his usual serious tone, 'That was a posh wife.'

Despite his great intellect, he made what seemed to me to be one glaring political misjudgement, which greatly helped Labour to win the 2005 general election. Michael Portillo had been the darling of the Conservative right. It was widely expected that once Hague resigned, Portillo would emerge as the anti-EU candidate, against Ken Clarke, and would win. Early in the contest, I was called by a spread-bet company who were predicting that Portillo would be the runaway winner of the first round of the election, when only Tory MPs had a vote. Out of kindness, I warned their PR man that the firm could lose a lot of money, whereupon he suggested that I bet on it. If I had, I would have walked away with rich winnings, but it would have been equivalent to insider trading.

I knew that Charles Moore had decided to put the weight of the *Telegraph* behind a campaign to knock Portillo out of the race altogether and hand victory to Iain Duncan Smith, with David Davis as a fall back. In an election in which only Conservatives had a vote, no one was likely to win against opposition from the *Telegraph*. Duncan Smith had never held government office. His first five years as an MP had been spent in open opposition to John Major. He told me proudly that during those years, the Conservative Association in the north London seat he represented had refused to hand any money over to party headquarters, keeping members' subscriptions for local use. Once, when we were taking the train to an annual Conservative conference, he told me that in an ideally run society, they would rip the rail lines and everyone would travel by car. I found Iain Duncan Smith impossible to dislike, because he was consistently himself, but I thought it blindingly obvious that a Conservative Party led by him was a sure-fire election loser. He was to the Conservatives as Jeremy Corbyn was to Labour. Alistair Darling told me that there was a fear in government that he was such an obvious loser that he would make it harder for the Labour whips to control their MPs.

Charles Moore maintained later that he helped knock out Portillo because, above all, he wanted to prevent Ken Clarke from winning and feared that he might have a better chance against Portillo than he would have against Duncan Smith. But I suspect he had assessed that Portillo was a follower of fashion, who was Thatcherite in the Thatcher years but would change with the weather, while Duncan Smith would always be himself. For the *Telegraph*'s ideologues, making sure that the party had a reliably anti-EU leader mattered more than anything, including getting back into office.

My older son, who was eleven, finished primary school while the leadership contest was on. To mark this watershed, I told him he could spend the day with me. As we walked into the Commons, we were waylaid by Ken Clarke and his campaign manager, Andrew Tyrie. Clarke went into a tirade about the *Telegraph*'s behaviour, telling me angrily that he and Portillo were the only credible candidates in the field and that to promote Duncan Smith or Davis was destructive mischief.

Being on the receiving end of his well-justified fury did not worry me, but I was concerned that my son might be upset, so I introduced him in the hope that it would calm the furious Clarke. He paused, looked down, remarked in surprise, 'Oh, a little McSmith!' and carried on ranting. Later that day, my boy and I visited Madame Tussauds. In the main cafe, he wandered off while I queued at the counter, only to come running to exclaim, 'Dad, you know that man who was shouting at you – I've just seen his waxwork!'

During August, we were enjoying a family holiday in brilliant sunshine on a beach in the south of France when my phone rang. It was head office. The newspaper wanted to interview each of the candidates in the leadership contest, but Clarke would not speak to them. They had an idea that he might relent if I were put up as the interviewer. I dutifully put in the request, knowing that if it was accepted, I was going to have to break off our holiday, fly to London, leaving Sue with four young children, and fly back after a day or two. It was a relief when Clarke obstinately stuck by his refusal to be interviewed by anyone from the *Telegraph*.

Charles Moore's unwavering opposition to the EU received its reward in August 2020, when Boris Johnson granted him a life peerage. He decided to be 'non-affiliated', rather than take instruction from the Tory whips. For many months, Covid restrictions and other commitments prevented him from visiting the House of Lords or contributing to its debates. That was a mercy in its own way, because Charles Moore is so very upper middle class that I feared that having to associate with some of the people who had been granted peerages would be a bit of a social comedown for him.

23

ETON BOYS

A short walk across the Thames from Slough, a town famous as the location of *The Office*, the classic comic study of boredom at work, and for John Betjeman's plea, 'Come friendly bombs and fall on Slough', there is Eton, home of the nation's most prestigious boarding school. When I worked in Slough in the early 1970s, I used to see the Eton boys about the town in black tailcoats, white ties and starched collars and noted that they all walked with their hands deep in their pin-striped trousers. At my old school, we were not allowed to be seen in public with our hands in our pockets. No such ban applied to the young Etonians.

No doubt, some of the boys who passed by on the pavement went on to be of great renown. They would not have included Boris Johnson or David Cameron, who were too young, but it is possible that I may have unknowingly seen a school-age Charles Moore or Oliver Letwin.

At Cheltenham, I worried about what the local townsfolk thought of us college boys. Some thoroughly disliked us, and it showed. I did not notice any such tension in Eton, where the locals seemed to tolerate these privileged youngsters as if they were part of the architecture. They are all that makes Eton famous. A section of local opinion revered them. The first time I covered the Marlow Regatta, the murmur of conversation suddenly ceased as the Eton rowing team took to the Thames, to the sound of the Eton boating song blaring out over loudspeakers, and a respectful crowd burst into applause.

On the *Evening Mail*, I was sometimes given the entertaining task of checking out the latest Eton newsletter. Every story we carried about Eton College had to have the phrase 'I say chaps!' in the headline, because our subeditors were sure that this was how Eton boys talked. There is a sport unique to the school, called the Eton Wall Game, with its own vocabulary. A contributor in one newsletter bewailed a recent increase in 'sneaking' and 'furking', which, in another language, said that contestants were committing fouls by putting both feet in front of the ball or heeling it backwards. This news was shared with the readers of the *Evening Mail* under the joyful headline: 'I say chaps, play the furking game!'

When Buckinghamshire County Council announced a planning decision to change the designation of several acres of field into housing land, I could not resist turning this rather mundane information into a story about Eton. First, I checked how many of the relevant acres belonged to the college, then looked up the difference in the market prices of farm land and building land and calculated how much money the college stood to make from this little adjustment to the map of the county. The answer was in six figures.

George Orwell claimed to have had a terrible time as an Eton scholarship boy, whose parents could not have afforded the fees.

There is so much honesty in Orwell's political essays that I have to assume that this really was his experience, but I am surprised. I was a scholarship boy at Cheltenham College. I was never seriously bullied because of it. It came with a clutch of small advantages. Perhaps in Orwell's day there were no black or Asian pupils for the school bullies to torment, so they picked on the scholarship boys instead.

Cyril Connolly was another Eton scholarship boy, three months younger than Orwell, whose memoir was serialised in a Sunday newspaper in about 1976. At around that time, I was an afternoon guest at the Northumberland home of a retired judge, Sir Geoffrey Wrangham, whose daughter I knew. He was highly amused by Connolly's description of the awful time he had had being a prefect's 'fag', a position analogous to an officer's batman. Sir Geoffrey proudly informed me that he was that very prefect who chose young Connolly to be his fag.

As the judge spoke, I realised that I must be in the presence of someone who knew the young George Orwell, whom I revered so much that while I was still at school I compiled a list of all his novels and ticked them off as I read them in sequence.

'Oh, young Blair!' said the judge, in reply to my question. 'Yes, I remember him.'

He spoke as one retrieving an unusual and agreeable memory from long ago. He seemed to think that young Blair and young Connolly were interesting boys, different from your average Etonian but worth knowing. His tone did not suggest that scholarship boys were inferior or unwelcome at Eton.

This was during the strike-ridden 1970s, when middle-class families had suffered inconveniences such as power cuts, or weeks with no post, and it was not unusual to hear someone make a sweeping remark about the supposed idleness and greed of the unionised working class. There was another man of my age present that afternoon, trying to make a good impression, who made some derogatory comment along those lines. I noted the blank reaction of the judge and Lady Wrangham. They were too secure in their social positions to want to sneer at people further down.

In the Houses of Parliament, the Conservative who strides through the building with an angry countenance, ready to spew right-wing vitriol, is not an Old Etonian. The Old Etonian is tolerant and polite. He was told as a child that he was born to be important and has never experienced a sense of social inferiority. Some are not even Conservatives. There was an interlude when there were more Old Etonians in the lobby, reporting on Parliament, than in the Tory shadow Cabinet. One went to work for the Labour Party. The last Old Etonian Labour MP was a Tory MP's son, Mark Fisher, who retired in 2010.

Another Old Etonian, the eccentric and incorruptible Tam Dalyell stepped down in 2005, after forty-three years as a Scottish Labour MP. He is remembered principally for the way he harried Margaret Thatcher in Parliament over the sinking of the Argentinian warship the *Belgrano*. It was for that reason he was invited to speak to party members in Portsmouth, but when he arrived, he had a new obsession and delivered a talk on the natterjack toad, which I am told was fascinating but not at all what the audience had come to hear.

That much-missed former Labour leader John Smith told me about going canvassing at election time with Tam Dalyell. One lady invited them in for a cup of tea, which they gladly accepted. Inside, Dalyell, who spoke very slowly in a deep voice, asked her, 'Do you mind if I have a boiled egg?' John Smith thought it was a bit much to ask her to feed him – but that was not in fact his request. Dalyell had a raw egg in his pocket. All he wanted was for her to boil it.

Generally, though, an Old Etonian's natural habitat is the Conservative Party – but, not, as a rule, its hard-right, anti-immigrant, Brexiteer wing. Boris Johnson might appear to be an exception, but at heart he was a liberal Tory opportunist who attached himself to the right for self-advancement. When twenty-one Tory MPs were purged for their opposition to a hard Brexit, during Johnson's premiership, in September 2019, three Old Etonians were on the casualty list – Nicholas Soames, whose mother was Winston Churchill's youngest child, Oliver Letwin and Rory Stewart. A fourth, Jo Johnson, was spared excommunication, although he resigned from the government and withdrew from the Commons to avoid being in open opposition to his brother.

Another anecdote I owe to John Smith was enacted in the Commons on a Friday morning, when a contentious private member's bill had brought MPs to the House who would not normally be there that late in the week. They included Tim Sainsbury, a mild-mannered, middle-ranking minister so inconspicuous that few people would have known that he ever existed had his great-grandparents not founded the supermarket chain that he called 'the family firm'. But no one could out-grandfather Nicholas Soames, who was also present that morning but was hoping to get away early to go shooting and was dressed accordingly.

'Going ratting, Nick?' Sainsbury asked.

Soames was not in the mood to be mocked. Back came the response, 'Fuck off, you grocer! You don't tell a gentleman how to dress on a Friday!'

Soames sometimes behaved as only someone from his background could. Women complained that he was rampantly sexist, though I do not think he intended to be. During part of my time in the lobby, I teamed up with a female journalist from ITN to invite politicians to lunch with us. I was pleased when Soames accepted our invitation – though afterwards, I learnt that I owed this privilege to the fact that he fancied my lunch partner. She was uninterested, and strictly told me that I was not to spread this gossip. In a Covent Garden restaurant, Rules, Soames was on the point of telling us both something confidential, when a man inconveniently sat at the adjoining table, within hearing range. Not wanting to be overheard, Soames turned his head and stared, silently, with mouth half open, until the discomforted guest stood up to ask to be moved to another table, after which he turned to us and carried on talking, as if he had done nothing unusual.

The second of the Old Etonians to have the whip removed from the party in 2019 was Oliver Letwin. He was cerebral, clever, kind and innocent. He and Charles Moore were old school and university friends, though they parted company over Brexit. When Letwin was a Cabinet minister, he liked to walk to work in the morning through St James's Park, reading the documents in his red box on the way and throwing those he did not need to keep in the waste bins provided for public use – until a photographer from the *Daily Mirror* followed him and retrieved the discarded papers, which of course, being government documents, were headed 'Strictly Confidential'.

I first encountered Oliver Letwin soon after he entered Parliament in 1997, when we were guests on a live discussion programme on BBC radio that ran from 11 p.m. to 1 a.m. The late hour was a hazard, all the greater for the fact that there was a generous supply of wine, to which we were free to help ourselves. One guest, a

Labour MP, was in a poor state emotionally, because her marriage had just fallen apart. She soaked up so much of the free wine that the BBC switchboard took calls from listeners complaining that she was drunk. She was eyeing Letwin with interest, but he was too engrossed in the political discussion to notice. When she suggested that they share a taxi home, at 1 a.m., he innocently thanked her. I could see a disaster in the making and wondered if I should try to take him aside and advise against getting into a taxi with a woman in that disturbed state, but that was not necessary: the BBC had booked one taxi for each guest.

Rory Stewart, the third member of that trio, was much newer to the Commons, having been first elected in 2010. I did not know him well but found him very easy to like on the occasions when I spoke to him. After he had resigned from the Conservative Party, he co-starred in a regular podcast with Alastair Campbell. On the twentieth anniversary of the Iraq War, listeners heard Campbell defend the decision to go to war, while Stewart described it as a 'catastrophic error'. On this, the ex-Tory sounded more 'left wing' than the Labour Party stalwart.

● ● ●

The United Kingdom somehow muddled through for forty-six years after the 1964 general election without an Old Etonian Prime Minister, until along came David Cameron. I remember almost nothing about my first conversation with him. In 1999, a mischievous insider told me that the Conservative Party organisation was suffering from an exodus of bright young officials, who could see that it would be many years before there was another Tory government, so were heading off to begin new careers in other sectors. One name he mentioned was David Cameron, who had made a promising start as a young special adviser to the Chancellor of the Exchequer but was now director of corporate affairs with Carlton Television and, I was told, had no ambition to return to politics.

I had no trouble getting through to Cameron. We talked at length. He seemed very friendly, over the phone. My frantic short-hand notes filled two pages, but no matter how I tried, I could not get a satisfactory answer to the question of whether he had or had not given up on a future in politics. Afterwards, I scoured my notes for a single useable phrase, but there was none. Cameron therefore was not included in the piece I eventually wrote about ambitious young Conservatives who had given up politics for good.

It is, by the way, a rare skill to talk to a journalist in an apparent-ly open and friendly manner without giving anything away. That encounter with Cameron reminded me of when I cornered Peter Mandelson in the Commons to try to get him to say how he would vote on the bill that was going to ban fox hunting. My understand-ing was that he was against the ban, but to say so would only add to his unpopularity in the Labour Party. Peter told me, very pleasantly, that he had an engagement in the House of Lords and suggested that we walk through the building together. As we walked, he plied me with procedural questions about the bill. I suspected that he already knew all the answers and was marking time, but I played along thinking that if I answered his questions, eventually he would have to answer mine. After several minutes, we reached the Lords and Mandelson very politely told me that our conversation had to end there. 'I trust I have been unhelpful,' was his parting comment, as he walked away.

Listening to David Cameron speaking outside a London school, on his first outing as Leader of the Opposition, I had an eerie illusion that I was hearing Peter Mandelson again. It was that tone of voice which said, 'I'm cleverer than you and superior to you in many ways, but let's put that to one side, because I'm going to talk to you at your level.' The impressionist Rory Bremner, a greater expert in such matters, also heard the hint of Mandelson in Cameron's voice. Cameron was not as intelligent as Mandelson but had a steadier temperament and was better at avoiding making enemies. He tried so hard to be like Tony Blair but succeeded only in being like Blair's favourite courtier.

By chance, I was a witness to the first exchange to take place between Tony Blair and David Cameron when one was Prime Minister and the other was about to be Leader of the Opposition. It was on 19 October 2005, the day after the result of the first round of voting in the Conservative leadership election. Cameron had come a very strong second in a field of four, seven votes behind the leader, David Davis, and was clearly on the way to winning in the final round. I was standing in Portcullis cafe, talking to a Labour MP, Jim Cousins, about primary care trusts when there was a disturbance nearby. I made a note in a private diary:

I was aware of an entourage sweeping past, centred around the tall, unnaturally elegant figure of Tony Blair. As I watched their progress, David Cameron emerged from the lift in the far corner and it became apparent that their paths could not fail to cross. In fact, they stopped to speak courteously to one another. I hurried across to earwig their conversation. TB: 'Are you enjoying it?' DC: 'Yes, I am actually.' Historic exchanges I have overheard…

I am glad that I made that note of this encounter, because even with the written account in front of me, I have no memory of it.

I had mentioned David Cameron in print a few months earlier, in December 2004. Then, there was a general expectation that the Conservatives would lose the impending election, their leader, Michael Howard, would resign and be succeeded by David Davis, whose campaign had been long in preparation. In 1990, when John Major popped up from nowhere to win the Tory leadership, two political columnists – Alan Watkins, in *The Observer*, and Alastair Campbell, in the *Sunday Mirror* – simultaneously took a punt that Davis would lead the Tory Party one day soon. The *Telegraph* considered backing him in 2001, but Iain Duncan Smith had a stronger base. Davis entered the 2005 contest as the recognised front runner, with the ambitious Iain Dale as his chief of staff; but I had been tipped off by someone well placed in the party that Davis's time had passed and that Howard's successor would be one of the new MPs, first elected in 2001. I checked out the shadow Cabinet and came up with three names – Mark Field, George Osborne or David Cameron.

Mark Field is not a recognisable name now, but then he had a brilliant future, which came to grief after he was assigned to mentor a promising wannabe Tory candidate, Liz Truss. His mentoring, which endured for eighteen months, was more intimate than the party intended. Truss's marriage only just survived and her ambition to be a Tory MP was put in jeopardy. Field's wife divorced him and his prospects of being a Cabinet minister nose-dived – but he told me how much he appreciated seeing his name in print alongside the two most important figures in the Tory government of 2010–19. It showed that he could have been a major player, if only he had kept his trousers zipped up.

George Osborne, who was thirty-four years old in 2005, sensibly calculated that his best option was to hitch his wagon to Cameron's, whose smooth self-confidence and shrewd reading of the Conservative Party, and a speech skilfully delivered to the annual Conservative conference without autocue or notes, carried the day.

There was one political skill in which Cameron outshone Tony Blair. That was his ability to work a room. He would go from huddle to huddle, with a protective aide at his side, addressing people by name and engaging in easy-going small talk without ever saying anything contentious. At the first Downing Street reception he hosted for the lobby, he came up to me and greeted me by name. I will never know whether he had actually remembered who I was, or whether someone had whispered in his ear, but I was impressed.

But under that smoothly competent exterior, there was nothing much. He was not as cynical as Boris Johnson; he worked harder to master detail and was a better family man by a very long stretch, but, like Johnson, he approached politics like a sporting contest, in which trophies were won by being clever. I witnessed him being flippant about something very serious, in a way that John Major, or Tony Blair, would never have been.

In January 2011, Cameron visited Oldham, where a closely fought by-election was under way. The former Labour Home Secretary Alan Johnson was also in town. On that same day, an assistant editor of the *News of the World* was suspended over his role in the phone-hacking saga, a criminal conspiracy that implicated Cameron's director of communications, Andy Coulson, as that newspaper's former editor.

Alan Johnson told journalists, 'There is a very long fuse on this, and I believe the very long fuse leads to Andy Coulson.'

I repeated this comment to Cameron later in the day, when we were allocated a few minutes of his time, standing in a circle in an echoing car workshop. But he was forewarned. He knew both that Johnson was in town and that earlier in the week, paparazzi had snatched a picture of him at lunch in the Savoy Grill, with alcohol on the table.

'Presumably he said it over a long lunch,' Cameron replied.

Michael White, of *The Guardian*, pointed out that I was quoting what Johnson had said that morning, in Oldham.

'A bottle of claret or two? Pink champagne?' Cameron added, like a man delighting in his own cleverness. He may have thought that a few slick remarks could chase the problem away but the law disagreed. Coulson was later arrested, charged and sentenced to eighteen months in prison.

Speaking at the Bath Literary Festival, in 2016, I said that Cameron might win the EU referendum, due in a few months, and if he did, he would be given credit for putting the issue to bed for a generation. But my understanding was that he had not expected to be in this position. He had expected the 2015 election to produce a hung parliament, like the one before, leaving him in coalition with the Liberal Democrats, whom he could rely on to spare him the hassle of a referendum. So, I predicted that if the public voted for Brexit, Cameron would go down in history as the Prime Minister who won an election by mistake, destroyed the Liberal Democrat Party by mistake, took Britain out of the EU by mistake and then probably caused the break-up of the United Kingdom by mistake.

I was not expecting all this to happen, but it raised a laugh.

David Cameron left office on such a wave of glib self-congratulation that he churned out a tedious memoir that filled as many pages as Margaret Thatcher used to cover her extraordinary life story. The only way that anyone so shallow and short on self-awareness would ever get to be Prime Minister for six years was by having good family connections and being told from an early age that he was born to be important. Cameron's career was forged on the playing fields of Eton.

24

JEREMY CORBYN

In moments of crisis people are caught in characteristic poses. A tabloid journalist was at Jeremy Corbyn's door, the phone was ringing, and his estranged wife, who never invited publicity and who had small children to worry about, was handling the crisis on her own, because he was out of the country. Of course he was, because a hundred years earlier, in May 1899, delegates from twenty-six nations had assembled to meet in The Hague to draw up the first international set of rules about the conduct of war. In May 1999, about 9,000 people had gathered from across the world to talk about peace. Jeremy Corbyn was one of them.

In the same month, bombs were dropping on Belgrade, because NATO had intervened to avert a possible genocide in Kosovo, a province that the Serbian government claimed as sovereign territory, though more than 80 per cent of its inhabitants were Albanian Muslims. Western governments, notably the UK and USA, were not prepared to risk a repeat of the 1995 massacre of Bosnian Muslims by Serb militia. In The Hague, there was a lively argument between those who thought that the intervention was a necessary precaution and those who believed that NATO was an imperialist aggressor intent on installing a more compliant government in Serbia.

We can surmise which side Corbyn was on. Preserved on Parliament's website is an Early Day Motion sponsored by Corbyn, which condemned NATO's 'fraudulent justifications for intervening in a "genocide" that never really existed'. History does not contain an example of a military action involving British troops since 1945 that had the support of Jeremy Corbyn.

But he was not able to make much of a contribution in The Hague because he was constantly on the phone trying to deal with the problem that had blown up back home. Someone had tipped off the *Daily Mail* that a small boy named Benjamin Corbyn, who was a pupil at a grammar school in Barnet, was the son of the man who was arguably the most left-wing MP in the land. The Labour Party opposed selective education. The only grammar schools were in areas where Conservatives controlled the local education authority. The chairman of Labour's backbench education committee had resigned in anger in 1996, when Harriet Harman and Jack Dromey sent their son to St Olave's grammar school in Kent. Corbyn's life-long ally and ex-lover Diane Abbott complained that Harman had 'made the Labour Party look as if we do one thing and say another'. (That was before her own son was sent to an expensive private school.) Corbyn lived in Islington where he had been a local MP since 1983. The *Mail* wanted to know why his son had not been sent to an Islington comprehensive.

Though it was a fair question, Corbyn did not think that the *Daily Mail* had given the family fair treatment. Back in London, he agreed on a plan with his ex-wife Claudia Bracchitta, with whom he was still on amicable terms, though they were filing for divorce. They had been very protective of her privacy. In those days, the best source of information on individual MPs were Roth's *Parliamentary Profiles*, but in the volumes brought out during the 1980s, Corbyn's marital status was recorded with three question marks, after he refused to say whether he was even married. But her cover was blown now, after she had been interrogated by a journalist on her doorstep, and they agreed to go public.

That week, I was surprised to hear from Jeremy Corbyn, whom I did know but only slightly. He suggested that I should interview him and Claudia, separately, so that they could tell their story through the sympathetic medium of *The Observer*. He and I met on a Friday afternoon in Portcullis cafe, in Parliament, where Jeremy was very tempted by the spaghetti Bolognese but had to refuse it, because it contained meat. He told me that his marriage had ended months earlier, for a number of reasons that he did not want to discuss and one that he did. He and Claudia had had an unresolvable disagreement over where their oldest son should go to secondary school. He argued that on principle they should accept the place Ben had been offered in a local comprehensive, but she would not hear of it, because it was a failing school, in a borough that was then ranked as the country's third worst education authority. As the marriage disintegrated, he conceded that the decision was hers.

On Saturday morning, I met Claudia in the spartan house in Islington where she and her ex lived, in separate flats under one roof. They had met at a political rally, of course. One of the events that drew Jeremy Corbyn into radical politics was the atmosphere he soaked up when Salvador Allende was elected President of Chile in 1970. Corbyn was there, aged twenty, and marched with Allende's jubilant supporters on May Day. Three years later, Allende was overthrown in a military coup and ended his life in the presidential palace. Claudia's uncle was also in the palace but escaped alive, and her family fled into exile. She was then aged eleven.

The picture I have of Claudia is of her sitting on bare floorboards, amid exposed wires and other signs of upheaval in this none-too-comfortable flat, her home life in chaos, her weekend ruined, reluctant to be talking to a journalist, while a photographer snapped her as she talked, but feeling that it was something she had to do.

She told me:

I am concerned Jeremy has been portrayed as a hard-left MP who couldn't care about his children, which is absolutely not the truth. I was put across as the pushy parent who wanted a grammar school place for her son and nothing else.

It isn't a story about making a choice but about having no choice. I couldn't send Ben to a school where I knew he wouldn't be happy. Whereas Jeremy was able to make one sort of decision, I wasn't. It's a position you are pushed into rather than one you choose.

Back at head office, Roger Alton read the piece, looked at Claudia's photograph and angrily wondered aloud why a hard-left MP like Corbyn should ever have been married to such an attractive woman. He sounded aggrieved.

Jeremy Corbyn was pleased with what I had written and would greet me warmly by name when our paths crossed, even after I had written and spoken publicly about why I thought he was unfit to lead the Labour Party. But he grumbled about one paragraph:

He is a quietly spoken, gentle individual who does not demand you listen to his opinions. They are the sort of opinions a lot of people hold when they are young, like wanting an end to poverty, hunger, unemployment, imperialism and wars, and wanting the children of poor families to have the same chance in life as middle-class children. What makes him unusual is that he will be fifty in ten days.

He did not like the reference to his age.

Jeremy Corbyn was not a complicated character. One of the reasons Labour did so much better than predicted in the 2017 election was that part of the public warmed to this strange politician who did not pretend to be anyone other than himself. During a television interview when he was challenged for the party leadership by Owen Smith, Corbyn and Smith were both shown photographs of well-known television personalities and invited to identify them. Smith, looking very pleased with himself, replied that they were Ant and Dec. Corbyn admitted that he had no idea who they were. At the end of the debate, the vote for Corbyn among members of the studio audience had gone up while Smith's support had shrunk.

The stupidest book ever written about Corbyn was a biography by the right-wing polemicist Tom Bower, which bore the absurd title *Dangerous Hero: Corbyn's Ruthless Plot for Power*. During his first thirty-two years as an MP, Corbyn was not dangerous, he was not a hero, he was not plotting and he was not interested in exercising power. No one knows more about a man's worst qualities than the wife he is in the process of divorcing, and yet Claudia was prepared to put aside her dislike of publicity to speak to a journalist she did not know in defence of her estranged husband. That answers anyone who claims that Corbyn was fundamentally a bad person.

But what the story shows is very telling about Corbyn in another way. On this important matter, of where his oldest son should go to school, Corbyn stated his principled position then stood back while someone else took the responsibility of deciding what was actually going to happen. That is pretty much the story of his political life, up until the extraordinary day when, without meaning to, he became leader of the Labour Party.

• • •

I first heard the name 'Jeremy Corbyn' in July 1984, in the Camberwell home of Stuart Holland, the MP for Vauxhall. In May of that year, P. W. Botha, the Prime Minister of South Africa, set off on a tour of European capitals, hoping to spread a message that the apartheid system was not as bad as it was made out to be. His receptions in Lisbon and Bonn were restrained. On 2 June, he met Margaret Thatcher in Chequers, the first South African to be treated so courteously in twenty-three years, but the reaction in the streets was not welcoming. There was a week-long picket of the South African in Trafalgar Square, and a rally in the square that drew a huge crowd, who heard the Labour Party's deputy leader, Roy Hattersley, repeat the party's call for a boycott of all trade with South Africa. That autumn, the African National Congress (ANC) President, Oliver Tambo, appeared as a guest speaker at the Labour Party annual conference, where he paid tribute to Neil Kinnock as 'an old and long-standing member of the anti-apartheid movement', adding that 'we find great hope in the fact [sic] that he will be the next Prime Minister of this country'.

After Botha had returned to Pretoria, the commissioner of the

Metropolitan Police issued an order banning any more protests outside the South African embassy, effective from 8 June. Leaders of the Anti-Apartheid Movement protested the ban but agreed to abide by it, because the leaders of the ANC in exile did not want a conflict with the police. But the ANC, like so many organisations made up of political exiles, was divided into factions. The leading opponent of Tambo and his allies, who included the imprisoned Nelson Mandela, was a formidable woman named Norma Kitson, who had moral authority because she had recently been reunited with her husband, David Kitson, who had been released after twenty years in a South African prison, the longest sentence served by any white opponent of apartheid. Norma, who was a communist, ran the City of London branch of the Anti-Apartheid Movement, which resolved to carry on picketing the South African embassy. On day one, 8 June, around two dozen young people were arrested but released without charge after a couple of hours in a police station. There were more pickets, and more arrests, opening up an unpleasant rift within the ANC, until eventually, the Kitsons had their membership suspended and they emigrated to Zimbabwe.

Meanwhile, Stuart Holland, who was then Labour's shadow Minister for Overseas Development, and another MP, Tony Banks, decided to go to Trafalgar Square, on 21 July, to see if they could talk the police into allowing the picket to continue peacefully without anyone else being arrested. Their mission failed, spectacularly, with the two MPs being bundled into a police van. Stuart Holland told me all about this, sitting at his kitchen table. He was annoyed with the police, of course. He was also a little put out by the behaviour of Jeremy Corbyn.

The arrests of two MPs naturally captured the attention of the national press, who tuned in the next day, in case there were any more interesting developments, and were rewarded by the spectacle of Jeremy Corbyn arriving with a huge protest sign draped around his neck demanding that the police respect the right to demonstrate. The unwritten message was 'go on, arrest me', which the police obligingly did. Holland was mildly annoyed by this grandstanding. He thought it would have been more collegiate of Corbyn to tell other MPs that he planned to stage this stunt.

Thirty years later, a photograph of Corbyn being led away by the police resurfaced, to be widely shared on social media by Corbyn's young admirers, who saw it as proof that their hero had been committed to the anti-apartheid cause like no other Labour MP. In reality, opposition to apartheid was one issue on which the entire Labour Party was united. When Mandela met Neil and Glenys Kinnock for the first time, he surprised them both by recognising them on sight: he had had their photographs pinned on the wall of his cell in Pollsmoor Prison. He also instantly recognised the mother of the Labour MP Peter Hain, because he remembered the white woman who sat through his trial in 1963. He even recognised the Labour MP Bob Hughes, who was barely known outside Parliament but whom Mandela knew to be a founder of the Anti-Apartheid Movement. But none of these people was photographed while being arrested on an anti-apartheid picket. That was Jeremy Corbyn's special contribution to that struggle.

'If you look at the Iraq War, who was on the right side of history in that? Jeremy Corbyn was,' the Labour MP Barry Gardiner declared, on the *Today* programme, in December 2019. From declarations such as these, which abound on social media, you might think that Corbyn was some sort of lone voice speaking truth to power in 2003. Actually, he was part of a crowd. Tony Blair was the first Prime Minister ever to seek a vote in Parliament before taking the UK to war. That vote on 18 March 2003 saw the biggest rebellion Blair ever faced, when 139 Labour MPs backed an amendment put by two former ministers, Chris Smith and Peter Kilfoyle, that 'the case for war against Iraq has not yet been established'. The Liberal Democrats also opposed the war. Their leader, Charles Kennedy, spoke to the mass anti-war rally in Hyde Park in February 2003. There were even a few Tory rebels, including the former Chancellor Ken Clarke.

The size of the Labour rebellion was in part down to a Labour MP named Alice Mahon, who diligently collected the signatures for an Early Day Motion tabled in March 2002, a whole year before the invasion, expressing 'deep unease' about the possibility of war. It was signed by 134 Labour MPs, some of whom were distinctly embarrassed a year later, when confronted with a choice between breaking a three-line whip or explaining how they had got over their 'deep unease' about the war. A fair few tried to duck the issue by abstaining.

The biggest drama of 17 March was the resignation speech by the former Foreign Secretary, Robin Cook, which ended to spontaneous applause and dominated that evening's news bulletins. Cook wanted to pitch his appeal to the mainstream of the Labour Party, so arranged that while he was speaking, he was flanked on either side by the former Cabinet ministers Frank Dobson and Chris Smith. What he overlooked was that the camera would also pick up whoever was sitting behind him, and there, in full view, was the unmistakable bearded profile of Jeremy Corbyn, dressed in a distinctive green corduroy jacket. No one asked whether Corbyn was for or against the war, because no other Labour MP voted against the Labour government as often as he did.

MPs do much more than talk in the main debating chamber. Parliament has a legion of select committees, including to shadow each government department. For every bill that passes through Parliament on its way to becoming legislation there is a committee that exists to scrutinise it in detail. Every government minister has at least one 'shadow' on the opposition benches.

Jeremy Corbyn was not an assiduous parliamentarian. He was never a 'shadow' minister of any description while Labour was in opposition; neither was he part of the Labour government at any level of seniority while Labour was in power. His committee work, such as it was, is recorded on the authoritative website TheyWork-ForYou, according to which he sat on only the Social Security Committee before Labour was in power, and during the thirteen years of Labour rule, the only select committee on which he sat was the London Regional Select Committee, of which he was a member for only the last five months of the Labour government before it fell. In the years 2001–15, according to the same source, Corbyn spent a grand total of thirteen days as a working member of one of the committees scrutinising legislation – less than one day a year. This abstemiousness may not have been voluntary, because to get onto a committee he had to be chosen by the whips or in some cases elected by his fellow Labour MPs. Corbyn put his name forward for election to the shadow Cabinet, when it was elected annually, before 1997, but with no prospect of success.

But he was never idle. After his election as Labour leader, I spent a day in his Islington North constituency and had no difficulty coming across people who knew of him as an active local MP. And whenever activists came together to talk about peace, disarmament or solidarity with the oppressed somewhere in the developing world, and wanted a British MP as a speaker, if Tony Benn was not available, the next best go-to MP was Jeremy Corbyn.

So, when he accidentally stumbled into the leadership of the Labour Party in 2015, he came with decades of experience in addressing rooms full of people who agreed with him. This expertise served him well during the 2017 general election, when the nation saw images of a Conservative Party making a pig's ear of its campaign, while Corbyn toured the country delivering his message to supportive crowds.

There are people who still mourn that election as the time when the country came close to choosing a Prime Minister who would have given the capitalist system a shake-down such as no British government has ever done. But I think that if, by some startling fluke, Corbyn had been projected into Downing Street, those who invested their hopes in him would have been terribly disappointed, precisely because he was not a ruthless plotter. His life, up to the age of sixty-six, had been spent setting his principled position on whatever issue drew his attention and leaving decision-making to others.

Corbyn had believed in nuclear disarmament all his adult life. In September 2015, during his first party conference as leader, he told the BBC that nuclear weapons are 'immoral' and declared that he would never use them if he were Prime Minister. As a lifelong Campaign for Nuclear Disarmament (CND) member, he had probably said this in different words hundreds of times, but suddenly, in his new role as Labour leader, he was being heard by skilled, unionised workers in the armaments industry. Members of his shadow Cabinet stepped forth to point out that what he said was not the party's policy. Corbyn's greatest union backer, Len McCluskey, was trapped in a difficult position. His union, Unite, had thousands of members in the arms industry. There was a risk that they might all defect to the GMB, whose leader, Sir Paul Kenny, had no compunction about attacking Corbyn's position. Kenny and McCluskey went in together to tell Corbyn, in effect, to keep his opinions on disarmament to himself.

In 1983 and 1987, Labour had fought elections on manifestos that promised to remove all nuclear weapons from the British Isles. The 2017 manifesto declared that 'Labour supports the renewal of the Trident nuclear deterrent'.

Early in 2016, junior doctors held a series of one-day or two-day strikes over working hours, which threw into sharp relief a fundamental disagreement within the shadow Cabinet over what the Labour Party was for. To the shadow Health Secretary, Heidi Alexander, Labour, as a potential party of government, could support the junior doctors' claim for better pay and working hours but should not be seen endorsing a strike. She was furious, therefore, when on her television she saw John McDonnell, the shadow Chancellor, standing on a picket line with the junior doctors, because he believed that Labour was or should be a socialist party that supports workers in their struggles. Later, she heard that there were junior doctors' representatives in McDonnell's office and barged in, demanding to be part of the conversation. She also complained to the shadow Cabinet. She told me that what stuck in her memory of this confrontation was the silence. Andy Burnham, a former Health Secretary, was sitting next to McDonnell, saying nothing. Corbyn was also silent, until Alexander rounded on him to suggest he show some leadership. Corby's plaintive response was, 'Can't we talk about this later?'

An incident that attracted a lot of publicity was when the Labour MP Margaret Hodge confronted Corbyn in a corridor in the House of Commons and called him an antisemite – though contrary to what was reported, she did not swear at him. Speaking for myself, I do not think Corbyn was an antisemite. I heard him speak admiringly at a wake in honour of the writer Mike Marqusee, who called himself a 'deracinated Marxist Jew' – coincidentally on the very evening when Corbyn was confronted by Hodge. I think that Corbyn had a blind spot. It was so basic to his image of himself that he was a lifelong anti-racist that he could not understand how anyone could honestly believe that he was antisemitic, even if he was photographed laying a wreath in a cemetery near the graves of two of the men who massacred Israeli athletes at the Munich Olympics.

But Margaret Hodge had lost close relatives in the Holocaust and deliberately set out to shock Corbyn by speaking to his face, in a part of the Commons where there were no journalists to overhear, but after others had spread the story to the media, she could see no point in denying it. As a former leader of Islington Council, Hodge had known Corbyn for almost forty years. She complained that in the old days when she approached him about some local problem, he would insist on talking about the civil war in Nicaragua. She also said that his reaction to being called an antisemite was curiously subdued. All he said was 'I am sorry you think that'. No other Labour leader in living memory would have reacted so tamely to such a serious insult.

Corbyn was a loner, who for years could be seen around the Commons, walking from here to there by himself, deep in thought. Even when he was supposedly a Prime Minister-in-waiting, he could be spotted alone. When he lost the Labour whip in 2020, no Labour MP went with him out into political isolation. The idea that he was equipped to lead the Labour Party, let alone run a government, was bizarre. When he had put his name forward in the leadership contest, without any expectation that he would win, I asked the chairman of the Parliamentary Labour Party, John Cryer, whose politics were not much different from Corbyn's, what would happen if he accidentally won. Cryer just laughed at the idea. 'Don't worry,' he replied, 'if Jeremy ever thinks there's any danger of him winning, he'll be on the first plane to Caracas.'

In a similar spirit, I came across Corbyn on the day he announced his candidature, wandering along a Commons corridor alone, as usual, and looking scruffy. In the 1980s, he was named as Britain's worst-dressed MP, after he had refused to wear a tie in the debating chamber.

'Jeremy,' I said, 'how can you lead the Labour Party when you don't know how to tie a tie?'

'That's my secret weapon,' he replied.

He was right about that.

25

CORBYNISTAS

Most of Jeremy Corbyn's supporters were young. It was the great achievement of his time as leader that so many were drawn to politics for the first time. But not all. There were some who had been around for decades, as he had, never expecting that they might one day hold important positions at the top of the Labour Party. I was at a private function where I heard John McDonnell, the shadow Chancellor, joke that if Corbyn had not been elected leader, the two of them would have spent their twilight years talking about how much better it would have been if only they had been running the show.

But there was one figure on the edge of the Corbyn operation with real experience of running a major organisation, who had nursed dreams of leading a resurgent socialist movement into government. This was Ken Livingstone, who ran London for five years as leader of the Greater London Council (GLC) and eight years as the capital's first directly elected mayor. No other British council leader in the entire twentieth century was as famous, or notorious, as Livingstone. He had not been in office long when, in October 1981, *The Sun* designated him as 'the most odious man in Britain'. Two months later, he was on the front page of *The Sun* again, decked out in a Santa Claus costume, under the headline 'the most odious Santa in Britain'. The first full-length biography of him, by the *Guardian* journalist John Carvel, came out in 1984, in the same year that a West End theatre staged *The Ratepayers' Iolanthe*, a political satire after the Gilbert and Sullivan opera, in which Livingstone was the main character, played by an actor named David Kernan, who mimicked his voice and mannerisms to perfection.

When the Conservative government decided to abolish the GLC and six metropolitan councils, making London Europe's only capital not covered by a local authority, it was commonly assumed that they did so to deny Livingstone his platform. I visited the offices of Tyne and Wear County Council during its dying days, hoping that an archivist there might be able to turn up information on the arrest of a young Russian travelling through Newcastle in July 1915 under the weird, false name of Moshe Dolgolevsky, who was in fact Lenin's friend, Nikolai Bukharin, in disguise. The mission was a failure, but I talked with the archivist about what he would do next, since his job was about to go. 'It's a bloody expensive way to get rid of Ken Livingstone,' he complained.

The House of Commons is not always a welcoming venue for new MPs who arrive with an established reputation. Livingstone was an outcast from the day he arrived, in 1987. On the morning after the election, I was with Neil Kinnock and Alastair Campbell at Labour headquarters when Livingstone appeared on screen, giving his take on why Labour had endured another heavy defeat. Kinnock was so angry that he started punching the air with both fists.

The Labour whip in charge of accommodation picked up the vibe. After a week or two, Livingstone called a press briefing to say that he had been told there was no space for him anywhere in the building, not even a corner of a table. Afterwards, he left the building. His fourteen unhappy years as an isolated MP ended with him being expelled from the party. He had opposed the creation of a directly elected mayor, but once the role had been voted into existence, he put himself forward to be the Labour candidate, on a promise that if he was not selected, he would not run against Labour as an independent. He was not selected, and he did run against Labour as an independent. Being expelled did not bother him. I saw him soon after it happened, at a reception in the Irish embassy. He predicted, correctly, that he would soon be back in, because 'I'm an engaging little worm'.

The day after his election in May 2000, I was called in as the only mainstream journalist to be granted an interview with the new mayor. As we talked, he welled up. Tactfully, I pretended not to notice. He did it again, and this time took out a handkerchief to wipe his eyes, and I realised that the old fox wanted me to notice. He wanted his tears recorded in *The Observer*. But they seemed to be genuine, so I obliged with a portrait that began 'It is not often you see a grown man cry...'

Livingstone was a better civic leader than he is given credit for. No one else would have risked introducing the London congestion charge, but no one has since seriously suggested removing it. He commissioned the feasibility study that led to the introduction of the capital's highly successful scheme for hiring bicycles, known as the 'Boris bikes'. He was thinking constantly about how to alleviate London's housing shortage. When I met him in his office in the new city hall, he flipped through a large, detailed London atlas that lay on his table, pointed to a triangle of land coloured green and went into detail about why it should be used for housing and who was preventing its development. On another occasion, standing outside Southwark underground station, which was opened in 1999, Livingstone looked up at its roof and remarked that if the planning authority had been more alert, they could have had homes built above the structure.

But being a civic leader was never enough. He craved attention. He was not frightened of bad publicity; he just longed to be noticed, and where other politicians minded their words carefully, he would deliberately make cruel or careless comments, just for the adrenaline rush. At the end of his first day in office in July 2000, I was invited to the celebration in Tate Modern. When I arrived, he spotted me and declared in a loud voice, 'Hello darling, you look so disreputable you don't even look like a journalist.' Then he summoned a security officer and proclaimed, 'Arrest this man: he's a journalist!'

I knew him well enough not to mind, but he landed himself in serious trouble after another alcohol-fuelled celebration when he likened the journalist waiting outside to a Nazi concentration camp guard and refused to back down on being told that the target of this pleasantry was a Jew. Some committee or another that nobody knew existed moved into action and disqualified Livingstone from the office of mayor, only to be overturned by a high court.

Personally, I had no reason to object when Livingstone invited the President of Venezuela, Hugo Chávez, to come to London and sound off against US foreign policy. When Livingstone saw me on a press bench at the back of the room in city hall, he sent a press officer to invite me to move to the front and be the first to ask Chávez a question. It was interesting to see Chávez close up, but the event contributed nothing that I could see to the good governance of London. Nor did it help Livingstone's campaign in 2008, when he was up against Boris Johnson, the only rival he ever encountered with an even greater need to be noticed.

I rang Livingstone in September 2015, thinking that he might have something interesting to say about the sudden rise of Jeremy Corbyn. In those early days, even commentators who were on Corbyn's side, such as Owen Jones, in *The Guardian*, pointed out that he was vulnerable because he had no solid political base. Livingstone and Corbyn had known one another since the 1970s. Ideologically, they were on the same page, but one of them had spent almost thirteen years running one of the greatest cities on earth, while the other had not been in charge of anything for thirty-two years, and before then, not much. I thought Livingstone might say something to the effect that Corbyn would need to go on a steep learning curve, or surround himself with experienced advisers, but without hesitation or reservation, he served up prepared lines on what a great leader Corbyn was sure to be in opposition before becoming a great socialist Prime Minister, a notion Livingstone was far too experienced and intelligent to actually believe. It was like a voice from a parallel reality.

He was hoping to make a comeback as a major player in the Corbyn-led Labour Party. But too many people knew that he did not have the temperament to play a supporting role. Livingstone's life was an endless drama, centred on him. Had he taken a modicum of care, he would have been elected back onto Labour's National Executive in 2016, but before voting began, he had disqualified himself by indulging his compulsive need to be in the eye of a media storm, by making an absurd and offensive remark that Hitler was a Zionist 'before he went mad'. The day after he said this, I found myself having to explain to a live radio audience that a Zionist is someone who wants a homeland for Jews ruled by Jews; a person who hates Jews and wants them removed to somewhere far away is not a Zionist. The reaction did not bother Livingstone. Watching him barely able to move amid a thicket of cameras, microphones and recording machines, I could see the look on his face which seemed to be saying 'this is fun: this is like my old glory days'. Even his friend Corbyn could not protect him after that episode. He avoided the risk of expulsion by resigning from the party, and so ended the political career of the once-renowned Ken Livingstone.

●　●　●

Jon Lansman was another outsider, who brought something to the party that very few people on the left could offer: he had a shrewd business sense. I first encountered him in March 1984, when he was a volunteer on Tony Benn's team in the Chesterfield by-election. He was then in his mid-twenties and had the job title 'business manager' of the weekly left-wing paper *Tribune*, which did not sound impressive to me, but Chris Mullin, who edited *Tribune*, told me he was 'very competent'. Lansman had been famous for a day in 1981, during the Benn–Healey deputy leadership contest, after Denis Healey had been barracked at a couple of public meetings and accused Lansman of orchestrating the disturbances but had to back down. Actually, Lansman was nowhere near the scene of either crime. I was there as Healey entered a room full of Benn supporters, during the Chesterfield by-election, spotted Lansman, and said, very loudly, 'I did a terrible thing to this fellow: I mistook him for somebody better looking.'

As Benn's political fortunes declined, most of the political figures who had been closest to him drifted away, preferring to co-operate with Neil Kinnock, but Lansman stayed on the outer edge of the Labour Party for decades, holding the same views at sixty as he had when he was twenty. In 2015, he held a Commons pass as a researcher for Michael Meacher, another old Bennite who by then had been an MP for forty-five years. In 1981, Meacher was known as 'Benn's vicar on earth'. When Benn visited the Days of Hope bookshop in 1982, he told Bob Clay and me what a 'good man' Meacher was, but they parted company, politically, in the mid-1980s. Meacher was a minister in the Blair government but rediscovered his radicalism after Blair sacked him.

Lansman moved in smartly to create a company to hold the data collected during the Corbyn leadership campaign, from which he launched Momentum. He was the first person I heard talking seriously about the possibility that Corbyn might win. But his only reward for the enormous service he did the campaign was a seat on the National Executive. He described that as a 'disappointing experience', which we can assume was an understatement. Though he was not religious, he had been brought up as a Jew and observed some Jewish customs and was driven to near despair by Corbyn's failure to deal effectively with antisemitism in the party.

Lansman also had a vision of Labour as an activists' democracy, which was the model on which he created Momentum. There is an opposing mindset also found on the radical left which says that 'if you have the power, use it' – words I heard Livingstone utter when he was leading the GLC. That was an attitude that Len McCluskey, leader of Unite, Labour's biggest union backer, brought to the party.

In summer 2015, just before the rise of Jeremy Corbyn, McCluskey was on a visit to Birmingham, where Unite's West Midlands regional organiser, Gerard Coyne, urged him not to run for a second five-year term as general secretary, warning that if he did, he would be challenged. According to the version of this conversation I heard from Coyne, McCluskey's response was to warn that running against him would cost Coyne his job. Even before the contest had begun, Coyne was hauled before a disciplinary tribunal because he had accepted an invitation from Jack Dromey, a former deputy general secretary of Unite, to address a meeting of Labour MPs in the Commons. Most of the MPs in the room were not Corbyn supporters. Unite's political conference had put the union squarely behind Corbyn. Unite contributed more than £250,000 to Corbyn's two leadership election campaigns. Coyne was consequently in breach of union policy, for which he was given a final written warning.

Despite that shot across the bows, Coyne went ahead and challenged McCluskey in 2017, running him much closer than anyone expected, knowing that defeat would be the end of his twenty-six years as a full-time union organiser. He was suspended as soon as the ballot had closed and sacked because his campaign had used some data that belonged to the Labour Party. The charge sheet was drawn up by Andrew Murray, Unite's chief of staff, who warned that this abuse of data could damage relations between the union and the party. Coyne has been a Labour Party member all his adult life and even went canvassing when Corbyn was its leader. Murray was a communist for forty years but joined the Labour Party after

Corbyn's election. In March 2003, I wrote a piece for the *Independent on Sunday* marking fifty years since the death of Stalin. Stalin did not have many admirers any more, but I was able to name three – Andrew Murray, Arthur Scargill and Saddam Hussein.

I ran the media side of Gerard Coyne's campaign, which, I confess, involved meeting people who would not normally be interested in an internal trade union election. We had an interesting meeting in a private house in Kensington, valued on Zoopla at £42 million, where a maid brought in tea on a silver tray, while Richard Sharp, a donor to the Tory Party and future chairman of the BBC offered us free advice. From there, we walked around the corner to meet Geordie Greig, editor of the *Mail on Sunday*. Coyne was prepared to meet people other union leaders would have avoided on principle, but he was not like the hard right-wing union leaders of the past. His opinions on most subjects, including for instance gay rights, would have marked him out as a *Guardian* reader, but then most of the leading journalists on *The Guardian* would count as being on the outer edge of the right wing in Unite's internal politics.

McCluskey's influence in the Corbyn-led Labour Party was not restricted to giving money. As a new leadership team took shape, it included his lover, Karie Murphy, who was appointed executive director of the Leader of the Opposition's Office under Corbyn – though at the time, anyone who identified them as lovers risked a libel action. He made the relationship public in a memoir he published after he had retired. No sooner had Andrew Murray switched parties than he was seconded part time to the leader's office. His daughter, Laura Murray, was also enlisted in the leader's office, before being promoted to the post of head of complaints. When there was a vacancy for the general secretary of the Labour Party, in

March 2018, Jennie Formby, a Unite official and the mother of one of McCluskey's children, put her name forward. This struck Lansman as so blatant an example of 'machine politics' that he threatened to run against her but was persuaded to back off.

My last conversation with Tony Benn was at a family gathering, on the day that the other, better-known Andrew Murray won Wimbledon in 2013. Talking of the future of the left, he did not mention Jeremy Corbyn or any of the big names of the Corbyn era, but he asked if I knew someone who had greatly impressed him, named Owen Jones.

I had first heard of Owen Jones when I was visiting the office of a left-wing publisher, Verso, where the historian Thomas Penn had a day job. He told me that they were about to publish a book called *Chavs*, and that its author would be a very big name soon.

At that time, *The Independent* had a left-wing columnist called Johann Hari, who had an enormous following online, drawing the young readers that all newspapers were desperate to attract. He was very talented but flawed. He has been described many times as a 'plagiarist', though he was not guilty of stealing anyone else's words or ideas. What he did, when interviewing writers for *The Independent*, was to take slabs of text from their books and pretend that they had said those words to him, in conversation. That created a scandal, as diligent Twitter users dug up example after example. It also later transpired that he had been obsessively editing Wikipedia using a false name to run vendettas against other journalists. After that second scandal, *The Independent* dropped him, creating a hole that was quickly filled by Jones. He was then twenty-seven years old but looked at least ten years younger. He was a pleasant, self-effacing colleague, who told me that, despite his spreading reputation, his parents thought him a touch too centrist. His father had been a full-time employee of the Militant Tendency.

After Corbyn's victory in the 2015 leadership election, I was invited by Goldsmith College to debate with Jones, who was by now a celebrated *Guardian* columnist and star of social media. Every seat in the lecture hall was taken. There were students sitting on the stairs, and on the floor at the front, and standing against the walls. They had not poured in to hear me, of course. Owen Jones was the attraction. At the start, the chairman asked everyone who had voted in the Labour leadership election to raise their hands, and up went a forest of hands. He then asked how many had voted for Jeremy Corbyn, and up went the same hands again. Still, I was heard out politely as I suggested that Corbyn's only achievement would be to hand victory at the next election to the Conservatives. I would have liked to stay and talk to Jones afterwards, but there was a long queue of young admirers wanting a word with him.

Either then or later, he passed through a portal that so many others who are continually in the public eye go through, after which he was constantly aware of being observed and finding it hard or impossible to switch off his public persona and hold a normal conversation. During a Labour Party conference, I spent lunch with someone who knew Jones's father from their shared time at Sussex University. I told Owen this when I saw him that afternoon, but I was not talking to someone I knew, I was addressing a public figure. I was informed that Owen Jones was born during the miners' strike. I already knew that, and even had I not, I would not have felt that I needed to be told. If I had responded by saying that I was born in the year that the NHS was founded, I do not think it would have added lustre to my life story.

But after the Corbyn experiment had collapsed, and its big names had slipped into obscurity, Owen Jones was still on the up and up. Benn was right to suspect that he was the best hope for the future of socialism in Britain. That reminded me of hearing that wise old bird Ken Clarke issuing a warning to a fringe meeting at a Conservative conference in 1999 against investing their hopes for the future in a journalist. 'We live in an age when politicians are weak, and journalists are strong,' he complained. The Tory Party did not know how they were ever going to regain power against a party led by Tony Blair. It worried Clarke that anyone should be foolish enough to think that the answer was that journalist, Boris Johnson.

26

TWO CAMPAIGNERS AND THREE POLITICIANS

There has rarely been a Prime Minister with so narrow a political base as Boris Johnson. He was the darling of the Conservative Party rank and file, but loyal supporters among his fellow MPs and the professional political advisers were few and far outnumbered by those who lent him their support while he appeared to be a vote winner. His most famous adviser, Dominic Cummings, turned against him and embarked on a savage campaign of revenge. There were perhaps just two members of his Cabinet who were committed in their loyalty to him personally – Nadine Dorries and Jacob Rees-Mogg.

The other Dominic – Dominic Raab – also owed his sudden promotion to very high office to Johnson, but unlike Dorries or Rees-Mogg, he stayed on in office as Rishi Sunak's nominal second in command. Raab's political career took a downturn when Theresa May became Prime Minister, in 2016. He had been a junior minister under David Cameron. He was offered a job by May, but whatever job it was did not appeal to him, and he returned to the back benches. From that weak position, he managed to effect a change in the law, with no help from the government.

Early in his time as an MP, Raab had formed a working relationship with a remarkable man named Bill Browder, a British citizen by adoption, who was born into an unusual American family. Every male Browder seems to have been a work-driven obsessive. Earl Browder was general secretary of the Communist Party of the USA. His son Felix, father of Bill, was one of the leading mathematicians of his generation. Joshua Browder, one of Bill's sons, devised an app when he was eighteen that made him a millionaire. Bill Browder's first known obsession was trading in shares in postcommunist Russia, after he had spotted that the privatised industries were being sold at prices far below their true value. Having made a vast fortune, he discreetly pulled all his and his clients' money out of Russia when spreading corruption made it impossible for him to continue. His parting act was to pay $230 million in tax, the largest single payment Russia's Treasury had ever received. All of it was then stolen by a network of criminals and corrupt officials. The crime might have gone unnoticed, except that Browder had engaged a Russian lawyer named Sergei Magnitsky who, with unbelievable courage, traced and named the thieves, for which he was arrested and so badly mistreated that after a year in prison, he died.

Bill Browder's next obsession was to punish the people who murdered his friend. He seemed never to stop thinking about this mission, day or night. When I got to know him, I would sometimes feed him a snippet of political gossip and could almost hear the cogs turning in his brain as he decided whether this new information was relevant to his life's mission. If yes, it was stored in one silo in his capacious memory; if not, it was discarded into another.

Magnitsky's killers could not be touched inside Russia, after they had, no doubt, handed over a slice of the loot to President Putin; but Browder reckoned that having robbed the Russian public, they would want to move their wealth abroad, where it was safe from other criminals, and where there were properties and luxury goods and holidays for sale. That was something Browder could frustrate and prevent. In the USA, he persuaded Senator John McCain to introduce a 'Magnitsky' Act, which passed through Congress and was signed off by Barack Obama, giving the State Department the power to ban the Russians implicated in the Magnitsky affair from entering the USA or using its banking system. Later, it was upgraded to a Global Magnitsky Act, applicable to abusers of civil rights anywhere in the world. In the UK, Browder lobbied politicians and briefed journalists and created the annual Magnitsky Awards, at which campaigners against injustice and censorship from across the world were honoured. Guests at this annual event would find themselves in fascinating company. There I encountered Vladimir Kara-Murza, who survived two attempted poisonings and went back to Russia after the invasion of Ukraine, in order to be on Russian soil as he denounced the 'regime of murderers' who had started the war, knowing that he would get a long prison sentence; Marina Litvinenko, widow of the murdered Federal Security Service defector, and her son; the sons of the murdered Maltese journalist Daphne Caruana Galizia; Anaïse Kanimba, adopted daughter of Paul Rusesabagina, Rwanda's best-known political prisoner; Richard Ratcliffe, campaigning to get his wife, Nazanin Zaghari-Ratcliffe, released from an Iranian jail; and many more.

But Browder struggled to find a way through Parliament's complicated processes to get a Magnitsky law passed in the UK. I had written about him while I was at *The Independent*, and when its print operation closed in 2016, and I was no longer employed full time, he offered to pay me by the hour if I would help him navigate the British political system. After some false starts, I hit upon a workable idea. Theresa May's government was committed to introducing a Criminal Finances Bill in 2017, to combat money laundering and corruption. I suggested that we might be able to tack on an amendment to the bill that would bar the people Browder was targeting from using the British banking system. I enlisted the aid of Margaret Hodge, one of the most formidable parliamentary operators on the Labour side, but she rightly pointed out that if the amendment was to succeed, it would have to be presented by a Conservative. Bill Browder called upon Dominic Raab.

The government was passively opposed to what Browder was trying to do. The Foreign Office was more concerned about Islamicist terrorism and global warming than about Russian corruption and wanted to keep its lines open to the Kremlin. The Treasury was happy to have Russian money enriching the economy. Some Russian money was funding the Conservative Party. None of this deterred Dominic Raab, who gathered sufficient support from fellow Conservatives to be able to tell the Home Office minister, Ben Wallace, that he could force a vote when the bill had its Third Reading, and with the opposition parties behind them, the rebels had the numbers to inflict defeat. The government decided that, in the circumstances, they could live with a Magnitsky amendment.

Indeed, after the Novichok poisonings in Salisbury, in 2018, when Theresa May was challenged on the BBC about Russians being able to enter the UK to commit murder, she replied that Parliament had recently passed a Magnitsky law, as if it had been her government's idea all along.

That amendment gave the government the power to ban people implicated in abuses of civil rights, such as Magnitsky's tormentors, from investing their money in the UK banking system. A year later, with the help of the Labour peer Helena Kennedy, another piece of government legislation, the Sanctions and Anti-Money Laundering Bill was amended to include the power to ban them from entering the UK. Although the law was on the statute books, the power it conferred was never used until Raab became Foreign Secretary.

Though Raab drew ridicule when, as Foreign Secretary, he confessed that he 'hadn't quite understood' how much of the UK's trade passed through Dover, he never cut as ridiculous a figure as Jacob Rees-Mogg. Wandering around in a double-breasted suit, with strange mannerisms and a head full of Catholic theology and ancient history, he was often aptly compared to a throwback to a bygone century. He achieved passing notoriety before he even arrived in the Commons, when he was asked on television whether there were too few candidates in safe Tory seats who had been to state schools and replied magisterially, 'The Tory Party', he replied, 'is not going to be able to form a government if it has potted plants as candidates.'

I confess that I liked Jacob Rees-Mogg then, because he had very good manners and was so isolated and odd and seemed harmless, because I did not suppose any Prime Minister would ever offer him even a minor job in government. He was the first MP to utter the word 'floccinaucinihilipilification' in Parliament, making it the longest word ever to appear in Hansard. It was invented in Eton by stringing together four Latin words to mean 'setting at little or no value'. Reporting on it for *The Independent*, I contrived to use the word four times in my opening paragraph. Kevin Maguire, of the *Daily Mirror*, who presented that week's edition of the Radio 4's *What the Papers Say*, delighted in having this paragraph read out by an actor, who had to pronounce the word four times on air. Then the BBC's *Sunday Politics* show, fronted by Andrew Neil, invited Rees-Mogg into the studio so that viewers could hear an Old Etonian fluently pronounce 'floccinaucinihilipilification', an achievement greater than anything Rees-Mogg accomplished as a Cabinet minister.

If there was one Cabinet minister more devotedly loyal to Boris Johnson than Rees-Mogg, it was the Culture Secretary, Nadine Dorries. I had a curious online spat with her when she was relatively new to the Commons, which began after I spotted two very similar reports in the weekend press, in which she complained that the police and criminal prosecution service had failed her, because one of her constituents was harassing her and she wanted him arrested. It took me no more than half an hour to establish the identity of her nemesis. He was an obsessive user of social media named Tim Ireland, who stood against Dorries as an independent at a subsequent election and gathered 384 votes to her 32,544. I never met or communicated with Tim Ireland, but someone who knew him, whose judgement I trusted, told me that he was no danger to anyone, so I wrote a piece for *The Independent* mildly suggesting that the police had made the right call. I also wrote that Dorries's word could not always be trusted. That was because of a well-documented mismatch between the blog that she wrote about her life as a newly elected MP and the £24,000 she had claimed for running a second home in her constituency. When questioned by the standards commissioner, Dorries replied, 'My blog is 70 per cent fiction' – meaning that she had been systemically misleading those who read it.

The next morning, I discovered that I had chalked up a long list of notifications on Twitter. I had put something out on Twitter and late in the evening – at 11.29 p.m. on 17 September 2014, to be exact – Dorries responded, 'Back on Twitter you inadequate misogynistic bully? I'm delighted to provide you with an opportunity [to] vent your woman hating bile.' After doing some research, she added, 'Your book is doing really well Andy, 190,000 on Amazon. Maybe you should achieve something in life before you criticise others.' This referred to *No Such Thing As Society*, a book I wrote about the 1980s, published in 2011.

In another tweet, she called me a 'pathetic little man', and a tabloid journalist I did not know took up her case and accused me on Twitter of being someone who 'liked to stalk women'. She also complained to the editor of *The Independent*, Amol Rajan, and to the broadcaster Iain Dale, who contacted me and politely urged me to leave her be, because she was very upset. Out of respect for Iain Dale, I did, for a time. When I wrote about her again, she retaliated by calling me her 'journo stalker'.

One of Nadine Dorries's tasks as a Cabinet minister was to legislate against online abuse. It has been suggested that some of the comments she had left on Twitter meant that she was not the best person to be judging what constituted abuse, but she told the BBC's *Breakfast* programme, on 5 February 2022, that 'nothing I've ever put on Twitter has been harmful or abusive'.

She was not the most objectionable person to work with Boris Johnson. In my experience, that honour goes to his former chief adviser, Dominic Cummings. He was the main character, played by Benedict Cumberbatch, in a 2019 television drama by James Graham about how Brexit was won, and he became even more famous later that year as the man who drove to Barnard Castle after testing positive for Covid, with his wife and child in the car, because, he said, he needed to test his eyesight.

Dominic Cummings is an example of a certain type found on the right-wing of politics – the privileged rich boy with an Oxford degree, who purports to be 'anti-establishment'. Just as Jeremy Corbyn was Britain's worst-dressed MP, so Dominic Cummings was Westminster's worst-dressed paid adviser. He was born into the elite he claimed to despise as surely as the Russian anarchist Mikhail Bakunin was of noble birth, and he shared Bakunin's sentiment that 'the passion for destruction is also a creative passion'.

Cummings had not been out of Oxford University for long when I was at the *Daily Telegraph*. Then, he was running a campaign entitled 'Business for Sterling', which was dedicated to preventing the UK from joining the euro. He was a shrewd organiser of political campaigners, and I had heard that Charles Moore thought highly of him. I also believed that I detected the hand of Cummings behind an unusual phone call I received at home, from the newspaper's business editor. I had written a factual summary of a report put out by a 'think tank'. It was a pretty standard piece of reportage, approved by the news editor, to which no one with authority over the news pages reacted, but the business editor was telling me that the piece should never have been written or published, because the think tank in question was pro-EU. When I next saw him in the office, he accosted me and suggested I seek his advice in future before I wrote on matters relating to the EU. 'I'm here to help,' he said. This was unusual behaviour by a fellow journalist, and though I cannot prove it, I suspected that he had had his ear bent by Dominic Cummings, who meticulously read the newspapers, sniffing out anything that might cause a reader to think there were any benefits to being in the EU.

I decided that I had better get to know Cummings properly, so a colleague from the *Financial Times* and I invited him to lunch. We arrived at the restaurant, as arranged, and talked to one another as we awaited our 29-year-old guest. He turned up twenty or thirty minutes later, did not apologise for making us wait and decided that we had chosen the wrong table. We moved to a table that suited him. I should say that, so far, I had been luckier than a more senior colleague at the *Telegraph* who also made the mistake of arranging lunch with Cummings and waited alone for about an hour for a guest who never turned up.

The *FT* journalist was, like Cummings, clever, very sure of his intellectual ability and much closer in age to Cummings than to me: their combined age was about ten years more than mine. Once we were settled at a new table, the pair began discussing how the world ought to be run, while I listened in silence, thinking that no matter how long I lived or how much I studied, I could never hope to know as much as these two young men thought they knew. There was nothing I could say because, if you do not know everything there is to know, you cannot add much to a dialogue between two young men who think they do. Now and again, I gazed longingly at the restaurant door, thinking what a release it would be to get up and leave – but to have done so would have invited another irate phone call telling me that I had disrespected the young hero of the anti-euro campaign. This torment lasted for more than an hour.

Here I should say that there are other journalists who rate Dominic Cummings as a top contact. The year after that ghastly lunch, he popped up as director of strategy at Conservative headquarters, when Iain Duncan Smith was leader, and certain lobby journalists were delighted to receive tips from him about the uselessness of Duncan Smith. After Cummings lost his position in Downing Street, he again became a valued source, as he devoted himself to taking revenge on Boris Johnson. There are people who think that Cummings is a not a dreary, joyless, hyperactive narcissist, born into wealth and playing at being a friend of people, but a brilliant eccentric visionary, like the crazy scientist in *Back to the Future*.

I once met Benedict Cumberbatch, at an event to publicise a television film about the physicist Stephen Hawking, fifteen years before he played Cummings in *Brexit: The Uncivil War*. We did not speak for long, so I cannot claim to know him well, but it was, I think, an unusual case of a famous actor being less up himself than the real-life character he was playing.

27

AN EMPTINESS KNOWN AS BORIS

When I was young, I found it strange that famous people could feel anything lacking in their lives. Most people I knew tried to have two lives: they escaped from their mundane jobs and everyday routine by switching on the television or opening a newspaper to dip into the lives of the famous. The first conversation at work would be about the programmes they had watched the previous evening, as they claimed a few vicarious minutes in the world of actors, sporting heroes, rock stars or even, perhaps, politicians. They might speak contemptuously about someone they had seen on screen – and they usually would if that person was a politician – but beneath the contempt there was a note of 'why is that person's opinion being broadcast and not mine?' But the famous needed none of this. They do not need passive involvement in other lives: they were living the life, so how could they not feel fulfilled?

But that was the wrong question. It is more to the point to ask whether someone who feels an emptiness within, perhaps for lack of a stable childhood, can fill the void by being famous. From observation, I would say that applause and acclaim will work as a temporary cure, as it brings on an adrenaline rush of success, but when that tide goes out, the problem stays, unsolved.

On the surface, I never met a more cheerful character than Boris Johnson. He was all fun and bonhomie as a colleague on the *Daily Telegraph*, and he had star quality. He was never 'Johnson', he was 'Boris'. When 'Boris' was Mayor of London, a teenage friend of one of my daughters, from a working-class family with no discernible interest in politics, offered me £10 if I would tell her the first digit of Johnson's mobile phone number. Perhaps she was hoping to prise out all eleven, at £10 a shot, but my daughter pointed out the first digit of his number was, obviously, zero, and there we left it.

On a crowded passenger plane to Delhi, which my wife and I boarded in March 2018, the last passengers to take their seats in economy class were the Foreign Secretary and his daughter, whose arrival created a frisson of excited recognition. Passengers went over to speak to him, as if he were a film star rather than a politician. Johnson was on his way to visit the in-laws – for the last time, no doubt, because later that year, it was all over the news that Johnson had begun yet another of his extra-marital affairs, this time with Carrie Symonds. His wife, Marina Wheeler, was intelligent, sociable, well connected. She was one of the UK's foremost civil rights lawyers, but that was not enough. Nothing was enough for Johnson. He had to have other affairs, one after another, until she called time.

When I first met him, he was one of the highest-paid political commentators in the land, and the editor of a prestigious magazine, but he insisted on being an MP too, while holding to his other roles. One day in 2002, I fell into a conversation with him, shortly after he was elected MP for Henley, and he seemed unusually gloomy.

In an attempt to cheer him up, I remarked that *The Spectator* had achieved a healthy increase in its circulation while he was its editor and therefore nominally in charge. This attempt at a compliment invoked only an exasperated sigh. 'To think I've wasted my time editing a magazine,' Johnson lamented, as he turned his back and walked away.

His political rise was a disaster foreseen. While I was on *The Observer*, in 1999, I was surprised that the former Chancellor Norman Lamont questioned me about what other journalists thought of Boris Johnson, as if it were a matter of importance. I was not then well enough informed to give an opinion. A few months later, I heard Ken Clarke warn a fringe meeting at the Conservative annual conference that the party should not make the mistake of calling upon Johnson to be the leader who would rescue them from defeat. That was twenty years before it happened.

The difference between Boris Johnson and a politician such as Ken Clarke is not just that one of them was honest; it is illustrated by that comment that Denis Healey made about Tony Benn – 'In those days, for politicians, politics was almost all that mattered.' Clarke was a politician from 'those days'. He looked at political problems and thought about how to deal with them, for good or ill. He was the Health Secretary who introduced the internal market into the NHS, in part to see off right-wing Conservatives, including Margaret Thatcher, who were leaning to the idea of a US-style insurance-based system. I visited him at his London home, when he was eighty-one years old and was still taking a close interest in the perennial problem of how to fund the health service. When he stood for the Conservative Party leadership, aides advised him to say as little as he could about the EU, but he ignored them and began his pitch with a powerful statement on why EU membership served British interests – as if the nation's future mattered more than the passing question of who would be Leader of the Opposition.

Boris Johnson was never one to let a political principle get in the way of his career. Politics was not his field. He was a performer, for whom policy details were the equivalent of the lines that an actor has to learn. Sometimes he fluffed them, but he always remembered to immerse himself in the role he was playing. On that flight to India, I tried to engage his attention about a matter that was within his sphere of responsibility, as Foreign Secretary. Before he was in government, Johnson had written eloquently about the need for 'Magnitsky' sanctions, but now that he was Foreign Secretary, and had the power to use them, after they were written into UK law, nothing happened. I tried to interest him in the thought that he could be the first to sanction some notoriously undesirable Russians. Johnson picked up what he thought was the cue and delivered the lines he had been given by his civil servants – but he was giving the correct reply to the wrong question. He told me that he was anxious not to damage the economy of the Virgin Islands. I could see the link. At the same time as Bill Browder was getting a Magnitsky amendment tacked on to the Criminal Finances Bill, the pressure group Transparency International was trying to use the same legislation to compel tax havens under British control, such as the Virgin Islands, to be less secretive. What Dominic Cummings described as Johnson's 'shopping trolley' mind had veered off onto a different topic.

Johnson's cavalier inattention to detail had a catastrophic impact on the life of Nazanin Zaghari-Ratcliffe during her six years in an Iranian prison, when he carelessly told a select committee that she had been in Iran 'teaching people journalism', which the regime cited as proof that she was there to spread propaganda. After her release, some right-wing blowhards attacked her for not showing gratitude to the UK government. When I met her at another event hosted by Bill Browder, all I could think of to say was that she owed no thanks to anyone in government, least of all Boris Johnson.

For as long as he could, he concealed this intellectual laziness behind a carefully crafted image of a man living in bumbling chaos. I had an 'oh god, oh crikey' telephone call from him one day, after he had failed to keep an appointment to interview John Monks, general secretary of the Trades Union Congress (TUC), for *The Spectator*. Johnson asked me to step in and do it for him. 'You know how to speak to these people,' he pleaded, from which I surmised that he had not forgotten the appointment, he just did not want to leave his comfort zone to go into the alien world of TUC headquarters. John Monks told me that he had discovered a long 'oh crikey'-filled Johnson apology on his answer phone, which he had played over the Tannoy system for the entire TUC staff to enjoy. 'These people with their expensive education who can't hold it together!' he remarked.

Actually, Johnson could 'hold it together' very skilfully, when he chose to. He made some comment as a shadow Higher Education Minister that conflicted with party policy – I cannot now remember what it was – and was required to retract and apologise. Journalists who rang him were treated to a full 'oh god, oh crikey' stream of confused sentences that tumbled out in no apparent sequence. But Johnson had made one more mistake. He forgot that political journalists record conversations, and they confer. Two of his callers played back his responses to one another and found that the bumbling expressions of contrition were word for word the same. It was a performance, by a constructed persona that concealed a sharp and calculating mind.

One day I encountered him by chance when he was parking his bicycle in the yard beneath Big Ben and was mulling over a problem familiar to anyone who has edited a magazine or worked on a news desk. The deadline for the next issue of *The Spectator* was nigh, and he was facing the white hell of a page with no content. Suddenly, a solution came into view. Standing by his bike, with his helmet in his hand and the clips still on his trousers, he called me over and asked if anything unusual had come to my attention recently. Under his prompting, I remembered hearing a day or two earlier that an active member of the Labour Party whom I knew well had decided to send her daughter to a private school. That was all he needed to hear. He asked how quickly I could deliver 750 words on 'Why do my Labour friends send their children to private school?', and, with his problem solved, he stowed his bicycle away and removed his helmet and clips. At no point did he bumble, or hunt for the right word, or run a hand through his blond hair.

But just because I saw that he could be acutely focused when he knew what he wanted does not mean that I thought he should be entrusted with running the country or anything else. Alistair Cooke, the Lord Lexden, the official historian of the Conservative Party, told me, 'I have never come across anyone – except, I suppose, Charles Moore – who worked with him and thought him fit to be Prime Minister.' I second that.

Lord Lexden also remarked that Johnson 'can certainly be sure of plenty of attention from future historians, which his selfish, attention-seeking ghost will relish'. Perhaps, but how miserable will his attention-seeking ghost be if future historians conclude that he was not a political titan like Winston Churchill but a poor player that fretted and strutted his hour upon the stage?

Johnson did once cause me a minor embarrassment, but it was before I knew him, and I was only collateral damage. The media had picked up a rumour that a journalist on *The Spectator* had become pregnant by Johnson, the editor, and had had an abortion. He issued an outright denial, describing the story as 'an inverted pyramid of piffle'. He was presumably counting on the woman to keep quiet but had not allowed for her mother, who had no compunction about telling the world that Johnson was a lying philanderer. He had not only lied to the media but also to the leader of the Conservative Party, Michael Howard, who angrily sacked him from his role as shadow Minister for the Arts and told his director of communications, Guy Black, to ring Sunday newspaper correspondents and tell them that Johnson had been sacked because it mattered 'when shadow ministers don't tell the truth'.

Early the next week, the political team at the *Independent on Sunday* had to answer an awkward question: why every other Sunday paper had quoted those words, except us. I might have been put on the spot, as political editor, had the night lawyer not nobly intervened to take responsibility for the omission. He was an experienced lawyer, who simply could not believe that Boris Johnson would tell a bare-faced lie and had struck out the spokesman's remark as defamatory.

But while I was on the *Telegraph*, an encounter with Johnson might brighten up a dull day. Soon after my novel *Innocent in the House* was published, Johnson rang to say that when he first heard about it, he had said to himself, 'Why should a fine journalist like Andy want to write a novel?', but he had flipped through the pages and had come across a seduction scene involving a younger man and older woman and thought 'this is rather good'. I took this as praise indeed, given the breadth of experience Johnson had of real-life seduction scenes. I suppose it would have been polite, if hypocritical, to return the compliment when Johnson's novel *Seventy-Two Virgins* was published three years later, but I never got beyond wondering why a successful and highly paid journalist should want to put his name to such garbage.

• • •

On 4 October 2000, the shadow Home Secretary, Ann Widdecombe, won a standing ovation at the Conservative annual conference by promising that a government led by William Hague would introduce automatic minimum £100 fines for anyone caught possessing cannabis. I thought that this was a very bad idea and said so to Johnson, and I was pleased to hear that he agreed. As the day progressed, it became known that Widdecombe was freelancing: she had not agreed this policy with William Hague nor anyone in the shadow Cabinet. Charles Moore decided that the *Telegraph* should come out against Widdecombe. There was a strange atmosphere among the political staff at that conference, who were not accustomed to working for a newspaper that was attacking an eminent Conservative for taking too hard a line on law and order. It provoked Ann Widdecombe to ring Charles Moore in a towering rage, accusing the paper of fabrication and misrepresentation. I was instructed to interview her, to restore some calm.

That evening, Charles Moore hosted a dinner for a select group of Conservative MPs whom he held in high esteem, including Iain

Duncan Smith, David Trimble, Nicholas Soames and Owen Paterson. I did not really want to be there, for the week had already been heavy on the belly: dinner on Sunday with the shadow Work and Pensions Secretary, on Monday with the Conservative Leader of the House of Lords and on Tuesday with the shadow Health Secretary. By Thursday, it was a pleasure to be in a pub eating cheap food with old friends from *The Observer*. I expected Wednesday's dinner to be dreary, but in the event I was very glad that Boris Johnson was there to lighten the mood. After we had all sat down, Charles Moore asked if anyone would like an aperitif. Johnson piped up, 'Got any spliffs, Charles?'

Nicholas Soames also told a funny story at the expense of one of the journalists at the table. Owen Paterson tried to amuse the company with a tale about an encounter he had had with someone who was working class. He seemed to think he was being satirical, in the style of Evelyn Waugh but without the venom. I thought the anecdote fell flat. The guests listened politely, then carried on talking.

Paterson struck me as a man of limited imagination, with very little idea of what life might be like for people whose families did not own a business in Shropshire where they could ease into employment after graduation. But he was without malice; he held unquestioningly to the political opinions handed down to him in childhood, and he was popular on the Brexit wing of the Conservative Party, because, to quote from Elfriede Jelinek's novel *The Piano Teacher*, 'people with a herd instinct hold mediocrity in high esteem'.

There was another dinner hosted by Charles Moore twenty years later, in the Garrick Club, to which former *Telegraph* journalists were invited. I was not there, but Johnson was, having flown back to London from the COP26 climate conference in Glasgow. Moore used the occasion to speak up in defence of Owen Paterson, who was going through a traumatic time. He was facing the public humiliation of having his Commons pass suspended temporarily as a punishment after the parliamentary commissioner for standards, Kathryn Stone, had judged that he had been wrongly acting as a paid lobbyist for private interests. Worse than that, his wife had committed suicide. On the morning after that dinner, Johnson ordered that Tory MPs were to be whipped to overrule Stone and rewrite the rules so that Paterson could continue his political and lobbying activities uninterrupted. After one day, Johnson was forced to back down. Paterson decided to quit politics. There was a by-election in North Shropshire, in which a 22,949 Tory majority vanished, to be replaced by a majority of 5,925 for the Liberal Democrats.

Hot on the heels of that blunder came the revelations of partying in Whitehall when other people were observing the lockdown rules that the government imposed during the Covid pandemic. While this scandal was news, Johnson was described several times as a 'party animal'. From what I knew of him, he was not a party animal; he was a loner. A party animal enjoys the company of others and will strike up instant friendships. When Boris Johnson enters a crowded room, he sees an audience for his long-running performance of Being Boris Johnson.

He is two years older than David Cameron. So through all their shared time at Eton, Oxford University and in the Bullingdon Club, Johnson could look down upon Cameron as a junior. Johnson was also much known among their fellow students. Fast forward two decades, and Cameron was a high-flying member of the shadow Cabinet, while Johnson had arisen only as far as the middle ranks and then been sacked. Cameron brought him back onto the front bench, but only as shadow Minister for Higher Education, which did not give him a place in the shadow Cabinet. I recall one Tory MP gleefully pointing out how awkward it was for someone with Johnson's breeding to be in a team led by John Hayes, who grew up on a council estate in Woolwich: they were like Captain Manwaring and Sergeant Wilson in *Dad's Army*, he said, laughing.

I encountered Johnson on 6 December 2001, the day before Cameron was due to make his debut at Prime Minister's Questions as Leader of the Opposition. Our exchange was so odd that I made a written note of it afterwards. It concerned a photo call that was scheduled that afternoon on the green below Big Ben, close to where we were standing, featuring David Cameron surrounded by his Conservative MPs. Johnson talked as if he knew nothing about it.

'What's going to happen?' he asked.

'There'll be a photo call – the new leader and his loyal supporters.'

'Do all Tory MPs have to be there?'

'I don't think that when Cameron's choosing his front bench, he'll be looking through the photo to see who was there.'

Johnson thought about it, then said, 'I think I'll give it a miss.'

He turned and walked away, alone, and that afternoon he stayed shut in his office, to avoid being part of a crowd when his old school fellow was the centre of attention.

CONCLUSION

AND SO...

Is it better to be alive now than it was when I was born?

That question is what they call a no-brainer. There is a cornucopia of reasons to be grateful to be a Brit, living now. The years that followed the 2008 banking crash were designed a time of 'austerity'. But imagine if someone had been whisked forward in a time machine from the post-war period into 21st-century 'austerity'. The time traveller would wonder why no one needs ration books, why nothing is ever delivered or collected by horse-drawn cart, why people are constantly talking into little handheld cordless gadgets... and on and on. This century has seen two decades of abundance, compared to what was available seventy-five years ago.

And society is also more tolerant. Racism, misogyny and bigotry in other forms are still with us, unfortunately, but they are not socially acceptable in the way that they used to be. Half a century ago, the Conservative government was offering to pay black and Asian immigrants to go away, because they were not wanted here. Prime

Minister Rishi Sunak's parents were among many who resisted the pressure and stayed.

It took years to convince public opinion that some people are gay and that their existence is no threat to the heterosexual majority. During the AIDS pandemic of the 1980s, which killed gay men in their thousands across the world, governments of the day had to make a choice: whether, in the name of morality and conservative family values, they should tell gay men that their sexual practices were lethal and that they should desist and understand that what they had been doing was wrong; or whether they should decide that saving lives was what mattered. Battling MPs, not all of them Conservatives, who believed that AIDS was a 'gay plague' and not a problem for the heterosexual population, Secretary of State for Health Norman Fowler and civil servant Romola Christopherson fought for a public education campaign about safe sex for all. They prevailed.

But it was only the terrible urgency of the AIDS crisis that provided Fowler and Christopherson the opportunity to persuade Margaret Thatcher that this was not the time for the government to be making a judgement about how people should live. Otherwise, it was normal for the government to make a matter of policy to encourage adults to marry and to take out a mortgage. No one now thinks that it behoves politicians to give the nation moral guidance, especially after Matt Hancock absconded from Parliament to appear on *I'm a Celebrity*, seventeen months after someone supplied *The Sun* with CCTV footage of him smooching his aide during the Covid pandemic, when less important people were being told that they must keep a social distance. Some might say that this removal of politicians from the role of moral arbitrator is progress.

So, what are we missing?

It is a matter of observation that our political leaders, who are watched more closely than they were a generation ago, are not of the same calibre as those who preceded them. It is less fun to be a journalist than it was when I joined the trade – despite all that Johnson and others have done to add to the merriment of political correspondents. Both are symptoms of a society with no sense of mission, that is breaking down.

Astronomers tell us that the universe is expanding and its stars and galaxies are forever moving further apart. Something like that is happening on the ground, in western society, where improved social mobility has produced the side effect that there are thousands of people living in isolation in a crowded conurbation surrounded by strangers, who must struggle to feel any sense of belonging.

One way that human societies have held together since the dawn of consciousness is through shared beliefs – the myths and doctrines and stories of how the world was created that delineated membership of the tribe. They were also, of course, a way of excluding outsiders. Our tolerant, loose-fitting age does not go in for exclusion. You can belong, regardless of your religion or belief system. That way we avoid the destructive conflicts and repression common in less open societies. But it has a downside. Now that the search for universal truth has stalled, we seem to be drifting towards anarchic intellectual chaos, in which the very concept of objective truth disappears.

You might be a trained scientist whose working life has been devoted to the study of contagious diseases, who has discovered through trial and analysis that vaccination can prevent the spread of Covid. I might be someone who does not fancy having a needle stuck in my arm, so I choose to believe that vaccination is a device by which the elite keep the people under control. Then that is My Truth, and in a post-truth world, my truth is as meaningful as yours.

Suppose I were the spare second son of a king who had written a memoir. I might lay down that what is written in these pages is My Truth. Not yours, mine. And if you were to point out that something that I have written conflicts with recorded fact, instead of acknowledging that memory is a faulty instrument, I might declare that there's just as much truth in what I remember and how I remember it as there is in 'so-called objective facts'.

It is a soft vision of hell to think that people might soon live in a world in which truth as a standalone concept has been driven out by legions of individually curated truths, each as valid as any other. In that dystopia, there would be no point in training to be a journalist. You could still be a commentator and influencer putting out your opinions, but what would be the use of an old-fashioned fact-gathering reporter when there is no truth to be reported?

The profession has taken a terrible knock anyway since the arrival of the internet, with local journalism worst hit. In the twentieth century, almost every journalist's career started on a local newspaper or local broadcaster, except for a tiny few who went directly from Oxford or Cambridge into the national media. Back then, no magistrates' court, inquest or council committee ever sat without a journalist or two on the press bench, taking shorthand notes, but now local journalism struggles to survive in any form. Paying journalists to go out into the world to observe and report is expensive, and the internet has sucked up the advertising revenue that used to make local newspapers profitable. It is so much cheaper to have reporters working online all day, watching for anything interesting that pops up onscreen and can be repackaged to hits on a website. John Wade, who owned the first newspaper I worked at, used to say that if he spotted a reporter in the office not on the phone, he would want to know why they were not out finding a story. Towards the end of my time at *The Independent*, a member of the public caused a minor disturbance in the public gallery at Prime Minister's Questions, which the *Indy* correspondent who was present thought was too trivial to report. But Christian Broughton, who ran the website, took a different view and sent a stern email that contained the striking phrase 'people who are allowed to leave their desks'. He meant us, the political correspondents, who enjoyed a privilege denied to the youngsters hired to trawl the internet.

It has been said often enough that the internet is like a wild frontier, where truth has been chopped up into individual portions and the deluded and dishonest can speak the same authority as people who have taken care to know what they are talking about. In this chaos, there can be no shared sense of purpose. It does not allow serious and detailed discussion of profound questions, such as where is our society headed.

Parliament used to be a forum for the exchange of serious ideas, where MPs made long, thoughtful speeches that aimed to persuade, which it is not any more. Anyone who doubts that can download the detailed, respectful argument over the 1966 Sexual Offences Bill, which, when passed, partially decriminalised homosexuality, and compare it with a contemporary exchange over, for instance, transgender rights. When Margaret Thatcher was removed from office, she signed off with an eloquent speech in Parliament defending her government's record. Boris Johnson, who was the best communicator of the post-2010 Conservative leaders, said his goodbye via the mass media, in a monologue that contained a couple of pithy phrases but amounted to nothing. But Johnson was not removed for political reasons. It was his frivolity that brought him down.

There were, of course, second-rate MPs before the twenty-first century, and too many who were lazy or dishonest, but Denis Healey's remark that 'in those days, for politicians, politics was almost all that mattered' is true of the stars of the political firmament, who were serious people who thought about how to negotiate the tricky road towards achieving what needed to be done. This was true right across the range. Tony Benn had books published about his version of socialism; Jeremy Corbyn's collected works are nowhere to be found. Enoch Powell was dangerous and malignant, but he was also a cultured, clear-eyed and accomplished public speaker; Nigel Farage, Powell's nearest contemporary equivalent, scarcely rises above the level of a pub bore. It is as if leaders with a vision are not needed any more, because of an underlying belief that human progress has reached the end of the line and human ingenuity cannot and never could devise a system superior to the liberal, market-driven democracy that we inhabit. But history suggests that it will not actually last for ever but will decay, collapse and be replaced by a different social order, which may be an improvement or may not.

There was that time in my life when, having seen the poverty and social deprivation in parts of Tyneside, I thought the whole rotten system needed turning upside down. A couple of vivid visual images from those days have stuck in my mind. A young NHS nurse once visited the Days of Hope bookshop with a colleague, who wanted her to see it. She was a twenty-something Malaysian, who had not been in the UK long. She stood in the shop for a long time saying nothing, looking around, bewildered, then suddenly exclaimed, 'If you ran a shop like this in Malaysia, you'd be killed!' For her, a society where you could be killed for your politics was normality; free speech was freaky and unsettling.

I also had a long conversation with a rather dull youth, who had been through higher education, unlike his working-class parents, but was in a low-paid job. He was talking volubly about the economic exploitation of the working class, in which he included himself. He was thirsty and occasionally interrupted his flow to take a gulp of milk from a carton he was holding, until it was empty and he threw it away. I became transfixed by watching this milk disappear and seeing the passing look of satisfaction it induced. It jarred with his vision of a proletariat ground down by market forces that there was always enough milk available close by, at a price he could easily afford.

There are people in the UK, of course, for whom finding the means to pay for basic necessities is a continual, debilitating grind, and not far away from where they are there will always be someone else basking in unearned riches. But though it is unfair, it is overall a wealthy, stable society in which most people never have to experience hunger, poverty, repression or violence. In the history of the world, we are the lucky few.

ACKNOWLEDGEMENTS

The bulk of this memoir was written while the country was in lockdown, but I will not thank whoever or whatever set off that pandemic. I am glad that when it reached me, it was in a mild form.

I am grateful to Olivia Beattie, editorial director at Biteback, for her decision to publish this book, and to my very methodical and demanding editor, Ella Boardman, and to Suzanne Sangster and Nell Whitaker, who handled the business side at Biteback, and, not for the first time, to my agent, Andrew Gordon.

There are hundreds more who unwittingly contributed to what is written here, not because they knew I was writing it but by impacting on my life and so giving me experiences to remember. Some are in the index, most are not – but thank you anyway.

INDEX

INDEX